Gender, Law and Health

Other titles in this series...

Gender Violence
Rekha Pande and Sita Vanka (eds.)

Gender and Management
Sita Vanka (ed.)

Gender and Work: International Perspectives
Sita Vanka, Rekha Pande and Bharat Kumar Chillakuri (eds.)

Gender and Structural Violence
Rekha Pande and Sita Vanka (eds.)

Gender and History
Rekha Pande (ed.)

Gender, Globalisation and Other Challenges
Rekha Pande, Sita Vanka and Jeevanandam S. (eds.)

Gender, Law and Health

International Perspectives

EDITORS

SITA VANKA

REKHA PANDE

RAWAT PUBLICATIONS

Jaipur • New Delhi • Bangalore • Guwahati • Kolkata

ISBN 978-81-316-0987-3

Published by
Prem Rawat for **Rawat Publications**
Satyam Apts, Sector 3, Jawahar Nagar, Jaipur 302 004 (India)
Phone: 0141 265 1748 / 7006 Fax: 0141 265 1748
E-mail: info@rawatbooks.com
Website: www.rawatbooks.com

New Delhi Office
4858/24, Ansari Road, Daryaganj, New Delhi 110 002
Phone: 0112326 3290

Also at *Bangalore, Guwahati* and *Kolkata*

Typeset by Rawat Computers, Jaipur
Printed and bound in India.

Contents

Gender and Health

The Prologue

Gender is a social attribute ascribing some characteristics or norms and modes of behaviour to the female and other to the male sex. The gender of a person is determined by a host of institutions like the family, educational institution, society, etc. Gender is, therefore, the result of the interplay of various factors – culture, religion, and similar factors of a society. It refers to historically defined identities, roles and behaviours of different groups such as men-women, girls-boys, old men-old women, etc. The female and male sexes are then socialized into being one of these groups. Gender roles refer to the expected duties and responsibilities, rights and privileges of men-women, girls-boys, etc. that are specified by socio-religious and cultural factors. The interplay of these factors determines their respective needs. The gaps, thus, result in inequality leading to discrimination.

The United Nations has spearheaded the movement to eliminate gender discrimination elevating the cause of gender equality to the centre stage of the global agenda. The UN held a number of meetings and conferences to bring the attention of the world community on the issue. The conferences have united the international community with a few common objectives and an effective plan of action for the advancement of women everywhere, in all spheres of public and private life. The inception of the United Nations in 1945 witnessed only the preliminary stage of the movement. There were only fifty-one member states of the UN to start with, only thirty allowed women equal voting rights with men or permitted them to hold public office. Nevertheless, the drafters of the United Nation Charter had the foresight to deliberately refer to the 'equal rights of men and women' as they declared the Organization's 'faith in fundamental human rights' and the 'dignity and worth of the human person'. None of the previous international legal documents had so forcefully affirmed the equality of all human beings, or specifically targeted sex as a basis for discrimination. At that moment, it became clear that women's rights would be central to the work that lay ahead.

The first three decades of the work of UN focussed primarily on the codification of women's legal, civil and human rights along with the gathering of data on the status of women around the world. Time, however, evidenced that formulating laws do not suffice to ensure the rights and gender equality for women. It is here that the UN took the lead to organize different conferences of member nations to follow the guidelines and enforce them. The Beijing conference in 1995 assured women of their rights. It is here that gender and law assumes significance and attracted scholarly attention to focus on the strategies and plans of action for the advancement of women in terms of their legal rights to fully participate at all levels of human activity.

The development of feminist jurisprudence has contributed immensely to the legal theory in recent years. The feminist writers have exposed the gender bias in the neutral systems of rules. According to MacCormick, the western theories believed that law is an autonomous entity, distinct from the society it regulates, unlike the political and economic system, which it applies universally irrespective of gender to ensure objectivity. Thus, law attains its special authority. This view was challenged by the radical school of thought who argue that law is a function of belief that make social, political and economic inequalities appear natural. Feminist jurisprudence builds the argument based on this strand of legal thought. It, however, focusses its foundations on the experience of the legal system, which has encouraged and perpetuated the unequal position of women. Since the feminist school of thought is of recent origin, it believes in the diversity of voices to express the reality of women's experience across the world and the gender inequality in law. Jack's Law Dictionary defines feminist jurisprudence as 'a branch of jurisprudence that examines the relationship between women and law, including the history of legal and social biases against women, the elimination of those biases in modern law, and the enhancement of women's legal rights and recognition in society'.

In addition to the legal rights, international agencies like the World Health Organization (WHO) has contributed significantly to formulate gender strategies to ensure equality in health. This strategy for integrating gender analysis and actions into the work of WHO was adopted by the 60th World Health Assembly in May 2007. It has developed tools to ensure systematic consideration of gender in the design, implementation and evaluation of health policies and programmes. In addition, the Gender Equity and Human Rights (GER) roadmap for action 2014–2019 was formulated. This action plan was proposed to integrate equity, gender human rights and social determinance into the work of WHO. Thus, an integrated approach for gender responsive, equity enhancing and rights based WHO programmes were planned for the five-year period.

There appears no problem per se in socially constructed differences between men and women, except that these differences limit their chances or resources needed to attain health, thus leading to discrimination and inequalities which might have negative consequences on health. Health disparity has been defined by the WHO as differences in health care received by different groups of people that are not only unnecessary and avoidable but also unfair and unjust. *Equity in health* refers to a situation whereby every individual has a fair opportunity to attain their full health potential, and that no one should be denied from achieving this potential. Health disparities or health inequalities are basically seen with gender as an access of difference in the social structure, which perpetuate marginalization of women in the form of cultural norms and legal codes. As a result, female life expectancy at birth, nutritional well-being, immunity against communicable and non-communicable diseases are often lower than those of men. Moreover, the male-female sex ratio, the female mortality, access to health care, cultural practices like son preference, etc. are all issues which perpetuate the inequity. This requires engendering the whole discourse on gender and health. Gender and health, thus, has also been brought into the research focus of scholars across the world. Violence and abuse, structural gender oppression access to the health care services and the system etc. are all forms of gender disparity. Gender main-streaming, women empowerment, and developing gender responsive health programmes are all certain strategies to ensure the physical and mental health of women and restore the gender equality to reassure women towards gender equality.

Taking clue from research, an attempt was made to discuss, deliberate and present multiple perspectives from various parts of the world in the Worlds Women's Congress-2014 conducted at the University of Hyderabad. Academics, researchers, NGOs and organizations working for gender justice participated and presented their perspective in a six-day congress held at the University focussing on *Gender in a Changing World*. The conference deliberated on an agenda for global gender policies and strategies, laying down a road map for gender-just society, gendered budgeting to empower women, engage with the industry to create awareness on gender issues and network with the stakeholders for engendered solutions. WWC was a significant event of the university, where a galaxy of 1,000 speakers spread across 850 panels and paper presentations from different parts of the world including Brazil, USA, UK, France, Germany, Korea, Nepal, Bangladesh, Canada, Israel and across India participated in the conference.

Varied themes such as *Gender and Culture, Gender and History, Gender and Management, Gender and Violence, Gender and Digital Divide, Gender and Globalization, Gender and Work, Gender and Law, Gender and Science, Gender and Health, etc.* were discussed and deliberated during the six-day event. The programme was structured in plenaries, presentation of papers, workshops, panels, discussions, along with informal interaction and networking along with exhibitions. The congress had a varied participant profile. There were researchers, scholars, government officials and policy-makers, NGOs, students, company representatives, feminists and many more who were interested in making positive contributions towards the cause of women's welfare and empowerment across the world, and becoming more useful to their own communities. Overall, the 12th Women's World Congress was aimed at each and every one interested in the creation of a gender-just society and provided unlimited resources and opportunities to interact with prominent leaders in the field of gender and women studies, so as to greatly expand on the global network of scholars and professionals.

Since, it is a worldwide perspective on *gender in a changing society*, *Gender and Law* along with *Gender and Health* were also important themes on which the participants deliberated, discussed and contributed their scholarly work, which is brought together in a volume. While the legal issues related to female foeticide, gender disparities in the law relating to the maternity benefits, the gender perspective on the unwritten customary law of different regions in India, the implementation of law from a courts's perspective, the legal norms at the intersection of social ethics and law in Turkey, the gender specific problem of refugees in Tibet and illustrative analysis of gender stereotyping and Indian legislation.

Scholars in their papers focussed on female foeticide, law and technological development in India from a human rights perspective. Science and technology have been the instruments of liberation of man. However, the indiscriminate industrialization might lead to gains of science as a harbinger of development and progress and in turn result in endangering human health and environment. Technology is like fire, it can be used both for constructive as well as for destructive purposes. Hence, the science and technology, which helps in enhancing the quality of life, simultaneously have the effect of violating human rights. Female foeticide is perhaps one of the worst effects of the development of science and technology and one of the worst forms of violence against women, where women are denied their basic human right – 'Right to Life'. The impact of science and technology on human rights, violence against women, law and practice of female foeticide in India are discussed with a human rights perspective by *Vishnupriya*. The issues related to female foeticide viz. causes, extent, consequences including the role of doctors, legal control and judicial response relating to female foeticide in India are discussed.

Scholars also highlighted the disparities in the law relating to the maternity benefits from a feminist perspective. Women often face allegations of being barren, lesser women, anti-family, anti-motherhood, aggressive etc. which is unfair and against the fabric of a civilized society. The discrimination meted out to them needs to be addressed as not having children is not a sin or a crime that one should be punished was discussed by *Neeta Khurana*.

The Khasi Society is a matrilineal society situated in the Khasi and Jaintia Hills of Meghalaya, in the North-Eastern part of India. Together it co-exists with another matrilineal society, that of the Garo people in the Garo Hills of Meghalaya. It is a tribal form of society with a clear set of traditional and customary laws though still unwritten in form. *Charis Mine P. Khonglah* highlights the nature of these unwritten customary laws in their socio-political context and the challenge of execution of such unwritten laws in traditional institutions as well as in modern constitutional bodies mainly from a gender perspective. An attempt was also made to discuss the consequential advantages and disadvantages of unwritten customary laws from this perspective.

Law has always been an important battlefield in the struggle of Brazilian women to underscore their rights. A law on the prevention of domestic and intra-family violence against women was in force in Brazil since August 2006. The Maria Da Penha Law is foregrounded on gender perspective and its implementation has been placed within a scenario featuring the deepening of policies, agreements and campaigns to guarantee its highest efficaciousness. *Isadora Vier Machado*, in her paper, attempts to critically evaluate the Maria Da Penha Law in Brazil and problematize the place of the Law's executors in facing violence against women.

Law and morality clearly share common aspects. It is a well-known fact that the both are the bearer of understanding of 'good' in a society. However, it is not always possible to claim that the transformation of each norm to a legal code widely accepted by a society and based on morality can lead to fair conclusions in every situation. *Zeynep Engin*, in her paper, examines the position of women in law and morality in the Turkish context.

Customary law especially in North-East India occupies a central place in the social, familial and political life of the individual and communities as a whole despite the presence of constitutional law. The practice of Christianity among the tribes has brought certain changes in their traditional practices. This results in multiple legal systems. The study by *Ruth Lalsiemsang Buongpui*, highlighting the relation between gender and law in general, has brought forward the partial nature of law towards women. It is important to understand the nature and functioning of customary law as it has its impact on women's status. Based on the study of the Hmar tribe, the paper highlights to unravel the ways in which gender relations gets constructed through the functioning and perpetuation of customary law.

Refugees are the resultant outcomes of either civil conflicts or natural calamities but lately gender-based refugees have increased over a period of time. International human rights law and international humanitarian law instruments complement the safeguards for the refugees specified in the 1951 Convention. Hence, the international refugee law applies to all forms of refugees. However, gender-based refugees were not much discussed and undermined in international relations. *Chime Youdon*, in her paper, dwells on the gender specific problem of Tibetan women refugees in a case study format. The paper argues that the laws and the conventions of international agencies like the UN are ineffective and needs to be relooked at.

'Gender stereotyping' as a way of thinking and attributing gender roles is deeply inculcated in the social psyche. As a result it has also found a profoundly disturbing position in the Indian legislation. The perspective on gender as a socio-cultural and personalized concept and understanding of the so-called 'gender roles' has crystallized the notion of 'gender role' and simultaneously made 'gender stereotyping' a strong fracturing concern. Indian legislation has been oscillating between deeply stereotyped and progressive gender neutral provisions. This has had a deep impact on the substance and direction of litigation and the judgments in the Indian Legal System. The primary concern of *Suvarna Pravin Damle*'s paper was to address language used in a certain legislation in view of gender stereotyping. Her paper attempted to study and identify provisions that indicate the deeply percolated essence of gender stereotyping in Indian legal system.

Female sexuality has been repressed, mutilated and distorted in the literary frameworks. Women have been depicted as the marginalized, undermined section of the patriarchal set-up. Their sexuality is feared, not desired in them. Female sexuality is a tabooed area, not to be discussed and analysed. Angela Carter, a self-avowed feminist, iconoclastic in her feministic stance takes up this rebuffed theme and dissects it to its very core. In her seminary, provocative work *The Passion of New Eve*, she breaks the mould of conventional female sexuality. She transforms it and catches its monstrous figments and draws a fresh iconography. Carter in her post-apocalyptic work takes a U-turn from the mythical representations and exonerates her Eve from the fretters of conventional sexuality. *Smrity Sharma* in her paper analyses the literary framework through Angela Carter's work to argue that sexuality has multifarious dimensions. She also highlights the need to not only redefine female sexuality but the male, as well.

Tuberculosis (TB) and Human Immunodeficiency Virus (HIV) are closely linked. TB is known to be the main opportunistic infection among people living with HIV, and HIV is the leading risk factor for developing TB disease. Gender issues are of extreme importance in health and for that matter in TB and HIV treatment. A study by *Hannah Benedicta Taylor-Abdulai, Patricia Akweongo* and *Philip Baba Adongo* explore the gender dynamics of TB treatment adherence with HIV co-infected patients in the greater Accra region of Ghana. The study revealed gender disparities in all spheres contributed to adherence to treatment.

The gender differences in the perceived health states of family care-givers in Japan and South Korea are very well known. However, these are important to improve the high levels of care of frail elderly and quality of life for family care-givers at home. *Jung Nim Kim* investigates whether the difference in family care-givers' gender affected their perceived health states and socio-economic status (SES) in Japan and South Korea.

Adolescence is stated as the period of transition from childhood to adulthood, which starts with the onset of puberty. It comprises the individuals between the ages of ten to nineteen years. It is a stage of behavioural and attitude formation. Sensitization and appropriate guidance helps them to take right decisions and develop healthy behaviours. Adolescent health needs are unique. If they are not well guided, they are likely to experiment with risky behaviours that could harm them and others. *Varalakshmi Manchana* attempts to assess the knowledge on sexual and reproductive health (SRH) and gender perceptions among school going adolescents in Hyderabad, India. The study concludes that gender balanced adolescent friendly health care approach is the need of the hour.

In Guwahati, homeless widows or divorced women live under severe stress because of their terrible circumstances. Their independent living is hampered owing to several stressors such as poverty, unemployment, lack of shelter and abuse. These stressors contribute to higher rates of mental illness, substance abuse and health problems among them. It is important for them to cope with persisting stress to prevent harmful impact of stress on health. *Sabiha Alam Choudhury* attempts to depict a picture of the level of stress faced by the destitute women in Guwahati city of Assam, India, and its overall impact on their health using various indicators based on primary and secondary data. The study reveals the condition or feelings experienced when a destitute women perceives that demands exceeds the personal and social resources and how it affects one's physical and mental health.

The HIV prevalence is considerably low in Kashmir as compared to other states of India. The factors responsible for such low prevalence to HIV/AIDS are not known but definitely this is being attributed to strong socio-religious factors prevalent in Kashmir society. In such a situation it is very important to know how Kashmiri women infected with HIV/AIDS are coping with their lives in a society strongly guided by strong socio-religious norms. *Khalida Gull* in her paper empirically analyses the social life of AIDS effected women in Kashmir, India. The socio-economic background of these women, level of awareness they have about the disease and social stigma attached are also analysed in the paper.

Violence is a common situation that one comes across in India. The inhuman brutalities of violence can lead to homelessness, deprivation of dignity and privacy, poverty and struggle for existence and survival. Violence specially occurred for political conflicts usually have a long-term impact on the overall well-being of people's life. Most of the violent acts that occur in our country are internal, between two groups of different communities. Assam usually undergoes certain political disturbances that create serious threat to the people's life who usually face it directly. Women are more prone to such violence in the state. Women facing these cruelty and inhumanity usually come under trauma and lose their mental as well as physical well-being. *Mousumi Mahanta* discusses the impact of political violence on women's mental health of Assam. The study is based on the fieldwork conducted on different areas of Sonitpur district of Assam, India.

Parenting assumes importance in the growth of a child. It assumes much more significance in parenting issue through personal experience and parental views. *Antoinette Zloty*, in her paper, outlines the issues in raising the mixed race children and suggests strategies for parenting such cross-cultural and mixed race children.

Soil and female body are synonymous in Indian culture, since both are productive. History shows that women, the primary producer of crops, dug the soil and sowed the seed by making a sowing shaft, which looked like a phallus. They knew the technology of birth by their own body mechanism. The paper by *Madhabi Maity* examined in detail how the female body and the body parts are respected in the daily life and how it is related to the mother earth.

Baby factories, a rapid growing business outfits in Nigeria, are churning out hundreds of babies for illegal adoption and for some other unknown purposes. Violence against women takes various forms, but the incidence of baby factories is a new phenomenon. The paper by *Jessica Ezekiel-Hart* highlights the relevant laws which protected the rights of women and children in Nigeria.

Odisha is classified as one of the 'High Focus States' under NRHM for the low status of health infrastructure. Among the three Revenue Divisions the maternal health of central division is alarming. To bridge the gap, a lot of programmes under NRHM have been taken up in Odisha. *Ranjit Kumar Dehury* and *Jagatabandhu Mohapatra* in their study evaluated the situation of maternal health in the central region districts of Odisha.

Healthy citizens are the greatest asset of a country. The statistics from World Health Organization (WHO), National Cancer Registry Programme (NCRP) and Population Based Cancer Registry (PBCR) records alarming rates of breast cancer prevalent in India. *Josephine Selle Jeyanathan* and *A. Shenbagavalli* in collaboration with the IGCAR, Kalpakkam organized medical camps to bring awareness and shed the shyness so as to prevent female mortality in India.

This book primarily aims at a compendium of articles and literature to the professionals, scholars and researchers on issues relating to gender, law and health. More specifically, the book seeks to include views of the experts on the gender issues and experiences of women from a multi stakeholder perspective – policy-maker, managers, academics and beneficiaries in the process of law and health from different parts of the world. The theme is contemporary and includes issues, perspectives, approaches, research studies/frameworks and emerging patterns relating to gender, law and health from across the world in a lucid way. The volume provides an excellent opportunity for all those interested to update their knowledge on the concept, processes, issues, emerging paradigms on gender, law and health from a multidimensional, cross-country perspective.

We place on record a deep sense of gratitude to a number of people who have directly or indirectly helped us in the completion of this volume. An event of the magnitude of the WWC-2014 and compiling the papers presented in the form of a volume would not be possible without the help and assistance of scores of people involved in it. The then Vice-Chancellor, Prof. Ramakrishna Ramaswamy, and the administration of the University of Hyderabad merits mention for their support and encouragement in our academic endeavours. We are thankful to the authors of the scholarly papers for patiently awaiting the completion of this volume. More particularly, the help, effort, time and editorial assistance of Ms Swati Singh and Dashimti Marwein, research scholars in the School of Management Studies, for their support in the finalization of this volume. The enduring support of our families have always enthused us in turning our dreams into a reality. Thanks are also due to Rawat Publications and the team of professional editors for their cooperation, excellent editing and the formatting of the work.

Sita Vanka
Rekha Pande

Contributors

Philip Baba Adongo, Head, Department of Social and Behavioural Sciences, School of Public Health, College of Health Sciences, University of Ghana, Legon.

Patricia Akweongo, Head, Department of Epidemiology and Disease Control, Department of Social and Behavioural Sciences, School of Public Health, College of Health Sciences, University of Ghana, Legon.

Ruth Lalsiemsang Buongpui, Research Scholar, Department of Humanities & Social Science, sIndian Institute of Technology, Guwahati, Assam, India.

Sabiha Alam Choudhury, Assistant Professor, Department of Psychology and Counselling, Don Bosco University, Guwahati, Assam, India.

Suvarna Pravin Damle, Practicing Advocate, Pune, India.

Ranjit Kumar Dehury, Research Scholar, Department of Humanities and Social Sciences, Indian Institute of Technology, Kharagpur, West Bengal, India.

Zeynep Engin, Associate Professor, Faculty of Law, Galatasaray University, Istanbul.

Jessica Ezekiel-Hart, Dean, School of Education, River State College of Education, Nigeria.

Khalida Gull, Research Scholar, Department of Sociology, University of Kashmir, Jammu and Kashmir, India.

Josephine Selle Jeyanathan, Research Scholar, Department of Electronics and Communication Engineering, National Engineering College, Kobilpatti, Tamil Nadu, India.

Charis Mine P. Khonglah, Research Scholar, Department of Political Science, North Eastern Hills University, Shillong, India.

Neeta Khurana, Assistant Professor, Gender and Literature, School of Liberal Studies, Pandit Deendayal Petroleum University, Ahmedabad, India.

Jung Nim Kim, Faculty, Graduate School of Social Welfare, Tokyo University, Gunma, Japan.

Isadora Vier Machado, Professor, Department of Criminal Law, University of the State of Parana in Maringa, Ab. Colombo, Maringa-Parana, Brazil.

Mousumi Mahanta, Research Associate, Chandrapraba Saikiani Centre for Women Studies, Tezpur University, West Bengal, India.

Madhabi Maity, Associate Professor, Department of Bengali, Midnapore College, West Bengal, India.

Varalakshmi Manchana, Assistant Professor, School of Medical Sciences, University of Hyderabad, Hyderabad, India.

Jagatabandhu Mohapatra, Research Scholar, School of Medical Sciences, University of Hyderabad, Hyderabad, India.

Smrity Sharma, Research Scholar, Department of English, Aligarh Muslim University, Aligarh, India.

A. **Shenbagavalli**, Department of Electronics and Communication Engineering, National Engineering College, Kobilpatti, Tamil Nadu, India.

Hannah Benedicta Taylor-Abdulai, Research Scholar, Department of Social and Behavioural Sciences, School of Public Health, College of Health Sciences, University of Ghana, Legon.

Y. **Vishnupriya**, Professor and Dean, Department of Law, Osmania University, Hyderabad, India.

Chime Youdon, Research Scholar, Centre for European Studies, Jawaharlal Nehru University, New Delhi, India.

Antoinette Zloty, Consultant, Winnipeg, Manitoba, Canada.

Gender and Law

1

Female Foeticide, Law and Technological Development in India

A Human Rights Perspective

Y. VISHNUPRIYA

Abstract

Science and Technology have been the instruments of liberation of man. The resources of science could be used for human welfare. However, the indiscriminate industrialization might lead to gains of science as a harbinger of development and in turn result in endangering human health and environment. Technology is like fire, it can be used both for constructive as well as for the destructive purposes. Hence, the Science and Technology, which help in enhancing the quality of life, simultaneously have the effect of violating human rights. Female foeticide is perhaps one of the worst effects of the development of science and technology and one of the worst forms of violence against women, where women is denied her basic human right – 'Right to Life'. In this paper, the impact of the science and technology on human rights, violence against women, law and practice of female foeticide in India are discussed with a human right perspective. The issues related to female foeticide viz. causes, extent, consequences, role of doctors, legal control and judicial response relating to female foeticide in India are discussed in detail.

Keywords

Science and Technology, Human Rights, Violence against Women, Pre-Natal Diagnostic Techniques, Female Foeticide, Sex-Ratio.

Introduction

The instinct for development is unique to human beings. Human intellectual capabilities are used to understand the dynamics of natural forces, interfere with and manipulate natural processes, with the ultimate objective of attaining security for life and then for making life comfortable. Science and technology have helped humans in umpteen ways. Right from the invention of making of fire and the wheel, to artificial intelligence, through invention of means of communication and mechanization of agricultural and manufacturing processes, all these developments have revolutionized human life and ushered in industrial civilization. However, every interference with nature has its own repercussions on human and environmental health. Similarly, medical advances that can save mankind from disease and early death have their own side effects on human health. Some of modern gadgets are claimed to be responsible for increased risk of different kinds of cancers and some of the diagnostic techniques have been proven to carcinogenic. Technology, which if properly used, could do wonders, would result in disastrous consequences if misused. What is quite alarming is that inventions like the modern weapons, or amniocentesis or pre-natal diagnosis of sex of the foetus are being used for destruction of life. Birth control measures and clinical experiments often impact human health. Biotechnology with the avowed object of creating food security may, apart from having negative impact on human health, also have the potential to wipe out biological diversity on earth. Every industrial manufacturing process and modern life styles in some way or the other threaten ecological sanity. Misuse of cyber space for criminal purposes is not uncommon. In summary, it could be said that science and technology which help in enhancing the quality of life simultaneously have the effect of violating human rights.

Violence Against Women

The earliest demonstration of discrimination and relationship of domination is said to be between men and women. Religion and culture could be different, but in terms of gender relationship, there appears an amazing similarity amongst all regions as well as religion. Patriarchy plays such an important role in shaping gender profiles that women themselves could not realize for a long time that gender relations are problematic. Even with the growing visibility of the problem, it was difficult to accept it as a 'problem' and much more difficult to think of solutions. Women who constitute more than half of a human population have been discriminated, harassed and exploited irrespective of the country to which they belong, unmindful of the religion which they profess. Everywhere women are confronted with many challenges (Misra, 2006). Female foeticide is one of the worst forms of violence against women where a woman is denied her most fundamental human right – 'Right to Life'.

Female Foeticide: Extent, Causes and Consequences

Female foeticide refers to the aborting of a foetus, purely because it is a female. It is important to identify as to how this practice started and why it continues to thrive in Indian society. The act of aborting or terminating a foetus while it is still in the womb, because it is a female, is known as female foeticide. This can be done after determining the sex of the child before she is born, through ultrasound scans. Although sex determination in India is illegal, the practice is rampant and has become a multi-million dollar industry. Coupled with prospective parents desperate for a boy child, and doctors who are carrying out these abortions, female foeticide has become a shameful and shocking reality of India. Advanced technology is increasingly used for removal of female foetus but it certainly affects the sex ratio. The misuse of modern science and technology by preventing the birth of girl child by sex discrimination before birth and thereafter abortion is evident from the census figures which reveal greater decline in sex ratio (*CEHAT and Others vs Union of India*, 2001).

The sex ratio in India has consistently been in favour of the boys since the beginning of the 20th century. The sex ratio has drastically dropped at birth according to 2011 census to a shocking 914 girls for every 1,000 boys born. The sex ratio at the national level has improved by seven points from 933 females per 1,000 males to 940 females in 2011. While in 2001 there were 927 girls per 1,000 boys, there are 914 girls per 1,000 boys in 2011, indicating a drop of 13 points. In some parts of the country, the sex ratio of girls to boys has dropped to less than 800:1,000. The most affected areas are mainly the state of Punjab, Haryana, Gujarat and Delhi. For instance the urban areas of Punjab, known for its prosperity, the overall sex ratio at birth has gone down to 761 females for 1,000 males. Similarly Chandigarh, the urban centre with the highest standard of living in the country, has a sex ratio of 771 females per 1,000 males (Census of India, 1991, 2001, 2011). The United Nations has expressed serious concern about the situation. The selective abortions are carried out in greater number amongst affluent families than under-privileged. They view the birth of a girl child as a bad omen for future. Moreover, they find the cost of raising a child to be normal with respect to the income that the child might generate. The reform needs to begin with the prosperous, educated class which aborts a female child due to their narrow patriarchal view where sons are considered to be the only hope of old age and even after life. Despite better literacy level and economic condition, gender discrimination against females is high due to prevalence of dowry system which makes birth of a girl child to be a burden even for educated people. Though formally outlawed, the dowry system is still prevalent in Indian society (Dayal, 1999).

The most important impact of female foeticide is the skewed sex ratio it gives rise to. The dearth of females leads to other complications like female trafficking, kidnapping and increase in assault and rape against women. United Nation's World Population Fund indicated that India has the highest sex imbalances in the world. Not surprisingly, demographers warn that there will be a shortage of brides in the next twenty years because of the adverse juvenile sex ratio, combined with an overall decline in fertility (Hameed, 2012). The decline in the child sex ratio is not a problem of numbers alone. It is the manifestation of low status of women in the society. The likelihood is that with fewer women in society, violence against women in all forms could go up. This atmosphere of insecurity would lead women to be confined within four walls of their home. This is the manifestation of the threat of serious disruption in social fabric. If this decline is not checked the delicate equilibrium of nature can be permanently destroyed. The increase in the imbalance between men and women leads to many crimes such as illegal trafficking of women, sexual assaults, polygamy and dehumanization of society. The *Hindustan Times* reported that young girls from Assam and West Bengal were kidnapped and sold into marriage in Haryana. Amartya Sen argued that sex selection both reflects and reinforces women's low social status, which beyond its intrinsic cruelty, impedes the development of democracy and prosperity in male-skewed nations (Singh, 2012).

From Female Infanticide to Female Foeticide

The traditional method of getting rid of the unwanted girl child was female infanticide, where the female baby was done away with after birth in various ways, either by poisoning the baby or letting her choke on husk, etc. With the advent of medical technology, sophisticated techniques can now be used or rather misused to get rid of her even before birth. Medical technologies have played a crucial role in reinforcing negative patriarchal systems that demand male heirs. Amniocentesis was first introduced in India in 1975 by the All India Institute of Medical Sciences (AIIMS), Delhi, for detecting congenital deformities in foetuses. By the mid-1980s, it is being largely misused to determine the sex of the unborn child and carry out sex-selective abortions in Maharashtra, Punjab, Haryana and Delhi. In subsequent years, the practice is spread to the rest of the country. As a result of selective abortions, about 40 million girls are found missing from the Indian population. Female foeticide is so widespread in some parts of the country that the mobile sex determination scan is more easily available than a clean water supply. Portable machines of sex determination scan are taken to remote villages on motorcycles. As a consequence of it, infanticide has given away to foeticide. Compared to infanticide, foeticide is probably a more acceptable means of disposing off the unwanted girl child. Infanticide can be an overtly barbaric and inhuman practice, while foeticide that is carried out by skilled professionals is a medical practice that uses scientific techniques and skills which reduces the guilt factor associated with the entire exercise (Mehta and Kothari, 2001).

Role of Doctors

Doctors can play a very important role in this respect and should act as torch-bearers for the nation and guide the people in the right direction. They can refuse to carry out pre-natal tests. Medical professionals, the medical associations, state and national medical councils have a larger role in ensuring medical code of conduct. Some doctors (obstetricians, gynaecologists) in cities, for instance Ludhiana, have a practice as they pioneer in the Ericsson method. They have laboratories with flourishing equipment for separation of the X and Y chromosomes from male sperm, by Ericsson method. The Y sperm is then injected back into the women's womb to ensure a baby boy. The doctors defend themselves by saying that they are preventing divorces and second marriages just for a son (Gurung, 2010).

Son–preference is a deeply rooted phenomenon in many parts of India and women who do not give birth to sons more often than not face social stigma, familial disapproval and even divorce or desertion by their husbands (Bajpai, 2006). Under the tremendous social and family pressure to deliver a male child, most often the women opts for pre-natal sex determination and decide to get rid of the female foetus. She does so at considerable risk to her own life as such abortions cause serious health problems. Two-third of women who undergo abortions suffer health consequences serious enough to affect their daily lives. Women are forced to internalize the pain and live with this crime (Hameed, 2012).

The Pre-Conception and Pre-Natal Diagnostic Techniques (Prohibition of Sex Selection) Act (PCPNDT Act) has been in existence since 1994. This Act has never been adequately enforced. Unfortunately, the administrative efforts have been entirely misdirected. They have been targeting women who undergo sex-selective abortions rather than the doctors who carry out the procedure. By leaving the doctors, when cases are filed against women, who have been compelled to undergo the tests, women are further victimized. This entirely defeats the spirit of the Act (Menon, 2010).

Section 23(3) of the PCPNDT Act holds guilty any person seeking use of the Pre-Natal Diagnostic Techniques on a pregnant woman, including such woman, unless she was compelled to undergo such diagnostic techniques. However Section 24 of the PCPNDT Act says that the court shall presume, unless the contrary is proved, that the pregnant woman has been compelled by her husband or the relative to undergo the Pre-Natal diagnostic technique. Besides, it is clear from Sections 23(1) and 23(2) that the law primarily addresses doctors and medical practitioners and ultrasound clinics, rather than pregnant woman. Under the PCPNDT Act, the primary culprits are doctors. On the contrary if the pregnant women are prosecuted, they are caught between the law that the state is using against them and their own family which threatens them if they give birth to a girl child.

Right to Life of Foetus

Right to Life is a well-established right and is recognized by various international instruments. The Indian Constitution has recognized the Right to Life under Article 21 as also recognized in several cases (*Maneka Gandhi vs Union of India, 1978*). The question that arises is whether foetus enjoys this right. There are no definite answers to this question. In India, the Right to Life is guaranteed to every person under the Constitution of India. The concept of personhood complicates the position of legal status of foetus. Often courts refrain from answering this question due to complex issues that arise in determining this question, like the time a foetus attains personhood. There is a desperate need for the courts to clarify clearly this vital issue and recognize the right to life of foetus (Prasath, 2005). There should be a legislation recognizing the foetus of a particular age as an individual and accord all the protection available to any other individual. Killing of a foetus, whether a male or female, should be declared as murder and be punished for the same. However, there are some statutes that indirectly provide protection to the life of a foetus.

Indian Penal Code

The Indian Penal Code (IPC) deals with various offences which may be committed against the body of women. Sections 312 to 318 of the IPC deal with the offences of causing miscarriage, injuries to the unborn child and exposure of infants. Whoever voluntarily causes a woman with child to miscarry shall, if such miscarriage be not caused in good faith for the purpose of saving the life of the woman, be punished with imprisonment of either description for a term which may extend to three years, or with fine or with both, and if the woman be quick with child, shall be punished with imprisonment of either description for a term which may extend to seven years, and shall also be liable to fine (IPC, Section 312).

If miscarriage is caused without the consent of the woman, whether the woman is quick with child or not, punishment is imprisonment for life or imprisonment of either description for a term which may extent to ten years and shall also be liable to fine (IPC, Section 313). Whoever, with intent to cause the miscarriage of a woman with child, does any act which causes the death of such woman, shall be punished with imprisonment of either description for a term may extend to ten years, and shall also be liable to fine (IPC, Section 314). Whoever before the birth of any child does any act with the intention of thereby preventing that child from being born alive or causing it to die after its birth, shall, if such act be not caused in good faith for the purpose of saving the life of the mother, be punished with imprisonment of either description for a term which may extent to ten years, or with fine, or with both (IPC, Section 315). Section 316 of the IPC punishes offences against children in the womb on the principle that a foetus gets life after twelve weeks of conception. Section 318 of the IPC says that whoever, by secretly burying or otherwise disposing of the dead body of a child whether such child die before or after or during its birth, intentionally conceals or endeavours to conceal the birth of such child, shall be punished with imprisonment of either description for a term which may extend to two years, or with fine, or with both. This is a very strict law in terms of punishment, but it is very difficult to implement, in the lack of evidences and non-availability of witnesses.

The Medical Termination of Pregnancy Act, 1971

The Medical Termination of Pregnancy Act, 1971 (MTP Act) is enacted to provide for the termination of certain pregnancies by registered medical practitioners and for matters connected herewith or incidental thereto. Section 3 of the MTP Act provides that a pregnancy may be terminated only if in the opinion of a medical practitioner the continuance of pregnancy would involve risk to the life of the pregnant woman or of grave injury to her physical or mental health or there is substantial risk that if the child were born, it would suffer from such physical or mental abnormalities to be seriously handicapped. Section 4 mandates that termination of such pregnancy shall be made only at hospital established or maintained by the government or a place approved by the government. Section 5 makes the provisions of Sections 3 and 4 non-applicable in some cases of serious emergency. Under Section 7, very wide powers have been given to the government to frame regulations for the proper enforcement of the MTP Act. Section 8 saves registered medical practitioners for an action taken by them in good faith.

The MTP Act does not confer or recognize any right on any person to perform an abortion or termination of pregnancy. Even the pregnant women cannot terminate the pregnancy except under the circumstances mentioned in the MTP Act. Even during the 'first-trimester', the woman cannot abort at her will and pleasure. There is no scope for abortion on demand. Section 3 of the MTP Act is only an enabling provision to save the registered medical practitioner from the purview of the Indian Penal Code. Termination of pregnancy under the provision of the MTP Act is not the rule and it is only an exception (V. Krishnan vs G. Rajanalia Madipu Rajan, 1994).

Code of Medical Ethics

The Code of Medical Ethics under the Medical Council Act, 1956, states that on no account, sex determination test shall be undertaken with the intent to terminate the life of a female foetus developing in her mother's womb, unless there are other absolute indications for termination of pregnancy as specified in the Medical Termination of Pregnancy Act 1971. Any act of termination of pregnancy of normal female foetus, amounting to female foeticide, shall be regarded as professional misconduct on the part of the physician leading to penal erasure besides rendering him liable to criminal proceedings as per the Indian Medical Council (Professional Conduct, Etiquette and Ethics) Regulations 2002. It is important to note here that the penalty for sex determination and female foeticide in the form of striking off the name from the register of doctors is apart from criminal action.

Pre-Natal Diagnostic Techniques (Regulation and Prevention of Misuse) Act 1994

The Parliament realized the grave implications arising out of the pre-natal diagnostic techniques and therefore, intended to regulate its use only for certain medical purposes. The Government realized that the abuse of techniques for determination of sex of the foetus leading to female foeticide is discriminatory against the female sex and also affects the dignity and status of women. Hence, the Pre-natal Diagnostic Techniques (Regulation and Prevention of Misuse), Act, 1994 (PNDT Act) was enacted to curb the indiscriminate act of foetal sex determination. The objective of this Act was to provide for the regulation of the use of pre-natal diagnostic techniques for the purpose of detecting genetic or metabolic disorders or chromosomal abnormalities or certain congenital malformation or sex linked disorders and for the prevention of the misuse of this techniques for the purpose of pre-natal sex determination leading to female foeticide. Section 3 of the PNDT Act provides that no place, including a registered genetic counselling centre or genetic laboratory or genetic clinics, shall be used or caused to be used by any person for conducting pre-natal diagnostic techniques except for the purposes specified under this Act. Medical practitioners, gynaecologists and paediatricians cannot conduct pre-natal diagnostic techniques at a place other than one registered under the PNDT Act. The provisions of this Act are mandatory and any violation of the same was punishable as prescribed under the PNDT Act. This landmark legislation evoked a lot of hope among all the stakeholders concerned about saving the girl child.

Despite this Act, a study of the census reports of 1991, 2001 and 2011 proves that the sex ratio has worsened in most parts of India. In 2001, the State Governments and Union Territories were directed by the Supreme Court in Centre for Enquiry into Health and Allied Themes vs Union of India, to supply quarterly reports to a Central Supervisory Board regarding action taken towards the implementation of the PNDT Act. Unfortunately, several states either dragged their feet in furnishing the reports or failed to initiate prompt action as per the guidelines. The PNDT Act for all the intents and purposes proved to be toothless piece of legislation as no significant impact was felt at the grassroot level because of the weak implementation of this Act. Consequently, to make it more effective, the PNDT Act was amended in 2002, and the amended Act came into force in January 2003. The Act has been renamed as the Pre-Conception and Pre-Natal Diagnostic Techniques (Prohibition of Sex Selection) Act, 2002 (The PCPNDT Act).

Pre-Conception and Pre-Natal Diagnostic Techniques (Prohibition of Sex Selection) Act, 2002

The PCPNDT Act provides for the prohibition of sex selection, before and after conception, and regulates the use of pre-natal diagnostic techniques for the purpose of detecting genetic abnormalities or other sex-linked disorders in the foetus. Under the PCPNDT Act, no person shall conduct or allow to be conducted any pre-natal diagnostic techniques including ultrasonography for the purpose of determining the sex of a foetus. The PCPNDT Act prohibits the use of any pre-natal diagnostic procedures and tests except for the purposes specified below (Section 4(2) of the PCPNDT Act):

1. Chromosomal abnormalities,
2. Genetic metabolic diseases,
3. Haemoglobinopathies,
4. Sex-linked genetic diseases,
5. Congenital anomalies, and
6. Any other abnormalities or diseases as may be specified by the Central Supervisory Board

And after specifying any of the conditions as under:

1. Age of the pregnant woman is above 35 years,
2. The pregnant woman has undergone two or more spontaneous abortions or foetal loss,
3. The pregnant woman had been exposed to potentially teratogenic agents such as drugs, radiation, infection or chemicals,

4. The pregnant woman has family history of mental retardation or physical deformities as spasticity or any other genetic disease, and
5. Any other condition as may be specified by the Board.

However, the person conducting ultrasonography on a pregnant woman is required to keep complete record thereof in the clinic, and any deficiency or inaccuracy found would amount to contravention of the provisions of this Act unless the contrary is proved by the person conducting such ultrasonography (Section 4(3) proviso of the PCPNDT Act). There is a prohibition on sale of ultrasound machine, etc., to persons, laboratories, and clinics, etc. not registered under the Act (Section 3B of the PCPNDT Act). Several offences and penalties have been included in this Act. Any medical geneticist, gynaecologist, registered medical practitioner or any person who owns a genetic clinic and contravenes any of the provisions of this Act can be punished with imprisonment for a term which may extend to three years and with fine which may extend to ten thousand rupees, and on any subsequent conviction, with imprisonment which may extend to five years, and with a fine which may extend to fifty thousand rupees (Section 23(1) of the PCPNDT Act). The name of the registered medical practitioner shall be reported and there may be suspension of the registration if the charges are framed by the court, and if convicted, his name may be removed from the register of the Medical Council for a period of five years for the first offence, and permanently for the subsequent offence (Section 23(2) of the PCPNDT Act). Even a person, who seeks the aid of any such genetic clinic for the purpose of sex-selection of the foetus, may be punished for a term of three years and a fine up to fifty thousand rupees for the first offence and for a term of five years and a fine up to one lakh rupees for subsequent offences (Section 23(3) of the Act). Under this Act, even a company or the director, manager, secretary or other officer of the company may be punished, if found guilty of contravening the provisions of this Act, unless it is proved that the offence was committed without the knowledge of such director, manager, secretary, or other officer or that he exercised all due diligence to prevent such an offence (Section 26 (10 of the Act). Every offence under this Act shall be cognizable, non-bailable, and non-compoundable (Section 27 of the Act). Although this enactment is a positive step, the enforcement of this law is weak. The reason for limited effectiveness of the law includes lack of political will to ensure enforcement.

Judicial Response

The Indian judiciary, as the guardian of the rights of people, played a dynamic role to protect the basic human rights of vulnerable sections of society. In 2001, Public Interest Litigation (PIL) was filed in the Supreme Court of India by health activists in *CEHAT vs Union of India*, urging inter alia effective implementation of the PNDT Act. In response to this petition, the Supreme Court issued notices to the central and State Governments to file replies. In this case, the Supreme Court pronounced laudable directions to the Governments to take serious steps to enforce the PNDT Act. Based on the directions of the Supreme Court, the PCPNDT Act of 2002 was enacted plugging the various loopholes of the Act of 1994.

The Gujarat High Court formulated several directions, viz. (a) every pregnant woman must be registered with the District Health Officer concerned within two months of pregnancy with a unique code, (b) the department of health must issue pregnant women a 'Mamta' card without which diagnostic sonography would not be conducted, (c) if a pregnant woman is advised to terminate pregnancy after having conducted an authorized diagnostic sonography, prior permission of the District Health Officer concerned has to be obtained, (d) within ten days after diagnostic sonography is conducted, medical practitioners must fill prescribed forms with detailed information on diagnostic sonography and any treatment/operations without disclosing details protected by patient privacy, and (e) the necessary paperwork as prescribed under the PNDT Rules must be submitted by medical practitioners online, in addition to paper filing. The Department of Health of the Government of Gujarat was asked to widely publicize these measures so that citizens of each district could be well-informed. However, there still exist a few ways by which errant medical practitioners have been able to circumvent the system, particularly with technological developments not known at the time this case was initiated in the Gujarat High Court in 2006 (Tanna, 2012). Taking a strong concern on female foeticide, the Supreme Court not only rejected the bail application of Dr Sudam Munde, accused of killing many foetuses in Beed, but also directed that he apply for bail only after six months (Lewis, 2012).

Conclusion

Despite various laws and judicial directions, the imbalance in the sex ratios in India appear alarming. The impact of legal instruments is inherently limited. They do not by themselves bring changes in attitudes and beliefs and they certainly do not address the deeply felt need for male children within the society. Additionally, the laws always lag behind rapid advances in medical technology. Female foeticide is a result of medical and scientific advancement. It should be controlled scientifically, by developing methods, devising the system in which sex could not be determined before birth. License of the guilty doctors in determining the sex should be cancelled forever. Media should expose such doctors who indulge in such unethical practices. Parents of the girl should be awarded with incentives by the government. Family welfare policies must be framed in such a way that the focus is on the value of the girl child, who should be guaranteed the right to equal education, equal employment and equal inheritance. Since the problem of dowry is the main cause for the evil practice of female foeticide, it should be eradicated effectively. There is an urgent need to alter the demographic composition of India's population and also to tackle this brutal form of violence against girls. People should be made aware of the ill effects of female foeticide and sex selection. Social efforts should be made to counter male-child preference and provide sensitization to gender equality. Sincere efforts are to be taken to make India free of the social evil of female foeticide to stop from being a daughterless society.

References

Bajpai, Asha (2006). *Child Rights in India*, New Delhi: Oxford University Press.

Census of India (1991, 2001, 2011). Government of India, New Delhi.

Centre for Enquiry into Health and Allied Themes and Others vs Union of India, AIR (2001) SC 2007.

Dayal, Vijendra (1999). *Human Rights and Women: Gender Violence and Crime against Women in India*, New Delhi: Ministry of Social Welfare.

Gurung, Madhu (2010). 'These Doctors Deliver Only Boys', *Social Welfare*, 56(11).

Hameed, Syeda (2012). *From Kashmir to Kerala: Addressing the Daughter Deficit*, New Delhi: Ministry of Social Welfare.

Lewis, Clara (2012). http://timesofindia.indiatimes.com/city/mumbai/no-bail-hope.

Maneka Gandhi vs Union of India, AIR (1978) SC 597.

Mehta, Swathi and Kothari, Jayna (2001). 'It's a Girl! Pre-natal Sex Selection and the Law', *Lawyers Collective*, November.

Menon, Sreelatha (2010). 'Mothers Sued, Doctors Go Free', *Social Welfare*, 56(11).

Misra, Preeti (2006). *Concept of Violence against Women, Domestic Violence against Women: Legal Control and Judicial Response*, New Delhi: Deep and Deep.

Population Foundation of India (2006). Government of India, New Delhi.

Prasath, S.J. (2005). 'Right to Life of Foetus', *AIR*, 92, Journal section.

Singh, Om Raj (2012), *Murdering the Girl Child's Right to Life: Female Foeticide and Infanticide*, New Delhi: Ministry of Social Welfare.

Tanna, Kartikeya (2012). 'The Menace of Female Foeticide: Gujarat's Initiatives', *Satyameva Jayate*, Zee Exclusive, 7 May.

The Constitution of India (1950) Article 21.

The Indian Penal Code (1860) Sections 312 to 318.

The Medical Termination of Pregnancy Act, 1976.

The Pre-Conception and Pre-Natal Diagnostic Techniques (Prohibition of Sex Selection) Act, 2002.

The Pre-Natal Diagnostic Techniques (Regulation and Prevention of Misuse) Act, 1994.

V. Krishnan vs G. Rajanalia Madipu Rajan (1994–1) 113 Mad. L.W.89 (D.B.).

2

Feminist Perspective on Maternity Benefits

Disparities in the Law

NEETA KHURANA

Abstract

The paper highlights the disparities in the law relating to the maternity benefits from a feminist perspective. An attempt is also made to focus on such questions as to why does motherhood define a woman's existence? Why is it that a woman is considered special, complete and worthy of respect when she becomes a mother? What about women who are unable to bear children because of various reasons and/or who choose not to have children? Does that make them any less special? Do they not have a right to the kind of benefits that are provided as maternity benefits, insurance covers, understanding atmosphere in the workplace, etc.? Should they not be given a reprieve to manage their emotional state of mind? These women spend more time working while others get benefits. There are laws of the Government of India which grant two year child care leave. What about advancing the same privilege to single working women or women who are married but do not or cannot have children? Such women often face allegations of being barren, lesser women, anti-family, anti-motherhood, aggressive, etc. which is unfair and against the fabric of a civilized society. The discrimination meted out to them needs to be addressed, as not having children is not a sin or a crime that one should be punished for.

Keywords

Motherhood, Existence, Privilege, Workplace, Discrimination.

Introduction

When law defines an individual category it does not necessarily always take into account the social compulsions over it. For a long time the word 'person' did not include within its ambit both the sexes. At stake, in the feminist debate of those days, were the benefits that were pursuant to a state of being. Women were unrecognized as beings or as persons until 1929 and were thus not entitled to any of the benefits forming part of the major laws. The biggest battles of gender inequality ought to be fought in the work domain and these pertain to an identical question of challenged and questionable existence. Broadly speaking, there are two arguments against motherhood. One simply advocated a voluntary childlessness and claims motherhood as a 'baby trap' bringing to an end a self-defined existence. The second, perhaps a more nuanced and recent is to do with the rights of women that accrue only from being a mother. While asking epistemological questions of law, this paper brings to attention how being is simply not enough in a society dominated by male ethos. One has to become to be. In other words, to be a women one has to be a mother.

One of the biggest curses of our times is identity politics. It is a curse not because it is retrograde or because it rewards divisive social engineering but because identities are not monochromatic, rather they are fluid and inalienable at the same time. This means one can be a minority and majority at the same time, for example: A Malayali male is minority in Kerala since the sex ratio in Kerala has more females to male, but if he is a Muslim, then he is minority by virtue of faith too, though he may be a majority when it comes to the national sex ratio. Therefore, the State must find ways and means to incorporate this difference and diversity. Since most of our politics revolves around identities, it is imperative to identify and celebrate difference. There is a tendency in the state apparati of most modern democracies to institutionalize injustice and alienation. This happens because our notion of equality does not celebrate diversity but tries to bargain for a 'unity in diversity'. The Maternity Benefits Act is one such crying example of the state perpetuating and institutionalizing misrecognition.

The task of post-socialist feminist theory is to emancipate differences within differences. Unlike liberal feminism, the post-structural or post-socialist feminists seek to remodel relationship within the oppressed gender. It does not presuppose the classical man/woman, master/servant dyad and goes much beyond it. This paper seeks to address some such similar, invisible yet very real oppressions, the law has arbitrarily imposed and nourished with regards to gender rights in India.

Understanding Inequality from a Gender Perspective

Laws seek to provide solutions to a society of neutrals, if not equals. It could be said, therefore, that there is a certain presumptive identity component in the way law looks at its categories. By securing equality before the law, feminists effectively sanctioned the expulsion of gender from the formal parameters of legal discourse, colluding in the idea that law was a neutral and autonomous space in which sex had no place. History, however, reveals a very different picture, in which law has long been complicit in the construction and maintenance of a gendered social order based on status and hierarchy (Connaghan, 2013).

In recent years, feminist scholars have rested their hopes of achieving gender parity within democratic societies. However, 'democracy' is, today, an intensely contested word (and not just in India) that means different things to different people, even as everyone claims to be for it. Since definitions restrict an idea and democracy is largely an idea, it is good to avoid restricting the understanding of the lived human experience to somebody else's definition or explanation.

Democracy, largely understood and widely publicized, is 'a process of communication across differences', where citizens participate together in discussion and decision-making to determine collectively the conditions of their lives.

Democracy requires three necessary conditions:

1. Social equality,
2. Recognition of difference, and
3. Absence of systemic dominance and subordination.

The concern of this paper is with the first two, as systemic subordination has been vigorously challenged and debated enough. The questions at the heart of radical feminist, like all radical democrats is the relation between equality and difference.

What are the differences that make a difference for a democracy, which differences merit public recognition? And more importantly, which differences should be treated irrelevant to political life and treated instead, as private matters need clarity.

To find a way out of misrecognition of difference, one must ask what is the effect of such misrecognition (for example, how does it matter if a woman who can't conceive is not a beneficiary of maternity benefits?). But the trouble with this line of thought is that the society does not treat oppression as oppression until it is in the broader theme of either equality or recognized difference. It means you are 'oppressed' only if you cannot avail maternity benefits and not if you are incapable of bearing and thereby, cannot avail these benefits. Effectively, the law has misrecognized the alienation that is deeply associated with childlessness. Law being 'an ass', like Shakespeare called, it does not allow subjectivities to claim the fruits of redistribution. But then experience can seldom be objective and, therefore, cosmetic attempts at establishing equality end up creating further alienations. One more problem is that due to their nature, subjectivities need representation and lung power to voice their difference. Thus, constructing a politics of sameness over difference is to be detested with.

Feminist scholar, Young, has offered an answer to this by defining oppression as 'incapacity to describe one's own experience' (Young, 2010). The present difficulties arise from isolating debates of recognition from debates of distribution. Radical democrats are unwilling to tie the Gordian knot between the two. One cannot be adequately addressed in isolation of the other. One must try and link the demands of social recognition with redistribution to bring cultural and social voices in the terrain of democratic equality. The life of the law has not been logic; it has been experience. The felt necessities of the prevalent moral and political theories, intuitions of public policy, avowed or unconscious, even the prejudices which judges share with their fellow-men, have had a good deal more to do than the syllogism in determining the rules by which men should be governed (Holmes, 1881).

Social action cannot have a guaranteed beginning and if at the heart of social action is redistribution then the understanding of equality and difference must take note of not just who has not benefitted from redistribution but also of who are less equal and misrecognized.

Gandhian Idea of Justice

Unlike in the West, India never experienced a full transfer of authority to the sovereign. This is because of the Gandhian notion of Swaraj which made the 'political' subservient to 'self'. In the broader sense, Gandhi speaking of justice referred to a State policy that provided for and facilitated:

1. Antyoday (Rise of the last person), and
2. Sarvoday (Progress for all).

This is precisely why the Constitution of India provided for a 'living wage' over 'minimum wage' He warned that the market driven forces cannot determine values. The argument is larger than just economics. If put to all social action, Gandhi being the anarchist that he was argued that state cannot define an individual's self-worth based upon how the individual may or may not add to society's net worth.

The concept of living wage is much broader than the concept of minimum wage as it talks about frugal comfort and expenses to be made on health, education and risk aversion. Living wage is more than fair wage, which in turn is more than minimum wage. In 1950, the Constituent Assembly opted for living wage and not minimum wage. The notion of living wage has been diluted in the last 60 years. It would be a death sentence to people if the government says it can't pay minimum wage.

One has to evolve a mechanism through which Sarvodaya does not obstruct Antyodaya and vice versa. The maternity benefit regulations seem to be caught in this very imbroglio. Gandhi succeeded because he backed it up with the philosophical fortitude of Satya and Ahimsa. The government seldom realizes how it prepares newer terrains of violence in its every attempt at curbing existing violence. This ill-conceived and myopic act is a testimony to the same.

Conclusion

Reference to values deprives law of its pretense to scientific character. This fetish with objectivity makes law turn a blind eye to unaccounted differences there may exist. Individual rights are paramount and it is the duty of the State to provide platform to every individual to express one's own experience from his or her subjectivities. Moreover, recognition and redistribution must go together. One cannot, therefore, ignore one at the cost of the other. A Pew Research Centre survey found out that 38 per cent Americans think childless mothers are bad for society.

Conforming to dogmatic social pressures based on outdated precedents must be certainly worse though. So a woman may choose to not become a mother. Being born with a uterus can't be controlled but one can control whether or not another life grows in it. Like success, a 'meaningful life' can only be subjectively defined.

Contrary to the very popular and annoying belief, an innate desire to reproduce is not present in every female. This law very dogmatically presupposes that a female is born with a uterus and hence it is natural for her to be a mother.

One can either ask normative descriptive or epistemological questions in conducting any social science research. One hopes to go beyond just explaining and prescribing the modules of gendered equality based upon legal rational. A society of thinking beings, therefore, shall indulge in knowing not just the meaning of being but also its value. Thus, while asking epistemological questions of law this paper brings to attention how being is simply not enough in a society dominated by male ethos. One has to become to be. In other words, to be a women one has to be a mother.

References

Connaghan, Joanne (2013). *Equality in the Feminist Turn to Law: Law and Gender*, UK: Oxford University Press.

Holmes, O.W., Jr. (1881). *The Common Law*, New York: Little Brown and Co.

http://www.pewsocialtrends.org/2010/11/18/the-decline-of-marriage-and-rise-of-new-families/ (Last accessed on 11 November 2014)

Young, Iris Marion (2010). *On Female Body Experience, Throwing Up Like a Girl*, UK: Oxford University Press.

3

Unwritten Customary Law of the Khasis

A Gender Perspective

CHARIS MINE P. KHONGLAH

Abstract

The Khasi Society is a matrilineal society situated in the Khasi and Jaintia Hills of Meghalaya, in the North-Eastern part of India. Together it coexists with another matrilineal society, that of the Garo people in the Garo Hills of Meghalaya. It is a tribal form of society with a clear set of traditional and customary laws though still unwritten in form. Constitutionally the society is classed under the Sixth Schedule to the Constitution of India where the autonomous district councils function as heads of traditional administrative institutions to safeguard the interests, customs and traditions of the people. In the Khasi social and administrative system, there is great struggle to define and redefine these unwritten customary laws to arrive at a system that presents balanced gender relations and roles. This paper highlights the nature of these unwritten customary laws in their socio-political context and the challenge of execution of such unwritten laws in traditional institutions as well as in modern constitutional bodies from a gender perspective. An attempt is also made to discuss the consequential advantages and disadvantages of unwritten customary laws from this perspective.

Keywords

Law, Customary Law, Gender, Clan, Codification

Introduction

The Khasis are a matrilineal community wherein lineage, descent and inheritance are determined along matrilineal lines. Like other tribes in the North-Eastern part of India, different aspects of their life are governed by customary laws which are unwritten in form, nor are present in any written form or format with any modern or traditional institution. These customary laws are adhered to by the members of the society. Within the society, men and women play or have different gender roles presented to them by these unwritten customary laws. While the unwritten nature of these customary laws present both advantages as well as disadvantages in relation to settlement of issues within the society, their codification is the need of the hour.

By looking at law from a legal perspective, 'law' refers to a set of public and enforceable rules that apply throughout a political community. It can be distinguished from other social rules on four grounds. First, as a law is made by the government and thus reflects the 'will of the State', it takes precedence over all other norms and social rules. Second, a law is compulsory; citizens are not allowed to choose which laws to obey and which to ignore, because a law is backed up by a system of coercion and punishment. Third, a law consists in published and recognized rules that have been enacted through a formal, usually public, legislative process. Fourth, a law is generally recognized as binding upon those to whom it applies; a law thus embodies moral claims, implying legal rules should be obeyed (Heywood, 2005). Hence, we can draw four concepts: state, coercion, legislation, obedience. It is clear, therefore, that the power to enforce any law emanates from the State. As Laski puts it, in explaining Austin's view, that law is simply the will of the sovereign (Laski, 2010). In a technical sense, customary law can, thus, be defined as a body or a set of rules and functions which a community practices and recognizes. As Becker defined, it is an established system of immemorial rules which had evolved from the way of life and natural wants of the people, the general context of which was a matter of common knowledge, coupled with precedents applying to special cases until forgotten, or until they became part of immemorial rules (Becker, 1989).

It is comparatively much easier, perhaps, to identify the sovereign that issues decrees or laws when aspect of such nature are discussed in the context of a modern civil society with a well-documented administrative machinery than when doing so in the context of a rudimentary form of society, such as a tribal society, as there is no such sovereign set as formally supported by the strength of a codified form of laws or decrees. Such unwritten customary laws or decrees govern the administrative as well as social life of the Khasis. The Khasi people, as a community, function under the guidance of these unwritten laws that shape the meaning of entire existence. The broadly cover traditions that include identity, property, family relations and public administration. In the modern context, though written materials are available on such laws to a certain extent, and works such as that of Cantlie, *Notes on Khasi Law,* have been used even in courts to reference customary laws in written record, they are not to be treated as exhaustive nor ever have been considered to be sufficient to have the strength of a legislated body of law in the modern administrative sense.

Gender is a very important notion when examining a society. Sex refers to biological characteristics, gender refers to social or cultural characteristics and that sociologists agree that women and men fit their gender roles largely because they are socialized to do so. Gender relations as a term can be used to refer to relations of power between women and men which are revealed in a range of practices, ideas and representations, including division of labour roles, and so on (Agarwal, 1997). Gender relations in the Khasi context, as in relation to most societies, can be viewed from a sociological and/or feminist standpoint, as well as from a political standpoint. It is almost a safe and given assumption today that the status of women in any part of the world is lower than that of men in almost all aspects of life. It is to be noted, however, that while gender conflict today has become a common problem world over, the form and extent of gender conflict varies from one society to another. As in India there are caste society and tribal society, the gender issues in both these societies are found at different levels (Banu). Compared to other tribal women in India, the Khasi women seem to be at a much better position as she can inherit property (Mann, 1987), but are bereft of real decision-making power in relation to that property and cannot play any role in the traditional and more grassroot administrative set-ups. Therefore, Nongbri writes that while it is understandable that many writers have deemed the Khasi as matriarchal, it is interesting to ask a Khasi whether the fact that women are central to the family and clan and have rights over property mean that they are matriarchal or conferred with superior powers, and went on to state that a close examination of the cultural notion of women and men, and the division of gender roles shows that the characterization of the Khasi as matriarchal is misleading, and more succinctly went further on to state that on the contrary, there are strong social pointers which show that the women are considered inferior to men (Kelkar et al., 2006). Moreover, some writers like Chacko went to the extent of stating that matrilinealism has, over a period of time, not done good not only to a man but also to a woman as well (Chacko, 2003). As such, the relation of gender roles and customary law in the Khasi society is an interesting aspect as it covers a unique feature of the socio-political structure of the society and underlines the fact that it is in relation to this very aspect that the society struggles the most in achieving its aim to function at a higher level.

The Unwritten Khasi Customary Laws and Gender Relations

Administration and Gender

Without indicating details, it is to be stated that the Khasis have many levels of administration. The lowest level is at the level of the village council. The *myntri* is the head of a village. The second and higher level is the *raid*, formed by a group of villages. The *lyngdoh* or the *basan* is the head of a *raid*. The third and still higher level of administration is the *kher* or *elaka*, the *sirdar*ship, and the *wahadar*ship, formed by a number of *raids* coming together under one administration of a *daloi*, a *sirdar*, or a *wahadar*, respectively. The highest level of administration is the *hima* or the traditional autonomous state formed by the coming together of many *elakas* and *raids* under one administration headed by the *syiem* (Bareh, 1985). It is to be noted that at every level, representation and participation in all councils is primarily the role of men. And, it is most certainly unheard of for a woman to have ever been assigned such roles, for ideologically women have always been seen as inferior to men and mainly reproducers (Nongbri, 2003); and neither has a woman any right to elect candidates to these posts (Chhakchhuak, 2002). And, in line with matrilineal principles, succession to power is always from a man to his maternal nephew and not to his son in case of higher offices such as that of the *syiem*.

Under the Constitution of India, the Khasis are governed under the Sixth Schedule to the Constitution of India, and the population falls under five districts, namely, the East Khasi Hills District, West Khasi Hills District, Ri-Bhoi District, East Jaintia Hills District and West Jaintia Hills District. Under such an administrative set-up, the district council functions as the head of traditional institutions that governs both as a legislative body and a tribunal head while the traditional heads today remain only as titular heads with no real administrative or legal authority (Gassah, 2002; Chattopadhyay, 2002), although some recent movements today, primarily the Ka Dorbar Ki Khlieh Nongsynshar Ka Ri Hynniewtrep, move for revival of administrative powers of traditional heads as per the Constitution. Nevertheless, the state legislature functions as the highest ruling authority in the present administrative system. Thus far, even in the modern administrative set-ups where women are given free access to participate and contest for elections, very less active participation has been seen so far. For example, in the Khasi Hills Autonomous District Council today, only three female representatives are there as against 29 male representatives (MDCs 2014). Also in the state legislative assembly, only three female representatives are present as against 57 male representatives in the entire state (MLA Profiles). The old saying is still heavily impressed on the Khasi psyche that 'when the hen crows, the world will come to an end, 'which indicates an axiom of understanding that a woman is to be silent in public affairs.

Corresponding to judicial authority, in the pre-British era, legal cases can be settled under traditional institutions like *ka sad ka sunon*, or the *dorbar hima*. Even the lowest council, the village council or *durbar shnong,* functions as a jury which adjudicates civil and criminal cases and the *syiem*, *lyngdoh*, *sardar*, *wahadar*, *basan* or headman as the judge. Similarly, higher councils, such as the *raid durbar* and *durbar hima* or state *durbar,* function as elected democratic bodies where the democratic principle is strictly followed, and are legislative, administrative, judicial or legal bodies in a very strictly traditional sense. All state matters are transacted after full deliberations on in open *durbar*. Every *durbar* is convened with prior announcement or proclamation and invitation to the people (Lyngdoh, 2004). *Durbars* at every level are capable of exacting punishment according to traditional practice. These punishments range from clubbing to death, imprisonment and fine, capital punishment to exile (Gurdon, 1977). Decision at every level is based on customary laws.

Even today, under the new forms of administration, courts have to rely heavily on customary laws which are largely unwritten. Laws that govern land and land use, family and family relations, religious rites and duties and state laws are derived from tradition. In explaining the sources of Khasi law, A.S. Khongphai writes, 'As the main source of Khasi law is custom, the duty of European Judges, formerly, the Deputy Commissioners, the Commissioners and the Governors were to inquire into the custom which is ancient, certain, reasonable, continuous, invariable and uniform' (Khongphai, 2003). Though many judgements have been passed based on court rulings as regards precedent cases, in cases where the court rulings of certain cases contradict a prevalent custom in practice, if challenged, the custom will prevail as precedent, even in cases ruled by higher courts like the High Courts or the Supreme Court.

Under the United Khasi Jaintia Hills Autonomous District (Administration of Justice) Rules 1953, there were three classes of courts for the trial of suits and cases between the parties all of whom belong to the scheduled tribes: (a) Village courts composed of criminal cases under purview of tribal laws and customs and offences of a petty nature, (b) Subordinate District Council Courts and Additional Subordinate District Council Courts introduced in the middle-tier and is presided by a judicial officer designated as magistrate and appointed by the executive committee with the governor's approval. The courts of the *syiems, lyngdohs, wahadars* or *sirdars* fall in this category, (c) District Council Court consisting of one or more judicial officers designated as 'judge' or 'judges', appointed by the executive committee with the approval of the Governor. The procedure of District Council Courts at various grades shall, in criminal cases, be 'in the spirit of the code of criminal procedure', and in civil cases, the court 'shall be guided by the spirit but not be bound by the letter' of the Code of Civil Procedure, 1908 in all matters not covered by recognized customary laws or usages of the district (Giri, 1998). As an underlining statement, it should be stated that in cases where the court rulings of certain cases contradict a prevalent custom in practice, if challenged, the custom will prevail as precedent, even in cases ruled by higher courts like the high courts or the Supreme Court.

Therefore, two underlying factors emerge from the above:

1. That the Khasis have their own administrative and legal procedures that are totally in line with the matrilineal system, and that women play most certainly no role in the traditional administration and in modern administrative set-ups their participation is still very less.
2. The modern administrative set-up is functioning alongside traditional institutions and that courts have to rely heavily on customary laws which are largely unwritten.

Identity and Gender

The identity of a Khasi is strictly governed by tradition. Cantlie writes, 'He is of the clan in life and in death' (Cantlie, 2009). Khongphai observes that Khasis reckon their *jait* from the mother and cannot take the *jait* of the father, and thus a son belongs to the mother, the mother to her mother, back to the primeval ancestress of the *jait*, known as *Ka Iawbei* or common ancestress (Khongphai, 2003), and further stated that there cannot be any Khasi without a *jait* and that *jait* is from the mother's clan and not from his father. 'As to who is a Khasi to which Khasi law applies, the non-controversial definition as stated before, is a person born of a Khasi mother' (Khongphai, 2003). Men cannot propagate the clan name. A mother who has only sons is considered to be *duh jait* or without descendants, especially if she is the only daughter with no other female siblings to propagate the family name, in which case, the family can adopt a female relative or clan member to serve as a carrier of family clan name called the *rap-iing*. In case of a Khasi father and a non-Khasi mother, the mother has to adopt a new clan name usually through the customary rite called *tang jait* whereby a new Khasi *kur* or *jait* is ordained. To this effect, the Khasi Lineage Act formed in 1997, encapsulates the above-mentioned aspects and elaborates further on the details of Khasi identity directly to be in line with the matrilineal system (*The Gazette of Meghalaya*, 25 February 2005). Consequently, women have a very high status as custodians of clan name or family name.

Nevertheless, therein lies one of the main causes of gender conflict in the contemporary Khasi society wherein men challenge this role of women and move to change the system altogether. With the changing social scenarios of urban settlement, more nuclear families coming up, and modern influences of lifestyle, there have been deviations from the matrilineal system, where there are some individual men who practice a patrilineal system of their own choice by registering their offspring under their clan name or, in certain rare cases, new clan name formed by their own choice. Some very active organizations such as the Syngkhong Rympei Thymmai were formed by association of men who wish to abolish the Khasi matrilineal system and are most critical of the above Act (Kelkar et al., 2006). Nevertheless, acceptance of such radical change in the society is at its nascent stage and has not yet reached a level of success as expected. In spite of this, the district councils are on a regular revision and supervision of such progress in society.

As another point of conflict, though matriliny places Khasi women at a higher plane than their counterparts in other societies, they are not isolated from atrocities and violence against them within the society, where male dominance is manifested in heinous acts of abuse and crime against women. From 2001 to 2013, for example, cases of rape have risen from 23 to 183 cases, kidnapping and abduction of women and girls from 11 to 33, molestation from 25 to 98, cruelty by husband or relatives from four to 23 (http://meghpol.nic.in). Dr Biloris Lyndem, a women's rights activist and a well-known educationist remarked that rural life is marked by poverty and alcoholism which has a fallout on women in the form of domestic violence and deserted wives and children, and what is worse is the complete silence around these issues, since women are ashamed to speak out (Chhakchhuak, 2002). Some writers have called this aspect within the Khasi context as the 'myth of the powerful matrilineal women', and about which some individuals have voiced their concern. Assistant President of the International Fund for Agriculture Development (IFAD) 2002–06, Phrang Roy, while quoting an IFAD study, says that the Meghalayan matrilineal societies are deteriorating the fastest; and added succinctly that though men here say that matrilineal society is negatively affecting the man's position, 'women are losing out faster' and warns that the state has to wake up to urgently address the special developmental needs of women in this peculiar situation (Chhakchhuak, 2002).

Three aspects emerge from this point:

1. That women play an important role in the Khasi society as custodian of a clan name,
2. That men feel deprived of their status and role in the family especially under changing social scenarios, and that there is an active attempt or movement of men to pressure for change of the matriliny, and

3. That higher status of women is only apparent as crime against women is on the rise in the society.

Distribution of Property and Gender

There are two main forms of property, ancestral (*nongtymmen*) and self-acquired (*nongkhynraw*). As land is one of the main aspects of property in the society, let us take as example what is the customary practice in relation to distribution and ownership of land. As original clans settled in certain regions of the land, they lay claim over vast stretches of land in that region. Such land is administered under ownership of original families of the clan settling in that region. As these families multiply, the land gets divided according to custom. Cantlie writes that division of property is more frequent than continuance in joint possession. A large area may be held by a clan, but it is divided into separate portions held by families. These portions are again sub-divided into holdings of stocks within the family. The mother divides her land among her daughters, usually on their marriage, reserving a larger share for ka *khadduh*. The older daughters hold these shares as property entirely separated from those of the rest of the family and without any control by ka *khadduh*. There is no obligation upon the mother to divide her property in equal shares among her daughters. Ka *khadduh*, who is given the largest share on account of religious and family duties, takes as custodian. What follows from this is the difficulty of keeping family and clan land undivided when nearness to a town makes it of value for sale or lease. Cantlie very remarkably noted that in such cases, ka *khadduh* and the managers of the branch of ka *khadduh* may claim that the profits from such land should go to ka *khadduh* and her branch, but the other branches do not admit this claim and demand a division of the profits or rental. Some families have made written agreements for the purpose of controlling such disputes, but without entire success. A right to partition, which is the remedy for disputes in a Hindu Joint Family, does not exist. Among the Khasis, the council of the family ought to settle such matters. This is done according to what seems just and expedient in the circumstances. The settlement in each case cannot and should not be taken as an exact guideline for other cases (Cantlie, 2009). In short, it can be inferred that as a general custom, inheritance of ancestral property is divided among daughters with the largest share for the last daughter as the custodian of ancestral property and religious rites and duties, and that sons do not inherit ancestral property, with an exception or variation whereby among the war sub-tribe, distribution is of equal portions to all the offspring including the male offspring and the *khadduh*, though she still serves as custodian of the ancestral property (Bareh, 1985). Even in today's context, where majority of the Khasis have converted to Christianity, the *khadduh*, in many families, though she no longer has to fulfil traditional religious rites and duties as in the traditional system, is still considered as custodian of ancestral property. However, management of ancestral property and decision-making power over such property is under the authority of the maternal uncle of the family as well as the brothers, as the last daughter does not have full autonomy over such property. O.D.V. Ladia, a prominent lawyer, explains that women are entrusted with enormous rights over property and important duties in performing family rites, but the actual ownership is not theirs; that, for instance, in contrast to men, women do not have the right to dispose of property on their own (Chhakchhuak, 2002). With this custom followed uniformly, Cantlie, in that period of time, bluntly stated that there is no power to make a will, and the power to make wills has never been recognized (Cantlie, 2009).

Self-acquired property, on the other hand, can be distributed among the offspring according to parent's wish and is not under strict customary laws, though there are some cases where the clan members of a man may claim back his self-acquired property from the wife, should the couple be barren (Cantlie, 2009).

It is here that the point of gender conflict arises whereby in general, men have raised concern in relation to inheritance. In general, men are seen as outside the fold for inheritance, especially of ancestral property, as whatever would belong to them might become property of another family with another clan name. It must be said that today, however, with the many changes that have occurred in the Khasi society, that have brought about changes from rural to urban, clan-based to family-based, agricultural to tertiary occupations, a will, at least in relation to self-acquired property is possible to a very large extent. But there is a thin line that divides ancestral and self-acquired property, as the latter is many a times is distributed in the manner of ancestral property whereby the last daughter provisioned with the largest share while sons are not considered for inheritance. Many groups, the most prominent being the Maitshaphrang Movement, have been fighting under this very same banner, for passing of a Bill for Equitable Distribution of Self-Acquired Property, and for implementation of the same.

There are at least two points that can be drawn from the above:

1. That distribution of property is along the lines of matriliny, and that importance of clan name or family name dictates the customary laws of inheritance both in traditional Khasi as well as in Christian families, but that women do not have full autonomy over ancestral property which is under authority of male members of the family.
2. That distribution of property is one of the main points of contention of contemporary movements by men who fight for equitable distribution of self-acquired property at least to both sons and daughters, because men feel deprived of opportunity and status in the family.

Conjugal Relations and Gender

The Khasis are a group of exogamous clans, i.e. they do not inter-marry within the same clan or *kur*. Khongphai writes, 'No marriage is valid if made between persons of the same *jait*' (Khongphai, 2003). Even in the case of Christians, they still adhere to the custom. Prohibited degrees of relationship are as follows: (a) if she is the daughter of his father's brother or brothers (*shipara kha*), (b) if she is the mother or sisters of his father (*sang kha*), (c) if she is the wife of his maternal uncle or uncles, (e) if she is his mother-in-law of her sisters, (g) if she is the sister of his living divorced wife (Khongphai, 2003). There are *jaits* (clans), although different in name but descendants from the common ancestress, for example the Diengdoh, Laloo, Lamin are prohibited from inter-marriage as the branches of the clan descended from the common ancestress. All Khasis, Christians as well as traditional Khasis, adhere to these customary unwritten laws very strictly, and deviation from these is considered a grave 'taboo' or *sang* in the most religious sense of the word. A person who commits *sang* is ostracized or even outcast by society and family if not by the church. Rarely, however, has the general population turned to full-fledged Hinduism, though a significant few have converted to Islam and other religions, nor follow other personal laws. As pointed in the Khasi Lineage Act mentioned above, should they adopt personal laws of other religions or other communities, they are no longer considered Khasis by definition.

Khasi traditional marriage has not been registered under any law. As such, traditional Khasi marriage does not have the strength of registered marriage as for Christians under the District Council adopted Christian Marriage Act, 1872 (Act XV of 1872) in the form of what is known as the United Khasi-Jaintia Hills District (Christian Marriage Act, 1954) (Khongphai, 2003) nor of the District Council adopted Special Marriage Act.

Nevertheless, among both Christians and traditional Khasis, cohabitation is more common than marriage through a registered ceremony. Consequently, many children are born out of wedlock and sometimes fatherless (Nongbri, 2003). Divorce becomes so much easier to obtain though it is frowned upon by the members of the society in general. The traditional method of divorce called *pyllait san shyieng* or, loosely translated, divorce by five cowries is by way of exchanging cowries or money in the presence of a witness. A wife once divorced from her husband cannot claim right for maintenance. O.D.V. Ladia, a prominent lawyer from Shillong, commented that women cannot claim maintenance if deserted by their husbands, as they do not have this right under matrilineal customary practices (Chhakchhuak, 2002). When it comes to modern or certified forms of marriage, however, divorce is settled in court. The main grounds for divorce are: (a) barrenness, (b) failure to live together happily due to dissolute habits or ill-treatment, (c) adultery, (d) lunacy, (e) incurable disease and unsound mind, (f) sodomy or bestiality, (g) desertion without cause and imprisonment for a period not less than a year (Khongphai, 2003). Adopted acts under the District Council such as the Indian Divorce Act and the Special Marriage Act, 1954 (Act No. XLIII of 1954) do include such provisions. But very few among Khasis would actually file for divorce and obtain rightful maintenance of children, as in the first place cohabitation is more common than registered marriage.

As such, the Meghalaya Assembly passed the Act in September 2012 to provide for compulsory registration of marriages in the state where it is mandatory for married men and married women to 'compulsorily' furnish marriage certificates for all 'official' purposes. However, the act is yet to be implemented with rules, and for which delay organizations such as the Maitshaphrang Movement have threatened an indefinite fast as on 20 November 2014 (*The Telegraph*, 8 August 2014). Christian organizations, such as the Khasi Jaintia Presbyterian Assembly, however, are against implementation as they feel there is no need as the society is matrilineal and children are the responsibility of the mother in case of divorce in any case. Yet, Rev. N.S. Phawa, the Senior Administrative Secretary, inadvertently admitted that though the ideology of a providing husband is very much part of the Khasi ethos, only a few men find it necessary to provide for their children once the marriage/union with the wife or children's mother is terminated. The customary law, too, is conveniently silent on this. Hence, there is no compulsion for the husband/father to provide for the children when he is estranged from the wife. Rev. Phawa claimed that it was a known fact that matriliny provides ample scope for errant husbands to shirk their responsibilities towards their wives and children even during the course of marriage (Clergyman questions marriage registration paras 2 to 11)

The following points can be drawn from the above:

1. That Khasi traditional marriage is not registered under any law, unlike for Christian and Civil marriage,
2. That if converted to any particular religion, following personal laws of any other community, one is no longer considered Khasi by definition,
3. That cohabitation is prevalent and that divorce is relatively very easy to implement in the traditional custom, and responsibility for maintenance of wife and children is not binding upon a man, and
4. That there is a move to implement the Compulsory Registration of Marriage Act, 2012, though opposed by the church.

Advantages and Disadvantages of Codification

In quoting Wharton's Law Lenicor, Mahanta and Wahlang wrote, 'Codification means the collection of all the principles of any system of law into one body after the manner of Codex justiniances and other codes' (Mahanta and Wahlang, 2001). The strength of the Khasi tradition and customs lies in the well-defined unwritten traditional laws and practices at every level of the society. That these customs have prevailed the test of time is an important factor. The Khasis, as a society, having had no written script of their own in the past also had no written records. With the coming of the British, written language of the Khasis is made possible through the Roman script with Sohra dialect as the standard. As mentioned above, till date, there have been only written materials that attempt to put into record customary laws. The power to legislate on such laws is still a distant goal.

Some of the advantages and disadvantages of codification are mentioned as follows:

Advantages

Many writers such as Chakrawarty feel that codification is urgently required to be carried out both in the private laws as well as in the public laws. Areas in private laws would include matters like marriage, divorce, maintenance, adoption, guardianship, inheritance to property, so on and so forth. Further, while codifying laws on these subjects, the guiding principles should be equality before law and equal treatment by the laws. Thus, while codifying the laws pertaining to inheritance, the concept of equal rights to inheritance of both the male and the female heirs must be introduced. Further, the idea of related Central Acts must also be accordingly altered in their applicability to the state. As far as public law is concerned, the laws pertaining to socio-political organizations must be codified, and in doing so, the guiding principles should be introducing certainty, serving the welfare of the people, providing for equal representation, and adult franchise. Thus, the age-old tribal institutions can be retained with that much qualification. Another area of public law requiring urgent codification is the law pertaining to land, its settlement, cadastral survey, registration, and produces of land including mines and forests. He also suggests that the basic prerequisite for bringing about codification of laws is just the political will to do justice. The leaders and the bureaucrats must have the intent to make sure that every person gets justice, and the desire to put in little efforts for that purpose .... To ensure that the codifications do not come from the top only, views and suggestions from the general public can be invited and also given serious consideration. At the same time, the pressure created by reactionary forces must be firmly resisted (Chakrawarty, 1999).

Suggestions for codification made by S.P. Mahanta and Mona Wahlang are:

1. In relation to property, equal distribution for man and woman in the family is to be considered,
2. Taking care of a widow by considering her losing deceased husband's property,
3. Women should be able to participate in Khasi traditional councils,
4. Some legislative enactments and/or judicial pronouncements for dangerous prevailing superstitious beliefs and practices, and
5. To debate whether traditional Khasis or the converted members benefit the most from the Scheduled Tribe status under the Constitution of India (Mahanta and Wahlang, 2001).

Disadvantages

Nevertheless, there are some writers who are of the opinion that codification will bring about far more harm than good to the tribal society. Writers like Nandita Haskar are of the opinion that codification of tribal laws will only enhance the power of the State over indigenous people and impose a totally alien legal system on them. Flavia stated that while the strength of customary law is that it adapts to the changing needs of a society but that it is wrong to assume that customary laws have existed unchanged from time immemorial, without any state intervention (Agnes, 2011).

Conclusion

Over and above, it can be stated, therefore, that, from a gender perspective, codification of customary laws in the Khasi society is to be given preference as, though it will empower the state to a large extent, it can be for a channelized purpose for the good of the majority. On hindsight, if advantages are to be mentioned in relation to the non-codified nature of the Khasi customary laws, it is only that the customary laws have so far been strong in the practice of the people. The traditions of the Khasis have proven to be strong in basic philosophy and consistent in logic which can be read from their customs and traditions, their folklore and festivals, their culture and religion, their manners and ways of life. However, it must be also said that if they remain non-codified in all their forms and variants, when in contact with other influences from other cultures, there is a greater chance that they might not stand the test of time. Moreover, if unwritten, there is greater chance of customary laws not being recognized as a legitimate form of practice in the long run. Codification will also lead to a smoother coordination of the traditional and the modern forms of administration and governance, as well as family laws. It will avoid foreseen and unforeseen strain on members of the community that will arise from probable and conflicting interpretations of customary laws. Traditional forms of administration, family and personal laws, gender relations, distribution of property and various other aspects, in case of codification, will get defined in a clear and thorough manner. Any interpretation or misinterpretation at individual and personal level will be checked for smooth functioning of society. And it is required with time to come up with formal written forms of the customary laws to engage society in a more positive manner for positive modifications and actions on customary laws. Such positive engagement will raise the level of the present tribal society closer still to a better form of civil society.

To outline some of the key areas for codification where it will help streamline roles and functions of both the genders, male and female, within the system, the following are some of the points for consideration:

1. In relation to administration, there is a need to incorporate women into the realm through methods of reform within the traditional councils. There is also a need to encourage more active participation of women representatives in state legislature, and at the district administrative levels, and movements and organizations at every level need to place this concern as priority on their agenda. To reiterate (Chakarwarty, 1999), codification of laws pertaining to socio-political organizations is a must, keeping in mind the welfare of the people, equal representation, and adult franchise.
2. In relation to identity and status, the concerns of both men and women need to be taken into consideration. As men feel deprived of role in the family as custodians of family name, their diminishing role and authority as maternal uncle in their ancestral home as well as their not-yet-defined role as father in their conjugal family, there is a need to address this issue primarily in the light of balanced share of roles in the society as a whole. On the other hand, the problems faced by women in the form of domestic violence and crime against women which are on the rise in the given matrilineal society, need to be addressed primarily in the light of the knowledge that matriliny is perfectly explicable on the absurd idea that it should have anything to do with social power or authority of women (Arnfred, 2011). There should also be a thorough and informed method of registration of marriage and divorce, with customary laws taken into consideration but improved to fit the needs and concerns of both men and women.

3. When it comes to property and inheritance, there needs to be a clear distinction between ancestral and self-acquired property and a clear outline of the role and status of sons, daughters, and the *khadduh* vis-à-vis factors of change in the society in relation to family structure, religious affiliations, gender sensitivity issues that have arisen. Especially in relation to self-acquired property, as there has been active movement towards legislation of equitable distribution of self-acquire property, there should be an accelerated move towards passing and implementation of the same. In rural families, there is not much pressure to change the system in a significant manner while in some families that have been urban-based, and/or that have changed religious adherence, there is some tendency to change distribution of property and not to concentrate property on daughters or the *khadduh* only. However, in general, it is safe to say that families still adhere to the sentiment of the tradition where they give sole importance to daughters or the *khadduh* as the ones who are responsible for taking care of ancestral property and/or self-acquired property of the parents, and in many cases understood heirs, but not the sons as they do not perpetuate the clan name. Therefore, proper codification and legislation of the law in relation to distribution of property is a must and needs to be in the light of an unbiased importance of male and female members in the family, and not to be based on clan identity alone.

It is appropriate to quote an example from the Land Reforms Commission, based on memoranda received from various citizens, where it is stated that there appears to be general agreement for codification of the land system in the light of present-day needs, demands and circumstances based, of course, on the foundations of the old, found good and true. In its recommendations, the Land Reforms Commission stated that in the course of their enquiry the Commission has been impressed by what appears to be the ambivalent attitude of an ordinary Khasi towards his customs. While on the one hand his immediate reaction to a proposal to any change is one of antagonism of varying degree, ranging from a voluble protest to a mere shrug of the shoulders, on the other hand, he feels, at the same time, that it is detrimental to his interests and growth to remain static or stagnant. The conservative side of his nature takes a no-change attitude, or if there must be a need for a change, it should be slow, while the progressive side of his nature takes a move-with-the-times attitude. Yet, through his whole being, there runs his laissez-faire philosophy of life, to let things be; time will take care of everything (Report of the Land Reforms Commission for Khasi Hills, 2012: 46). There must be a strong initiative on the part of every citizen to work out this positive change in the society where custom and progress go hand in hand.

References

'Activist Warns of Fast over Marriage Act', *The Telegraph*, 8 August 2014, http://www.telegraphindia.com/1140808/jsp/northeast/story_18697357.jsp#.vg-rm2czd7c.

Agarwal, Bina (1997). 'Bargaining and Gender Relation: Within and Beyond the Household', *Feminist Economics*, 3(1): 1–51.

Agnes, Flavia (2011). *Family Law*, Vol. 1, New Delhi: Oxford University Press.

Arnfred, Signe (2011). *Sexuality and Gender Politics in Mozambique: Rethinking Gender in Africa*, UK: James Currey, http://books.google.co.in/books.

Bareh, Hamlet (1985). *The History and Culture of the Khasi People*, Guwahati: Spectrum Publications.

Becker, J.C. (1989). *Seymour's Customary in Southern Africa*, South Africa: Juta and Company.

Cantlie, Keith (2009). *Notes on Khasi Law*, Shillong: Chapala Publishing House.

Chacko, Elizabeth (2003). 'Marriage, Development and the Status of Women in Kerala, India', *Gender and Development*, 11(2), http://books.google.co.in.

Chakrawarty, Subhash (1999). 'Application of Customary Laws and Prospects of its Codification in Today's Meghalaya', in Jeuti Barooah (ed.), *Administration of Justice in Meghalaya*, Guwahati: The Law Research Institute.

Chattopadhyay, S.K. (2002). *Tribal Institutions of Meghalaya*, Guwahati: Spectrum Publications.

Chhakchhuak, Linda (2002). 'The Myth of Matriliny: Empowerment Still Eludes Meghalaya's Women', *India Together*, Shillong, April (WFS), http://indiatogether.org/women/articles/matriliny.htm#sthash.zghgjlt0.dpuf

Gassah, L.S. (2002). *Traditional Institutions of Meghalaya: A Study of Doloi and His Administration*, New Delhi: Regency Publications.

Giri, Helen (1998). *Khasis under British Rule (1824–1947)*, Shillong: Akashi Book Depot.

Gurdon, P.R.T. (1977). *The Khasis*, New Delhi: Cosmo Publications.

Heywood, Andrew (2005). *Key Concepts in Politics*, Houndmills: Palgrave Macmillan.

'Incidences of Crime against Women during the Years 2001 to 2013', http://meghpol.nic.in/crime/crime_women_2001-2013.pdf.

Kelkar, Gobind, Dev Nathan, Rewati and Gupta, Swati Sain (2006). *Gender, Identity and Development*, New Delhi: Institute for Human Development.

Khongphai, A.S. (2003). *Principles of Khasi Law*, Shillong: Khasi Jaintia Press.

Laski, Harold J. (2010). *The Grammar of Politics*, New Delhi: Anamika Publishers and Distributors (P) Ltd.

Lyngdoh, R.S. (2004). *Chronicles of an Impossible Election*, New Delhi: Penguin Books.

Mahanta, S.P. and Wahlang, Mona (2001). 'The Application of Customary Laws and Codification', in Jeuti Barooah (ed.), *Administration of Justice in Meghalaya*, Guwahati: The Law Research Institute.

Mann, K. (1987). *Tribal Women in a Changing Society*, New Delhi: Mittal Publications.

MDCs 2014, http://khadc.nic.in/mdcs%202014.htm

MLA Profiles, http://meghalaya.gov.in:8080/megportal/government/mlas?page=1

Moniti, Chakravarthy-Kaul (1999). 'Common Lands and Customary Law: Institutional Change in North Eastern India over the Past Two Centuries', http://lccn.loc.gov/96902125.

Nongbri, Tiplut (2003). *Development, Ethnicity and Gender: Select Essays on Tribes in India*, Jaipur: Rawat Publications.

Oxford Dictionary and Thesaurus (2001).

Report of the Land Reforms Commission for Khasi Hills (2012).

The Gazette of Meghalaya, No. 22, 25 February 2005, http://khadc.nic.in/acts_rules_regulations%20_n%20_bills/acts%20n%20rules-arranged/khasi%20lineage%20act,pdf.

The KHADC (Khasi Social Custom of Lineage) Act, 1997, http://www.khadc.nic.in

The Law Research Institute, Eastern Region, Guahati High Court, 2001.

4

The Implementation of Maria da Penha Law in Brazil

The Courts' Perspective

ISADORA VIER MACHADO

Abstract

A law on the prevention of domestic and intra-family violence against women is in force in Brazil since August 2006. The Maria da Penha Law is foregrounded on gender perspective and its implementation has been placed within a scenario featuring the deepening of policies, agreements and campaigns to guarantee its highest efficaciousness. There were difficulties in its execution especially when flexibility to the juridical canon is required due to the different types of intervention (mainly psycho-social) suggested by this law. It is actually founded within a conflict dimension (between the genders), a theme which has been rarely discussed in the juridical milieu. The paper highlights the preliminary results of research on the systematization of the main critiques towards the Brazilian Courts within the working of the law. It also analyses the manner in which the principal controversies have been decided and the manner they have embodied the analytic category of gender to judge them. The paper starts with a review of the literature on Law, Sociology and Anthropology. The decisions available in the Brazilian Courts' websites were collected and analysed with the qualitative perspective and inductive method focussing on the manner in which the judges used gender to restrict or widen females' protection web. An attempt was also made to contribute towards the process of the critical evaluation of the Maria da Penha Law in Brazil and problematize the place of the Law's executors in facing violence against women.

Keywords

Maria da Penha Law; Gender; Brazilian Courts

Introduction

This paper is a preliminary analysis of the research work specifically concerned with a survey on the positions taken by Brazilian Courts on the issue of *gender*, particularly with regard to one of the most important gender laws in Brazil – The *Maria da Penha Law*. A set of decisions by the Court of Justice of the state of Paraná (south of Brazil) was analysed to investigate how the courts defined *gender*, within the decision process on the main controversies related to the implementation of the above-mentioned law.

The Context

Brazil has 27 state courts. In this context, it is highly significant that the state of Paraná ranks third in the number of murders of women in Brazil in 2012 (SENADO FEDERAL 524). Against this background, this paper aims to analyse the Court of Justice of the state of Paraná. This study investigates court decisions after the promulgation of Law 11.340/2006 (known in Brazil as Maria da Penha Law) upto 2014. The decisions may be accessed free on the internet (www.tjpr.jus.br) by consulting keywords, year or name of the judge. Search criteria employed were the terms *Law+Maria+Penha+Gender*, and only decisions comprising these terms were chosen. In all, 197 decisions were accessed but only 30 comprised the four terms mentioned above.

It should be underscored that Brazil already has a tradition in civil law. Law is the main source for the establishment, modification or extinction of rights in this country. However, jurisprudence had a secondary function and produces deep changes in the way the law is applied in specific cases. It is an important secondary source of rights. This paper does not intend to problematize Brazilian Law, concerning violence against women, rather it analyses the way this law is applied to situations focussing on the concept of gender.

Maria da Penha Law

It is important to make some remarks about this specific law. Brazilian feminist movements have struggled against violence against women in Brazil, mainly in the 1970s. It was a period of intense industrialization and the admission of women into the labour market. Law has always been an important battlefield in the struggle of Brazilian women to underscore their rights. This is due to the fact that up to the 1980s the country experienced a violent military dictatorship and at the end of two decades of military rule, the law, as the principal source of rights, was an important field for the guarantee of citizenship.

However, the criminal law was the only law that, until 2006, warranted drastically the defense of women's right against several forms of violence. Crimes of body injuries, threats and libels were the main items worked up in favour of women, with a series of limitations (which shall be analysed on another occasion). For instance, these crimes were subjected to a conciliatory policy which rarely brought about any real accountability and liability to the agents of violence. All ended within a culture of impunity. It has been registered that in 2001 a woman suffered violence in Brazil at every 15 seconds (Fundação Perseo Abramo).

In 2006, Law 11.340/06, also known as Maria da Penha Law, began to be enforced in Brazil. It is a landmark in feminist struggles and is considered the most important historical document within the vindications of the rights of Brazilian women. The law was called Maria da Penha Law to pay homage to a woman called Maria da Penha who, after two murder attempts by her ex-husband, had the courage to bring her case before the Organization of American States. The result comprised recommendations so that the Brazilian Government would modify the scenario of violence against women.

The Maria da Penha Law is a completely different law from those available for women since it has plural characteristics and does not consist of a mere increase of guarantee for cases of violence. It comprises three dimensions: it protects (protective measures ensue, coupled to educational proposals for people and others); it criminalizes (it not merely enforces the structures of punishment but incorporates proposals for the treatment of the agents of violence); it constitutes norms (through a definition of several types of violence against women; the acknowledgement that violence is a violation of human rights; the insistence that violence is based on gender) (Machado, 2013).

The most interesting section of the law concerns how the law constructs the idea of violence based on *gender*, underlining the urgency of social commitment with changes in violence indexes. The Fifth Article of this law states: 'For the effects of this Law, domestic and familial violence against women consists in any action or omission based on gender that causes death, injuries, physical, sexual or psychological suffering, coupled to moral harm and damage to property'. Not all types of violence against women result within the precise context of the Maria da Penha Law but events exclusively based on gender are the target.

The idea of violence constructed by the items of the law (especially Articles 5 and 7) comprises a set of indispensable requirements, among which may be mentioned:

1. Violence should be committed against women,
2. Violence should be foregrounded within power relationship based on gender,
3. Violence must cause one of the results indicated by the law, on the physical, psychological, property, moral or sexual stance,
4. Violence must occur within one of the spaces mentioned in Article 5, or rather, within the milieu of the home, family or in any other relationship of intimate affection, and
5. Violence has to be committed regardless of women's sexual orientation. In a nutshell, it shows that in affective or conjugal relationships, it does not matter, whether who commits violence against women is a male or another female (Machado, 2013).

Gender within human sciences integrates debates on the male-female, female-female and male-male relationships, especially as from the 1980s. The law was promulgated to comprise such relationships, especially based on the logic of power which changes over time and through place (Scott, 1995).

The legal experts have appropriated the gender category to problematize how law and legal discourse may be important factors of legitimation of power relationships that establish themselves within gender. Alícia Ruiz remarks, 'Law is a social discourse and, as such, provides meaning to the behaviour of human beings and transforms them in agents, while, at the same time, it works as the great legitimating agent of power that speaks, convinces, seduces and imposes' (Ruiz included in Birgin 2000). Carol Smart (included in Birgin, 2000), for instance, appropriates the term coined by Teresa de Lauretis to show that the law is similar to gender technology: 'We may readily say that we may begin analysing Law as the process of production of identities of a fixed gender instead of analysing its application to agents that already are bequeathed by gender'. In this way, if gender is 'the product and process of a certain number of social technologies or biomedical apparatuses', the law may be conceived as a cultural and social apparatus of codification and 'engendering' (De Lauretis *included in* Hollanda 1994).

When the law establishes a model that exceeds the repression stance, it naturally introduces difficulties in the deployment process since it frequently requires the flexibility of the juridical canon under the heading of interventions derived from other origins (especially, psychosocial origins). This is due to the fact that it is based on gender conflict, which is only slightly discussed or worked upon in the juridical milieu.

The Courts' Perspective

In the wake of criticism against the Brazilian judiciary in the deployment of the Maria da Penha Law, that the need to analyse how the Courts have decided on the main controversies related to its implementation and in what manner it has embodied the analytic category of gender for their solution assumes significance. Data was interpreted by a methodology of jurisprudential analysis in which it was possible to collect decisions on the problem within a time frame so that the stand, trends and possibilities of solutions, yet to be adopted, could be evaluated (Freitas Filho; Lima, 2010).

The first series of decisions starts with a highly specific category of cases, or rather, cases of violence occur between members of the same family without any affective-conjugal involvement. These cases of violence occur between brothers/sisters-in-laws, cousins, uncles and nephews.

Case 1: Conflict between Nephew vs Uncles and Grandparents

The case revolves around a nephew arraigned on the crime of threat (Art. 147 of the Criminal Law) against uncles and grandparents. Since he was refused money to buy illicit drugs, he threatened to kill them with a knife.

When the judge decided on the violence committed, he sentenced:

> [...] it is not enough that the specific behavior is against the person of a woman; violence must be conditioned against the person as a woman. In this particular

case, the Maria da Penha Law may not be applied since the crime had no connection whatsoever with the victim's female gender.

(TJPR-1ª C. Criminal-RSE-1115265-7-Peabiru - Rel.: Macedo Pacheco - Unanimous decision-J. 29.05.2014)

According to Miriam Grossi (1998), 'besides the different manners to interpret the situation of women in our culture, the categories *sex* and *gender*, *gender identity* and *sexuality* are very much equivalent in Brazil'.

It is interesting to note that this conceptual misunderstanding is reaffirmed in the case. While trying to eschew any eventual doubts on the inexistence of gender relationships *in casu*, the judge failed to establish a clear difference between sex and gender. This misunderstanding can clearly prevent the incidence of the law and leave women without adequate protection.

Case 2: Conflict between a Married Man vs the Wife's Friend

The case deals with an event in which a husband threatened (Art. 147 of Criminal Law) and slightly injured (Art. 129, *caput*, of Criminal Law) the female friend of his ex-wife, who was trying to call the police and notify a discussion that the agent of the crime was having with his wife (TJPR-1ª C. Criminal em Composição Integral-CC-730213–0 - Foro Central da Comarca da Região Metropolitana de Curitiba - Rel.: Telmo Cherem - Unanimous – J. 10.02.2011). The judge decided on the non-applicability of the Maria da Penha Law since the victim was not a vulnerable or hypo-sufficient person. Such conclusion has been very usual in Brazilian courts, preventing, for instance, middle or upper classes women to have adequate protection. However, the choice of the category gender as the first basis for the Maria da Penha Law and the requirement, as a counterpoint, of proof for female hypo-sufficiency and vulnerability, are contradictory since the very category already demonstrates a power structure in which hypo-sufficiency and vulnerability are presumable within the context of violence which involves women widely and extensively, and reinforces the logic of male dominance (Bourdieu, 2000).

Case 3: Conflict against Young Women and Elderly Females

Further, an important category of decisions is extant on the prevalence or not of the Maria da Penha Law above other special protection statutes, especially those involving children or the elderly. It should be admitted that the category gender should be interpreted with other terms, or rather, age, in this specific case, which triggers the immediate application of the Maria da Penha Law by widening tutelage to young women and to elderly females. Jurisprudence authorizes the application of the Maria da Penha Law concomitantly with the law on the protection of minors (Bianchini, 2006). However, it is not a prevalent trend within the court decisions under analysis. Cases involving elderly females or young women are generally removed from the application of the Maria da Penha Law.

The Maria da Penha Law is prevalent when the victim is a young woman or an elderly female within the following circumstances: (a) violence should occur within a context of close affection and relationship; (b) in the case of young females, they should be over fourteen years old. The above referential approaches the limits of gender and sexuality, excludes other relationships which do not involve affection and confuses more and more the limitation of the first category. In fact, it reinforces the difficulty that judges have to put the law in practice.

It is interesting to note that there were only a few court sentences foregrounded on a reliable theoretical perspective, with quotes from human sciences and from the laws of other countries (Spain, for instance). They were pronounced by an Associate Judge with a relevant academic formation (degrees in Accounts and Law; a Master's and a Doctoral degree in Law; more than ten published articles in important scientific journals; seven published books; numberless chapters in books) who concomitantly exercized his jurisdictional profession. These subjective attributes undoubtedly affected his stance for the implementation of the Maria da Penha Law.

Conclusion

The corpus of court decisions demonstrated an ambiguous trend in the application of the concept. On one hand, there is a position for the strict application of the legal resolutions and dispositions which, as shown above, brings about discussions and incoherent statements of the same judge. On the other hand, there are signs of a position abounding with a greater reflexive strictness, based on scientific and interdisciplinary statements which enable the application of the law according to its spirit and ideals.

There is a serious conceptual misunderstanding that prevent the judges to establish a clear difference mainly between sex/sexuality and gender. The existence of the law, by itself, does not guarantee the protection of women. If the Judiciary does not operate it properly, women are not protected, because gender violence will not be clearly identified.

The judiciary body should take hold of its primary role in the application of the legal document and find theoretical subsidies to optimize the exercise of its institutional role so that social justice could be implemented. The definition of situations of violence must be compatible with women's expectations (Gregori, 2006) so that adequate challenge could be undertaken.

Finally, the main step to be taken is to problematize the concept of gender, bringing to the judiciary the set of discussions built by the university, as an attempt to improve women's lives.

References

Bianchini, Alice (2006). Competência dos JVDFM nos casos de criança ou adolescente do sexo feminino vítima de violência de gênero. *Compromisso e atitude.* Disponível em: http: //www.compromissoeatitude.org.br/competencia-dos-jvdfm-nos-casos-de-crianca-ou-adolescente-do-sexo-feminino-vitima-de-violencia-de-genero-por-alice-bianchini/.

Birgin, Haydée (Org.) (2000). *El Derecho en el Género y el Género en el Derecho.* Buenos Aires: Bilbos.

Bourdieu, Pierre (2000). *A força do direito:* elementos para uma sociologia do campo jurídico. *In:* O poder simbólico. 3. Ed. Rio de Janeiro: Bertrand Brasil, pp. 209–54.

Debert, Guita Grin; Gregori, Maria Filomena; Piscitelli, Adriana (Orgs.) (2006). *Gênero e distribuição da justiça:* as Delegacias de Defesa da Mulher e a construção das diferenças. Campinas: PAGU: UNICAMP.

Freitas Filho, Roberto; LIMA, Thalita Moraes (2010). Metodologia de análise de decisões. *Anais do XIX Encontro Nacional do CONPEDI.* Conpedi: Fortaleza, pp. 5238–47.

FUNDAÇÃO PERSEO ABRAMO. *A mulher brasileira nos espaços público e privado.* São Paulo: 2001. Disponível em: http: //www.fpabramo.org.br/o-que-fazemos/pesquisas-de-opiniao-publica/pesquisas-realizadas/vinculo-com-o-agressor.

Grossi, Mariam (1998). *Body, Gender, Sexuality and Subjectivity Among Men who Practice Cross-dressing.*

Hollanda, Heloisa Buarque de (Org.) (1994). *Tendências e impasses:* o feminismo como crítica da cultura. Rio de Janeiro: Rocco.

MACHADO, Isadora Vier (2013). *Da dor no corpo à dor na alma:* uma leitura do conceito de violência psicológica da Lei Maria da Penha. Universidade Federal de Santa Catarina, Florianópolis.

Scott, Joan (1995). Gênero: uma categoria útil de análise histórica. *Educação and Realidade.* Porto Alegre, Vol. 20, No. 2.

Senado Federal. *CPMI Violência contra a Mulher.* Brasília (2012). http: //www.senado.gov.br/atividade/comissoes/comissao.asp?origem=CN&com=1580.

5

Women in Turkey at the Intersection of Social Ethics and Law

A Perspective

ZEYNEP ENGIN

Abstract

Law and morality clearly share common aspects. It is a well-known fact that both are the bearers of understanding of 'good' in a society. However, it is not always possible to claim that the transformation of each norm to a legal code, widely accepted by a society and based on morality can lead to fair conclusions in every situation. This paper examines the position of woman in law and morality in the Turkish context. Even though there is the principle of equality in Turkish Constitution, the visible prints of patriarchy can be observed in many laws, and the Constitution. Women face a variety of regulations due to the social/moral rules, from politics to civil rights, in many other fields. There are a number of reasons for this situation – the value given to women's chastity, the concept of women being a weaker sex compared to men, and the avoidance of seeing a woman as an individual. This paper highlights this issue through various examples. The differences between men and women will be analysed in the Turkish context.

Keywords

Social Ethics and Women, Women in Turkey, Women and Law.

Introduction

While there are numerous similarities between law and ethics, there are countless points that can stand as differences between the two. Ethical behaviour is defined as differentiating between 'good' or 'bad' in behaviour, thought, emotion and action. Legal behaviour is based on the difference between 'fair' and 'unfair', and the aim is to reach a just conclusion. Law aims to regulate the human relations according to the principle of justice. It, at the same time, lays the foundation of providing human goodness (Tepe, 2005). In the relation between law and ethics, the emergence of law as a target to establish an order, to provide some social peace, to be beside the practical benefit and to carry out justice embodies the main intersection with ethics. If the different points between law and ethics are left aside, it is well known that both include a 'good' and that law heads for a definite target of 'goodness' – which is known as justice – (Işıktaç, 2008). According to law, there is a 'good' or 'bad' and because of this reason it is confronted as a bearer of a definite understanding of value.

Law reflects the attitudes, priorities and values of those who obey the laws defended by the majority imposing them, and idealizes all (Billigton, 2011). At this point, it is possible to say that in many areas ethics, knitted by judgements of value intersects with law. In societies, there has always been a judgement on individual goodness, as well as societal goodness. That is the reason why it can easily be stated that there is a unity between law and ethics in terms of the subject and content, and that law creates the opportunity of establishing ethical codes, besides the fact that ethics supports law (Aral, 1992). In addition, a positive legal code can be claimed as contradictory to the Constitution because of its contradiction to the public interest, and in case of any attempt to do so, it will not be valid in long-term (Dabin, 1953).

Another common point between law and ethics is that both are not static, although they are accepted as ideal rules. It cannot be said that they are immortal, despite their emergence as unchangeable goodness in the first place and their longer life span than the others. The norms that can be named as cultural norms are different human understandings of definite natural, social conditions and different cultures, and because of this reason, in a specific area and time period, they are the reflections of existing human behaviour. The function of these norms is to establish order in a society and protect the existing order. As these conditions exist, they keep their functionalities, however when the conditions change, they lose their functions and their reason for existence disappears. It is obvious that the norms related to traditions are these norms (Kuçuradi, 2003).

There is another point that should be added when attracting attention to relation between ethics and law: the transformation of norms based on ethics to a legal norm does not guarantee reaching absolute fair conclusions. Here, the mentioned customs and traditions constitute a situation that they are appropriate for social ethics, but not for human rights. To illustrate, after the abolition of slavery in the USA, the attitude towards the African Americans was not named as discrimination.

Another issue is the possibility of the intervention of personal ethical value of the judges who implement these kinds of rules. There is a very striking example from 1987 that is still on our minds in Turkey: In a matter of dispute, a woman was harassed violently by her husband, and based on this she filed a divorce suit against her husband. The judge not needing to see the evidence given by the suitor, in his verdict, refused the demand with an old Turkish saying as thus: 'Do not leave a woman unbeaten and not pregnant in any way.'

Consequently, it is not possible to accept that every legal norm grounded on ethics is directed towards the ideal. When the established relation between ethics and law is transformed into a norm, it is also highly needed to filter this from the perspective of human rights. Under these, it would be possible that the norms would have longer life span and be closer to the ideal.

The Place of Women in Law: Ethics Relation

Social gender is not only related to the roles or identities of women in a society, because not only it influences the perception and communication of people but they are also closely related to the institutions such as army, law, health and education power relations and the power relations producing them, and exerts into every aspect of social life (Delice, 2008).

Actually, unless the world history had been reflected as 'his' story and the rules had been set by men, there would not be a requirement for gender discrimination between law and ethics. Women's 'establishing family' and men's 'establishing state' (Sancar, 2012) is an argument that is still valid in today's modern world. Because of this reason there are still traces of male dominated structure both in the fields of ethics and legal regulations. In the last 150 years, western societies have been trying to eliminate these traces that are parallel to the power that the women movement has gained. In Turkey, women movement is not as strong as the western countries, however, the western laws that were received after the foundation of Turkish Republic and the steps taken for the European Union have led way to women having great gains.

Today, in Turkish jurisprudence women and men are equal. However, it is also true that due to the settled social ethic laws much more different regulations are being implemented, and even if the mentioned equality is established through legal regulations, in this specific implementation there are significant diversions from this idea of equality. These diversions emerge because of the basic emotion of the men wanting to protect the women based on the idea of woman being seen as a holy motherly figure, and sometimes due to the chastity issue in which women are seen as a symbol, and sometimes it is just because of a woman being the opposite sex and it embodies a sexual connotation. This paper highlights the problems of women in Turkey at the intersection of social ethics and law. The regulations in which the traces of male dominated ethic understanding exist is also discussed using examples.

Women in Turkish Legal System

Women and Ethics in Turkish Constitutional System

In jurisprudence all the people are equal; therefore women and men are equal. Article 10 of the Turkish Constitution mentions the equality between men and women. Besides, state has the liability of this issue and in the Constitution it is stated that this equality is to be actualized. However, there are some articles that are against this equality. In Article 41, 'protection' of the mother and the child is mentioned. In Article 50, it is stated that 'minors, women, and physically and mentally disabled persons, shall enjoy special protection with regard to working conditions.' These statements lead to the following conclusions:

1. The word 'women' proves the masculine point of view, starting from the constitution.
2. The protection of the weak, the destitute and the bound is an ethical liability, in fact the related articles of civil law gives liability to the acquaintances and relatives in this situation (indemnity for the loss of absence). Protection of the child by the Constitution is a comprehensible situation because compared to the other species, a human child grows up very late, and needs care and protection for a long time. Nonetheless, protection of the mother means protection of 'women' with a child and in the case while 'men' with a child are not protected, the reason why this protection for women is needed stands as a question mark. For instance, if the state as a well-functioning social state provides kindergarten opportunity for the families with children, a very significant difference in work life between men and women would be closed.
3. The statement in Article 50 of the Constitution once more consolidates the point of view that 'women shall enjoy special protection' and 'women being weak'. Here, taking women differently from men and the idea that women shall be protected and the efforts being done for this issue includes an ethical concept of goodness. In the Article 50, women being taken with 'physically and mentally disabled persons' is an unfortunate mistake and social inequality has now gained legitimacy in the hands of the constitution.

Monitoring Woman Body through Social Ethics and Laws

With a large proportion of Muslim population, women circumcision does not exist like in some other Muslim countries, but on the grounds of ethics and religion, dominance was tried on the woman's body. One of the most disputable issues is abortion. Abortion in Turkey is an issue that has been discussed from time to time in medical, legal, ethical and religious terms and is barely accepted by the western countries. The ones that oppose abortion agree on the idea that a foetus is a potential individual and defends the order of 'no murder'. On the other hand, if the protected value is the decision of a woman to continue or not to continue unwanted pregnancy with her own free will, opposing this is to take away the control of a woman on her own body, and definitely means the deprivation of the right to make a decision on this issue (Billington, 2011). The most controversial subject is the situation of the woman getting pregnant from rape. The following example is related to a pregnant girl who is underaged and pregnant from rape: The mentioned event took place in a place called Edirne. It was understood that dumb and deaf 14-year-old girl got pregnant from rape, and through a judicial decision the foetus was aborted and the girl was held under protection by the state (Özmen, 2012). Another striking example is from Isparta. A woman who got pregnant from rape, murdered the man who raped her with a gun, cut his head off and threw it at the village square and did not want to give birth. But because the legal time limit of 20 weeks had exceeded, she had to give birth to the child. The victim did not want the child, so the baby was guarded by the state (Arkan, 2012).

Another control mechanism is that when a woman gets pregnant, upon a medical investigation, this situation is passed as a piece of information by a phone call to the pregnant woman's home number. This can lead to terrible consequences by alerting the chastity related codes: any male family member who knows about this pregnancy can murder the pregnant women. Although family planning is mentioned in the constitution, lately, because of the reasons based on social ethics, bearing many children is supported. Because of this reason, C-section is opposed; new precautions are being taken to prevent C-section in state hospitals.

State can object the individuals by the rules and ease governance through having a homogeneous population (Revel, 2012). By the drawn borders, the state defines some as exceptions and throws them out of the society. This features its masculine quality. The situation of the women who earn their living as sex workers illustrate this clearly.

State permits the existence of the places called brothels where women serve to meet the sexual demands of men, collect taxes from the owners of these businesses and makes regulations to monitor the health standards of the women working at these places. Above all, what is highly striking is that state regulates such a private area (Hatemi, 1976). This state regulation emerges as the continuation of social judgements related to chastity. Through the rules that the state executes, the coding of a woman's body is that it belongs to men or even to society and not the woman. Due to this, the women working as sex workers are accepted to be outside of this code and perceived as the bodies belonging to everyone (Zengin, 2011). The reduction in Former Turkish Penal Code Article 438 should be seen as an interpretation of this situation.

Apart from this, a woman being with numerous men (the number is not identified) can create the doubt that she can be a sex worker and in order to detect this she can be under surveillance unknowingly. Up onto the point where women sexuality and sexual attitude is visible in the society, all the authorities would find the category that the women fit in and set alarm to classify her in this category (Zengin, 2011). The monitoring of the state is not restricted to this: Only the women working in this brothel can enter these places, and it is not possible for other women to enter this place, especially the married women cannot work hereabouts, and cross-gender men are included (Zengin, 2011).

We know from a published work that permission had not been taken to enter the brothels even for doing an academic research on this field – in which the gender of the researcher being a woman is the reason (Zengin, 2011). The attitude of the state that prefers to stay silent to the extent that it can hinder a scientific study provides that this private place is known by a specific group of people. Also, it provides the anonymity of this field where the women are exploited, and aims at keeping women from the actual reality of these places, and thus 'protecting' them (Zengin, 2011). By this way, through keeping the citizens that need to be protected from prostitution, holds a part of the population in this border, and leaves the others out (Zengin, 2011). The ones who are out of the border cannot leave these houses. The relationship between prostitution and state, the daily acts of the state related to prostitution, how bio power and sovereignty cooperates and the sexual operation it has are striking indicators.

Regulation in Civil Law Related to Women

Testamentary Dispositions and Ethical Rules

Civil Law is a text that takes woman and man relationship in detail from one perspective. It can be easily run into some social ethics related restrictions as in related family law and inheritance law. If the added term to testamentary dispositions is against the law or the ethics, the testamentary disposition is invalid.

One of the most common problems arising, as an example of immorality, in testamentary dispositions is named as 'mistress will', whereby a married man legates the person he is in an actual extra-marital relationship with through a declaration of mind. This appears to have been a disputable issue long discussed by the Civil Law jurists. Here, the protected value is the 'married woman' and the 'family'. Bequeathing to a woman who is connected to the man romantically, which is also the reason for the destruction of a marital union, is a topic that is being discussed. However, the tough attitude has become much softer in the recent years, and the immorality of the acquisitions that the person involved in extra-marital relation gets is accepted under certain occasions: This acquisition is qualified to the condition of being done merely to continue the extra-marital relationship and that the mistress is aware of that acquisition (Serozan and Engin, 2014). And this can be a change, meaning that ethical value judgements should be reconsidered because in western societies the fact of living together has shown an upward trend.

Mother's Refusal, Incapability of the Father in a Union of Marriage

Lineage tie provides practical results in daily life. With this tie, not only the benefits of the child are looked after but also the peace of the family is established. In our legal system, the child-bearer is the mother. As the surrogate motherhood accepted in other countries is not regulated by our laws, there occurs no problem related to who the mother is. The father of the child who was born in the union of marriage is accepted presumably. The refusal of the lineage is first the right of the father. If there is no genetic connection with the child, the interest is on the husband when the child is not related to the husband (Serozan, 2005). In this way of regulating the law, it is understood that a fair solution has been found.

Nevertheless, the mother has no right to claim that the child she bears and the father has no lineage tie. In Italy and France, this right is given under the condition when there is a divorce and a marriage with the real, that is, the genetic father (Serozan, 2005).

Certainly, the identity of the father can be easily found by technological opportunities, but a mother – most probably – knows the identity of the father without using the technology. Then, what lies under the reason why a mother cannot use this right? A woman having an affair and a child is a situation that cannot be associated with a woman's chastity, and announcing it is also something totally unacceptable. Here, the adultery concept is different for women and men-male polygamy can be a reason for this (Hatemi, 1976) and in a case of woman 'adultery', there are very strict ethical codes against her. In this case, as the woman cannot refuse the father, the child should be of someone who is not the legal father.

Striking Examples in Terms of Labour Law

Women in work life and working in equal conditions with men in Turkey and western countries is an issue challenging the societies/cultures from the Industrial Revolution era. Women working in Turkish society arose after the First World War, when there was a situation when male population decreased. However, the social expectation is towards the denial of the same restricting to taking care of children, the elderly and the household. Modernization has led to women working as nurses or teachers. The absence of public welfare measure has had an effect on the continuation of the existing roles of women that have been borne by women related to the care of children, the sick, the disabled and the elderly (Kandiyoti, 1997; Kadıoğlu, 1998). In fact, the choice of women to these professions that can be regarded as the continuation of these jobs proves this. For instance, women are first thought as a nurse, not a doctor because medicine requires a long and scientific education, whereas nursing is regarded as a continuation of the caretaker roles that have been done for centuries.

In a research conducted in Turkish public administration that was done in 1978, the participants were asked the nine reasons why women were not ranked in high administrative positions and asked to order these. At the end of the research, the belief that the discontinuation of women in work life and the women's leaving the work life because of marital responsibilities were mentioned. The participants pointed traditional and social attitude as the second reason. In a research that was done by Turkish Statistical Institute in 2013, a group highlighted that the primary function of women is childcare and house work, another group commented that women working is against customs and traditions. As it can be clearly seen, in the last thirty years, there is a little change in the data related to the work life of women in the last thirty years and there is non-egalitarian and sexist attitude for every stage of hiring and promotion of women. Nevertheless, it should not be forgotten that there are no qualified women population reaching to high ranks. This reason enlarges the demand for women workforce that is ready to be recruited for low paid, part-time and temporary jobs that are at non-unionised little workshops, and in the form of home-centred and unorganized jobs (Kandiyoti, 1997). Another sexist attitude towards women employment is towards the women workers employed at night. Legal regulation is done in accordance with the Constitution and the aim of taking care of the women workers is protected.

A 24-hour functioning through a shift procedure is possible for a workplace on the condition that it takes care of the restrictions for the workers. While the former Labour Law No. 1475 prevented the night work, Act No. 4857 lifted the ban and regulated the working of women workers that complete eighteen in night shift through a special by-law (Official Gazette No. 25548 dated 8 September 2004 Regulation of the Prohibition of Women Employment in Night Posts). According to this, women workers cannot work for more than 7.5 hours, the liability of their transportation is of the employer, health report that is to be done every six months is a must, upon the request of the women, the night shift is regulated not to be in the same hours of the husband's night post and the request of husband and wife working at the same night post is compared in the rate of possibility of the employer. On the side of the men workers, health report and transportation of the workers is not required. Health report implies that women are weaker than men, and the transportation liability is based on an ethical code that 'honourable' women cannot be on the streets at night. Besides, what is being established by this is a positive discrimination towards women who want to work but hesitate to work at night.

Conclusion

Like law, ethics diverts itself to definite value judgements. The emergence of rules is formed by a consensus in both legal rules and ethical rules. A consensus on a norm can reflect the point of view of the majority, but it may not be democratic and not reflect the epistemological features. It is always possible that a norm of a consensus and unanimity can be against human rights (Kuçuradi, 2003). A norm that is based on and evaluated by this idea is required to be fair, equal and righteous, and the most important of all to be egalitarian. It has been well-known that women have been restricted by ethics and put in between the walls for centuries. Even the indisputably influential French Revolution done in the name of the human rights, with its thinkers establishing the foundation of this revolution, did not mention women's rights. The place of women has been next to her husband and children, and leaving this private area and appearing in the public sphere indicates a very tough process. Industrial revolution and wars turned the balance upside down and women appeared to be in the social arena more. Two weapons emerged when men saw the threat to lose their manhood: The first is ethics, and the other one is law. The norm-bearers are men, therefore it has not been hard for them to do so.

In the last decades, in our jurisprudence, it is needed to say that differences between men and women in the name of ethics are less, and that they are excluded from the laws. The products of masculine ethics like 'man is the head of the family', 'the last saying related to children is of man', 'virginity checks', the offences like 'deflowering by falsified marriage promises' or 'ban on wearing trousers' were excluded from the jurisprudence. What is needed in the contemporary organizations and society is the equality of men and women leading to positive discrimination.

References

Aral, Vecdi; *Hukuk ve Hukuk Bilimi Üzerine*, Filiz Kitabevi, İstanbul, 1992

Arasli, Oya; *Adaylık Kavramı ve Türkiye'de Milletvekilliği Adaylığı*, Ankara Üniversitesi Yayınları, Ankara, 1972.

Arkan, Havva Nur. 'Tecavüzcüsünü Öldüren Kadın: Bebeği İstemiyorum'. Hürriyet. 31.08.2012. Last Visited: 25.12.2014. <http://www.hurriyet.com.tr/gundem/ 21343825.asp>. (Web)

Bilir, Faruk; *Siyasi Partilerde Parlemento Adaylarının Belirlenmesi*, Yetkin Yayınları, Ankara, 2007.

Billington, Ray; *Felsefeyi Yaşamak*, Çev.: Abdullah Yılmaz, Ayrıntı Yayınları, İstanbul, 2011.

Çıtçı, Oya; "Türk Kamu Yönetiminde Kadın Görevliler", *Türk Toplumunda Kadın*, Der.: Nermin Abadan-Unat, Genişletilmiş 2. Bas*ı*, Araştırma, Eğitim, Ekin Yayınları, Ankara, 1982.

Dabin, Jean; *Théorie Générale du Droit*, Bruxelles, Etablissements Emile Bruylant, 1953.

Delice, Serkan, "Osmanlı'yı Bugün Nasıl Tefsir Ediyoruz? Tarih ve Toplumsal Cinsiyet Üzerine Düşünceler", *Cinsiyet Halleri*, Der.: Nil Mutluer, Varlık Yayınevi, İstanbul, 2008.

Eser, Hamza Bahadır-DİNÇ, Mehmet; "Kadınların Siyasal Katılımını Artırmaya Yönelik Bir Yöntem Olarak Kota Uygulamaları", http://idc.sdu.edu.tr/tammetinler/ demokrasi/ demokrasi9pdf (29.10.2011) (web)

Gender Statistics 2013". TÜİK. Ankara, 2014 Last Visited: 25.12.2014. <http:// www.tuik.gov.tr/Kitap.do?metod=KitapDetay&KT_ID=11&KITAP_ID=294>. (Web) 8.9.2004 tarihli 25548 sayılı Resmi Gazetede yayımlanan Kadın İşçilerin Gece Postalarında Çalıştırılmaları Hakkında Yönetmelik.

Güneş-Ayata, Ayşe; "Türkiye'de Kadının Siyasete Katılımı", *1980'ler Türkiye'sinde Kadın Bakış Açısından Kadınlar*, Der.: Şirin Tekeli, İletişim Yayınları, İstanbul, 1995.

Hatem, Mervat F., "19. Yüzyıl Mısır'ında Sağlık Mesleği ve Kadın Bedeninin Denetlenmesi", *Modernleşmenin Eşiğinde Osmanlı Kadınları*, Ed.: Madeleine C. Zilfi, Çev.: Necmiye Alpay, Tarih Vakfı Yurt Yayınları, İstanbul, 2000.

Hatemi, Hüseyin; *Hukuka ve Ahlaka Aykırılık Kavramı ve Sonuçları*, İstanbul Üniversitesi Yayınları, İstanbul, 1976.

Işiktaç, Yasemin; *Hukuk Sosy*olojisi, Filiz Kitabevi, İstanbul, 2008.

Kadioğlu, Ayşe; "Cinselliğin Ýnkârı: Büyük Toplumsal Projelerin Nesnesi Olarak Türk Kadınları", *75 Yılda Kadınlar ve Erkekler*, Tarih Vakfı yayınları, İstanbul, 1998.

Kandiyotı, Deniz, "Ataerkil Örüntüler: Türk Toplumunda Erkek Egemenliğinin Çözümlenmesine Dair Yönelik Notlar", *Cariyeler Bacılar Yurttaşlar*, Metis Yayınları, İstanbul, 1997.

Kuçuradi, İoanna; "Etik İlkeler ve Hukuk", HFSA, No: 8, 2003.

Özmen, Engin. "Sağır ve Dilsiz Kıza Tecavüz İddiası". Posta. 10.09.2012. Last Visited: 25.12.2014. <http://www.posta.com.tr/3Sayfa/HaberDetay/Sagir-ve-dilsiz-kiza-tecavuz-iddiasi.htm?ArticleID=139209%20%20%20%20%20%20%20%20%20 %20&Date=06.09.201 >. (Web)

Revel, Judith; "Kimlik, Doğa, Yaşam. Üç Biyopolitik Yapıbozumu", Cogito, S.: 70–71, 2012.

Sancar, Serpil; *Türk Modernleşmesinin Cinsiyeti. Erkekler Devlet, Kadınlar Aile Kurar*, İletişim Yayınları, İstanbul, 2012.

Serozan, Rona- Engin, Baki İlkay; *Miras Hukuku*, Seçkin Yayıncılık, Ankara, 2014.

Serozan, Rona; *Çocuk Hukuku*, Vedat Kitapçılık, İstanbul, 2005, S. 187.

Şimşek-Rathke, Leyla; *Dünden Kalanlar. Türkiye'de Hemşirelik ve GATA TSK Sağlık Meslek Lisesi Örneği*, İletişim Yayınları, İstanbul, 2011.

Tepe, Harun; 'Hukuk ve Etik: Hukukun Etik Temelleri', Hukuk Felsefesi ve Sosyolojisi Arkivi, İstanbul Barosu Yayınları, 2005.

Zengin, Aslı; *İktidarın Mahremiyeti*, Metis Yayınları, İstanbul, 2011.

6

Customary Law and Status of Women

A Study of Hmar Community of North-East India

RUTH LALSIEMSANG BUONGPUI

Abstract

Customary law especially in North-East India occupies a central place in the social, familial and political life of the individual and communities as a whole despite the presence of constitutional law. Christianity among the tribes has brought certain changes in their traditional practices, this results in multiple legal systems. Against the background, the study on the relation between gender and law, in general, has brought forward the partial nature of law towards women. It is important to understand the nature and functioning of customary law as it has its impact on woman's status. Based on the study of the Hmar tribe, the paper intends to unravel the ways in which gender relations gets constructed through the functioning and perpetuation of customary law.

Keywords

Customary Law, Gender, Tribe, Gender Relations, Status of Women.

Introduction

North-East India is one of the most ethnically and linguistically diverse region in India. The region has a high concentration of tribal population dominating the hilly states of Mizoram, Nagaland, Meghalaya, Arunachal Pradesh, Sikkim and the hill districts of the state of Manipur, Assam and Tripura (Shimray, 2002). Each tribe has its own distinct historical identity, linguistic, cultural practices and lifestyles that are carried forward from generation to generation (Fernandes and Barbora, 2009).

Customary laws are part of the tribal traditional customs and practices where the tribes considered it 'intrinsic to their identity and culture' (Fernandes and Bharali, 2009). Among the most distinctive features of tribal peoples are their 'unique cultural patterns, social institutions and legal systems. These features vary from place to place according to different social and political systems. Although indigenous peoples live within state systems with formalized constitutional and legal systems, many of their social and cultural practices continue to be regulated by their customary law' (Roy, 2005). The operation of customary laws acts as a powerful tool to define the roles of men and women and dictate acceptable standards of behaviour (Agarwal, 1994; Krishna, 2005). Customary law, which is derived from the morals, values and traditions, has its authority and control over the people. It regulates the 'entire spectrum of activities from birth to death' and governs their 'civil and criminal affairs including family relations, traditional authority, property rights and succession' (Frenrich et al., 2011). Such laws have been in practice since time immemorial and occupy a central place in the social, familial and political life of the communities as a whole.

It is important to understand law in its historic context to have an understanding of the present legal system (Tamanaha, 2008). The ordinary manner, in which law is understood, is a body of rules of conduct, which has binding force and controlling authority over the people. To understand the influences that went on to shape customary laws as it is today and the policies that led to the perseverance of customary laws despite establishment of state law, historical understanding of colonial rule can help in understanding how it continues to have importance in indigenous life. In the context of North-East India, as Christianity played a major role in social organizations, it also becomes important to understand the role played by Christianity in shaping customary laws.

Colonial Historical discourse in North-East India

With the annexation of the 'region in 1826, the British East India Company got a foothold in the North-Eastern region's political administration' (Nongkynrih, 2009). Before their annexation, the entire North-East remained 'outside all the great empires established in the Indian subcontinent' (Srikanth, 2000).

The diversity that exists in the North-East region is different from the mainland India social organization, which is based on caste structure. With the 'exception of Meiteis in Imphal valley and the Assamese in Brahmaputra valley, the hill people remained outside the orbit of Hindu influence and caste based societal formation' (Dena, 2008). The various ethnic communities lived in the hilly, isolated and segregated habitats (Chatterjee, 2010). They had their own language, social, economic, cultural and political institutions. Inter-tribe feud and the practice of head hunting were very common among the tribes (Downs, 1994). Each community in the region has their own 'decentralized and democratic government' (Chatterjee, 2010), and 'well-defined territory with clearly defined boundaries' (Khongreiwo, 2009). They were mostly under the control of their chiefs (Gangte, 2008).

The colonial rulers saw the region – the hills and the peoples – as very distinct from the mainland India, as their languages, their economy, their social organization, and even their physical features all marked them as distinct (Dena, 2008). The colonial rulers were not clear with the 'kind of policies to be adopted to deal with the tribes' (Srikanth, 2000). They perceived the region as lack of 'marked internal differentiation, the absence of advanced notions of private property, incidences of animistic practices and endogamous relations' (Srikanth, 2000).

They slowly brought in changes in the socio-economic life of the people. The colonial rulers introduced new systems such as enactment of new forest and wasteland policies, the replacement of *posa* (payment in kind) by cash, abolition of slavery, the expansion of tea plantations and agricultural activities up to the foothills, the control over markets (Srikanth, 2000). The introduction of money replaced barter system and brought a new system in the economy in the form of money transaction (Fernandes et al., 2005). Communication systems such as postal system, construction of roads and new forms of transport were also initiated by the British (Downs, 1994). As a result, the tribes were exposed to people from the plains such as the contractors, moneylenders, traders and bureaucrats. These affected the traditional source of livelihood of the indigenous hill tribes and the British felt the 'need to keep the tribal areas aloof from the plains for their own political and strategic interests' (Srikanth, 2000). Thereby, to segregate the hills and the plains, the Inner Line Regulation of 1873 and Scheduled Districts Act of 1874 were implemented to control the entry of the non-tribals into the tribal areas (Dena, 2008). As a result, North-East region remained aloof from the mainland India and the region was considered as a 'specially administered area' (Panmei, para 1, 2013).

The colonial regime initiated their new 'political policy of dividing the region administratively into hill and plain areas' (Nongkynrih, 2009). The 'hill areas were further separated into two categories based on their level of development and accessibility: Excluded Areas and Partially Excluded Areas' (Nongkynrih, 2009).

Due to the divide and rule policy of the colonial rulers, there was controversy at the verge of India's Independence; whether this portion of land should conglomerate to the Indian states in independent India. Various tribal communities demanded self-government as there was a fear in the minds of the tribal leaders that inclusion of the tribes into the mainland would result in the mainland culture and identity subsuming theirs (Nongkynrih, 2009; Pereira, 2009; Panmei, 2013). Subsequently, a 'plethora of efforts have been made by the Government of India to address these demands so as to integrate these tribal communities into the project of nation building' (Pereira, 2009). The Constitution of India assures the protection of their culture, tradition, customs and laws. As a result special articles were laid down for the different states such as Article 371 A (Nagaland), 371 B (Assam), 371 C (Manipur), 371 G (Mizoram) and 371 H (Arunachal Pradesh).

Christian Missionaries' Intervention and Social Changes

Although the British did not interfere in the administration of the hill tribes, however, they considered it necessary to 'civilize and humanize' the hill communities through the spread of modern education and Christianity in the 'western Christian mould' (Srikanth, 2006). The Christian missionaries were allowed to work among the people; although, the Inner Line Regulation was passed. The missionaries worked among the hills 'learned the local languages, developed local scripts and grammar of the people, started schools in the native villages and towns and taught them in their own languages' (Srikanth, 2006). In course of time, many of the tribes in North-East India are converted into Christianity. Though most of the tribes were converted to Christianity, the missionaries did not force them to give up their tribal customs and traditions (Shimray, 2002).

However, certain practices of the tribes which were very significant for the tribals were denounced by the missionaries. Changes were brought into their traditional institution and practices. The missionaries eradicated those practices which they felt does not fit into their religious teachings. Their methodology coincides with the colonial rulers who saw the people as uncivilized and their need of liberation from tradition to modernity (Sawmveli, 2005). For instance, they prohibited the practice of headhunting among the tribes (Dena, 2008; Downs, 1994; Lawmsanga, 2010).

Frederick Downs argued that the practice of headhunting was not just 'a matter of taking trophies in war'; it was rather a 'way of proving cleverness and daring of the ambusher in 'penetrating the inner defenses of the enemy'. It was associated with the 'image of manhood'. Haldipur commenting on the headhunting practices among the Nagas also writes that such practices demonstrated 'the theme of integration of culture .... It was the very core of the Naga culture based upon the concept of fertility ... their lives and their activities and behaviours were inextricably woven round this practice' (Haldipur, 1972). The disapproval of such practices by the missionaries with the conversion to Christianity resulted in the disappearance of the headhunting and ultimately 'changed the mode of life of all the tribes in the administered area' (Mills, 1992).

Youth dormitory was prevalent among most of the tribes in the region. Since inter tribe feud was very common among the tribes, ensuring peace and security to the people was an important task on the part of the youth. Such institution slowly came to an end. M. Horam is of the view that the missionaries disapproved such institutions on the assumed ground that the youth dormitory was a 'place of vices' (Horam, 1988). Though the missionaries cannot be accounted for the disappearance of such institution, yet it was through their teachings and the establishment of the schools that replaced such institution. It can, thus, be maintained that customary law continue to survive despite certain changes brought in by the missionaries. To understand how gender relations gets constructed through the functioning and perpetuation of customary law, the next section throws light on the Hmar tribe.

The Hmars

The Hmars are one of the various tribes of North-East India. They belong to the Chin-Kuki-Mizo ethnic group and are recognized as Scheduled Tribe under the 6th Schedule of the Constitutions of India. They are found today in Cachar and North Cachar Hills of Assam and the adjoining states of Manipur, Meghalaya, Mizoram and Tripura in India and Bangladesh and Myanmar (Dena, 2008). The present study is conducted among the Hmars of Manipur.

Pahnam (Clan Organization)

The Hmars social structure is based on Tribe-Clan-Sub Clan-Family-Individual category (Hmar Inpui). The Hmars have a clan organization where descent is traced through the male line called *Pahnam* (*pa* means father and *hnam* means clan). They have a strong social bond based on the *pahnam* (clan). *Pahnam* is an important institution of the Hmar society. Each *pahnam* is further divided into a smaller kinship based unit called *hnamsiper* or *hnam kaupeng* (lineage).

The members of the *pahnam* traced their descent from a common ancestor who is regarded as the founder of the clan (Sanate, 2010). In addition to the members who belong to the *pahnam* by birth, the women who are married to the man of a particular clan also become members of their respective husband's clan. Thus, a *pahnam* consists of men sharing a common ancestor, their wives and children born within the clan (Dena, 2008). Unmarried daughter remain as member of her father clan until her marriage. After her marriage, she joins the clan of her husband and becomes members of her husband's clan (Sanate, 2013).

Crossthang Sanate writes, 'the solidarity of the *Pahnam* is manifested in the performance of various customs and rituals within the life cycle of an individual. For instance in the event of death it is the duty of the members of the particular *pahnam*'s family to arrange all the necessary rites required as per the customs and practices. Thus, to ensure social security, the clan members of both sexes extend their maximum help socially, emotionally and economically to all its members' (Sanate, 2010). This sort of collective responsibility of the clan members makes it a strong force for social order (Varte, 2013).

Customary Laws of the Hmars

In Hmar dialect, customary law is called *hnam dan*. The major areas of the application of hnam dan are marriage, divorce and inheritance issues.

The different types of marriages in the Hmar society are:

1. *Sawngpuia Innei* (marriage with parental approval)
2. *Chawngmolaka Innei* (engagement of the girl child before she reached the age of maturity. However, only when the girl has attained the marriageable age, she is married with the approval of the parents)
3. *Kohran Dana Innei* (Church marriage)
4. *Inruka Innei* (Eloped marriage)
5. *Tluna Innei* (Marriage by intrusion)

Except for *Kohran Dana Innei* (Church marriage), the other forms have been practiced since the pre-Christian days. Church marriage began only after the coming of Christianity in 1910. Responses collected from the field study shows that Church marriage is the most preferred form of marriage. *Chawngmolaka Innei* and *Tluna Innei* types of marriage have disappeared today. In *Kohran Dana Innei*, all marriage formalities are conducted through the customary law such as payment of bride price *(man le muol)*. After completing such formalities, with the consent of the Church, marriage is held at the Church. Wedding takes place at the Church of the groom and not of the bride.

According to the Hmar customary laws, there are five forms of divorce such as:

1. Divorce due to adultery called *uire*,
2. Divorce initiated by husband called *mak*,
3. Divorce by agreement called *peksachang*,
4. Divorce initiated by wife called *suminsuo*, and
5. Divorce by mutual agreement called *inthrat thre*.

The Hmars follow the patrilineal system of inheritance. Certain Hmar clan like Faihrem, Leiri, Changsan and Khurbi follow the system of primogeniture whereby the eldest son inherits paternal properties; while other clans follow ultimogeniture, i.e. the youngest son inherits all property. If a man has no son to inherit his property, he may adopt a son, may be his brother's son or the son of a relative.

Customary Law and Gender Relations

The different roles that are ascribed to men and women are socially and culturally determined and influenced by traditional practices, institutions, customs and beliefs. The gendered notions of dominance have its roots in the traditional ideologies, which are manifested through the proverbs, division of labour and unequal distribution and access of power. Traditional gender roles have a great influence on gender relationship in the society. Despite the fact that youth dormitory was an important place of training, recreation for the youth, however, it was meant for the young men and women who were not allowed to have access to it. Such institution was restricted for the young men (Varte, 2013). Women were rather obliged to look after the welfare of the family as most of the domestic affairs and the household maintenance fall upon them. Today, even though such institutional practices have been done away, yet the attitude towards women, to quote Temsula Ao (2010), as 'benevolent subordination' continues.

The gendered creation of the Hmar community can be seen in the traditional sayings such as *Nuhmei varin tuikhur ral a kai ngai naw* which means the wisdom of a woman does not extend beyond the bank of a river. An old wife and old fencing can be replaced any time. Let a woman and a dog bark as they like. Women and crabs have no religion. Such sayings serve as a 'justifications for the distorted and stereotyped construction of gendered practices in the society' (Chakraborty, 2008). It also gives a picture of the patriarchal ideologies in the society. It can be noted from the above sayings that women are not regarded to have the 'wisdom and the reasoning power' and the capability of being given any power, be it in the private or public domain (Lalrinchhani, 2008).

Analysis of the existing customary laws shows that Hmar society being patriarchal society; women are excluded from participating in decision-making bodies. It is the *laibung* who decides issues related with marriage, divorce, child custody and inheritance rights. As mentioned earlier, women do not have a clan. Respondents' view also shows that not only are women allowed to participate in such decision-making bodies, their physical presence in such meetings is not permitted. It is men who are the interpreters of the customary law.

Gendered norms have assigned specific roles to men and women in society. While the management of the family and all the activities connected with it are considered to be the sole responsibility of women; men on the other hand are concerned with administration and management of the affairs of the community.

Conclusion

Christian missionaries succeeded in spreading Christianity thereby changing the traditional social institutions and practices. The British rulers left the tribes unadministered allowing them to be governed by their respective customary law (Verghese, 1997). The rule of difference policy of British, which they designed to preserved for their political expediencies led to the survival of the traditions of the tribes in North-East. The tribes accepted customary law as their form of governance, which they held it close to their identity. They felt that the continual reference to customary law is a way of preserving their traditional customs and tribal identities. However, as customary law is patriarchal in ethos, very often individual and gender choices got foreclosed and women are relegated to the lower status. Customary law, thus, needs to be grounded on equality and human rights such that both men and women are given equal rights.

References

Agarwal, Bina (1994). *A Field of One's Own: Gender and Land Rights in South Asia*, Cambridge: Cambridge University Press.

Ao, Temsula (2010). 'Benevolent Subordination: Social Status of Naga Women', in Preeti Gill (ed.), *The Peripheral Centre: Voices from India's Northeast*, New Delhi: Zubaan.

Chakraborty, Anup Shekhar (2008). 'Emergence of Women from "Private" to "Public": A Narrative of Power Politics from Mizoram', *Journal of International Women's Studies*, 9: 3–27.

Chatterjee, Sarajit Kumar (2010). *North-East India: Dispersion and Discontent: Historical, Cultural and Socio-Political Perspectives*, New Delhi: Abhijeet Publications.

Dena, Lal (2008). *In Search of Identity: Hmars of North-East India*, New Delhi: Akansha Publishing House.

Downs, Frederick S. (1994). *Essays on Christianity in North-East India*, New Delhi: Indus Publishing Company.

Fernandes, Walter and Barbora, Sanjay (eds) (2009). *Land, People and Politics: Contest over Tribal Land in Northeast India*, Assam: North Eastern Social Research Centre.

Fernandes, Walter and Bharali, Gita (2009). 'Customary Law-Formal Law Interface: Impact on Tribal Culture', in T.B. Subba et al. (eds), *Christianity and Change in Northeast India*, New Delhi: Concept Publishing Company, 93–108.

Fernandes, Walter, Pereira, Melville and Khatso, Vizalenu (2005). *Customary Laws in North East India: Impact on Women*, Guwahati: North Eastern Social Research Centre.

Frenrich, Jeanmarie, Galizzi, Paolo and Higgins, Tracy E. (2011). *The Future of African Customary Law*, New York: Cambridge University Press.

Gangte, Priyadarshni Meitei (2008). *Customary Laws of Meiteis and Mizo Society*, New Delhi: Akansha Publishing House.

Haldipur, R.N. (1972). 'Policy towards and Administration of the Tribes of North-East India', in K. Suresh Singh (ed.), *Tribal Situation in India*, Simla: Institute of Advanced Study, 305–15.

Hmar Inpui: Traditional Institutions of the Hmar Tribe, http://www.inpui.com/2009/02/traditional-institutions-of-hmar-tribe.html, Web 12 May 2013.

Horam, M. (1988). *Nagas Old Ways and New Trends*, New Delhi: Cosmo Publications.

Khongreiwo, Rammathot (2009). 'Understanding the Histories of Peoples on the Margins: A Critique of "Northeast India's Durable Disorder"', *Alternatives: Global, Local, Political*, 34(4): 437–54.

Krishna, Sumi (2005). 'Gendered Price of Rice in North-East India', *Economic and Political Weekly*, 40(25): 2555–562.

Lalrinchhani, B. (2008). 'Mizo Migration and Gender Relations, a Historical Analysis', Unpublished PhD Thesis, Department of History, North Eastern Hill University.

Lawmsanga, A. (2010). 'A Critical Study of Christian Mission with Special Reference to Presbyterian Church of Mizoram', Unpublished PhD Thesis, Department of Theology and Religion, University of Birmingham.

Mills, J.P. (1992). *The Lothas Nagas*, London: Macmillan Publishers Ltd.

Nongkynrih, A.K. (2009). 'Privatisation of Communal Land of the Tribes of North East India: A Sociological Viewpoint', in Walter Fernandes and Sanjay Barbora (eds), *Land, People and Politics: Contest over Tribal Land in Northeast India*, Assam: North Eastern Social Research Centre, 16–37.

Panmei, Pounamjuan (2013). 'Our Seven Sisters: A Utopia', http://www.mizonews.net/op-ed/seven-sisters-utopia, Web 28 August 2013.

Pereira, Melvil Victor (2009). 'Customary Law and State Formation in Northeast India: A Comparative Study of the Angami and the Garo of Meghalaya', Unpublished PhD Thesis, Centre for Political Studies, School of Social Sciences, Jawaharlal Nehru University, Delhi.

Roy, Raja Devasish (2005). *Report on Traditional Customary Laws and Indigenous Peoples in Asia*, London: Minority Rights Group International.

Sanate, Crossthang (2010). 'Social Change among the Hmar in Manipur', Unpublished PhD Thesis, Department of Sociology, School of Social Sciences, North Eastern Hill University, Shillong.

Sawmveli, V. (2005). 'Christianity and Gender: A Study of Protestant Mizos', Unpublished MPhil Thesis, School of Social Sciences, Department of Sociology, University of Hyderabad.

Sheleff, Leon Shaskolsky (2009). *The Future of Tradition: Customary Law, Common Law and Legal Pluralism*, New York: Routledge.

Shimray, U.A. (2002). 'Equality as Tradition: Women's Role in Naga Society', *Economic and Political Weekly*, 37(5): 375–77.

Srikanth, H. (2000). 'Homogenisation and Disintegration: A Study of Northeast India', *Journal of Assam University*, 1: 101–08.

—— (2006). 'British Colonialism and the Hill Tribes of Composite Assam', *Man and Society: A Journal of North East Studies*, 3: 79–116.

Tamanaha, Brian Z. (2008). 'Understanding Legal Pluralism: Past to Present, Local to Global', *Sydney Law Review*, 30: 375–411.

Varte, Immanuel Zarzosang (2013). 'Impact of Development on the Hmars of Tipaimukh in Churachandpur District, Manipur', Unpublished PhD Thesis, North Eastern Hill University, Shillong.

Verghese, R. (1997). *India's Northeast Resurgent*, 2nd edition, New Delhi: Konark Publishers Private Ltd.

7

Gender Specific Problems of Refugees

A Case Study of Tibetan Women Refugee

CHIME YOUDON

Abstract

Refugees are the resultant outcomes of either caused by civil conflicts or natural calamities but lately gender-based refugees have increased over the period of time. International human rights law and international humanitarian law instruments complement the safeguard for the refugees specified in the 1951 Convention. Hence, the international refugee law applies to all forms refugees in the world without any discrimination. However, gender-based refugees were not much discussed and undermined in international relations. Under the Chinese communist regime, Tibetan people continue to suffer from violation of human rights. Tibetans are victims of occupation, arbitrary arrest, torture, violation of freedom of speech and assembly, restriction on freedom of religion and freedom of expression. Women have to suffer gender-based torture such as forced birth control, sexual related torture, forced sterilization and abortions. Moreover, women political prisoners are raped, tortured and sexually abused, because of severe beatings and torture, many results in death. Tibetan women are discriminated in the field of education, employment and health. Chinese Government has proposed a birth control policy on Tibetan women, which controls women's right to live.

UNHCR guidelines for the protection of women's right are less clearly defined and fail to reach them and understand their core problems. Even though countries like China are party to UN Convention such as Convention against Torture and Other Cruel inhuman or Degrading Treatment or Punishment in 1988 and CEDAW-Convention on the Elimination of All forms of Discrimination against Women in 1981, but still they violate such conventions. In this case, it is the state that violates the rights of individual. Hence, UN Conventions and laws are ineffective and challenging. Against this background, this paper analyses the specific problem of refugees with a case study of Tibetan women refugees.

Keywords

Tibetan Refugee Women, Exile, International Refugee Law, Gender-Based Violence and Torture, Chinese Communist Regime.

Introduction

The term refugee was initially adopted in international relations within the context of post-war reconstruction. But with the change in the nature of international relations, there was an increase in the displacement of people not only caused by war, but also by colonization, gender violence, civil conflicts, climate change and so on and so forth. This has resulted in the rise of the refugees in international communities. The evolution of concept of refugee can be traced to the inception of the UN Convention of 1951. According to the United Nations Refugee Convention 1951, refugee is a person who has a well-founded fear of persecution; or a person who is a victim or potential victim of persecution because of race, religion, nationality, membership in a particular social group, or of a particular political opinion. According to the United Nations, more than 80 per cent of refugees are women and children who are more vulnerable to exploitation and deprivation of rights as compare to male refugees.

Most refugees are the resultant of either civil conflicts or natural calamities but lately gender-based refugee has increased over the period of time. International human rights law and international humanitarian law instruments complement the safeguard for refugees specified in the 1951 Convention. Hence, the international refugee law applies to all forms of refugees in the world without any discrimination. However, gender-based refugees were not much discussed and undermined in international relations. As a result, 'some states and jurisdiction continue to fail to apply a full interpretation of the refugee definition'. According to UNHCR, 80 per cent of refugees and international displaced people are women and children. Women in the resettlement are particularly vulnerable. Women experience gendered forms of violence and discrimination, such as inequality, abuses, rape and fear of rape, enforced pregnancy, slavery, sexual trafficking, enforced sterilization, and infection with sexually transmitted diseases and AIDS as well as relatively poor health. This abuse violates both women's rights to their own bodies and to their physical and psychological well-being. Moreover, women often face unemployment problem, hence, they do the most low skilled, least paid and most abused and dishonoured jobs. In the globalized world, patterns of trade, investment, and communication are dominated by the masculinity whereas women are treated as commodities and commercial objects. Women bear these problems while being a mother, nurse, teacher, breadwinner and physical protector of their families. Be it female refugees or poverty-induced displaced women, they all experience the same gendered specific violence in the globalized world.

After much discussion and debate, it was felt necessary to recognize gender-related refugee status. In 1990, skilled female interviewers were provided to women asylum seekers (Executive Committee, 1990). In 1991, UNHCR provided 'Guidelines on the Protection of Refugee Women', and stated that 'special efforts may be needed to resolve problems faced specifically by refugee women (UNHCR, 1991). Further, in October 1995 and in the subsequent years, the Executive Committee called upon the High Commissioner to support and promote efforts by States towards the development and implementation of criteria and guidelines on responses to persecution specifically aimed at women. In accordance with the principle that women's rights are human rights, these guidelines should recognize as refugees women whose claim to refugee status is based upon well-founded fear of persecution for reasons enumerated in the 1951 Convention and 1967 Protocol, including persecution through sexual violence or gender-related persecution (Executive Committee, 1995).

Even though, there are numerous Non-Governmental Organizations and Inter-Governmental Organizations who work to advocate on behalf of refugee women and children but those organizations' works are not clearly defined and fail to reach them and understand core problems of women. At the same time, women have not been regarded in mainstream refugee debate rather systematically excluded. The gender-based violence continues to be experienced by the women. UNHCR 1991 guidelines for refugee women is not a legal binding to all the states and communist regime like China still continues to torture and harass women, specifically Tibetan women, making them refugee in their own land. This paper proposes to identify the push factors that cause Tibetan refugee women and gender specific problem of refugee women. An attempt has been made to answer research questions that arise. They are:

1. Main causes or push factor which led to Tibetans fled to exile. What are the challenges and hardship refugee women face in life in exile.
2. What is it that the international community has done so far to protect marginalized people?
3. Are UN Convention 1991 guidelines effective for refugee women?

Tibetan Women

Under the Chinese communist regime, Tibetan people continue to suffer from violation of human rights. Tibetans are victims of occupation, arbitrary arrest, torture, violation of freedom of speech and assembly, restriction on freedom of religion and freedom of expression. Women have to suffer gender-based torture such as forced birth control, sexual torture, forced sterilization and abortions. Moreover, women political prisoners are raped, tortured and sexually abused, because of server beatings and torture, many result in death. Tibetan women are discriminated in the field of education, employment and health. Chinese Government have proposed a birth control policy on Tibetan women it controls women's right to live and their reproductive roles. Traditionally, Tibetan women enjoyed a great deal of freedom, economic condition was better and stable unlike conditions under the Chinese occupation. Women in Tibet are living in a low socio-economic class with limited access to education, which results in unemployment and poverty. Because of such acts of Chinese Government against Tibetans, thousands of women fled to exile, in order to escape from repression and restriction in life. Women in Tibet continue to suffer torture and harassment because everyone cannot run away like those who made it. It has resulted into both internal and external refugee. However, their burden was not reduced after coming into exile as they have to adjust new environment, new beginning without home and family. They have to start their life from the stretch.

Tibetan Women in Chinese Occupied Tibet

The status of women in traditional Tibet was remarkably good and Tibetan women usually enjoyed much more freedom and prestige in Tibet than other Asian countries (Rajput, 2012). After China occupied Tibet, Tibetans were tortured and their rights were violated. Tibetan women in Tibet face gender-specific violations such as torture, reproductive rights violations, and discrimination in the field of education, health facility, employment and human rights violation in one word. Women in Tibet live under severe restrictions to their political, religious, reproductive and social freedom (Rajput, 2012).

In the case of Tibetan women refugee, before going into the problems that they face, the main causes or push factors that led Tibetans women to flee into exile are discussed. Women in occupied-Tibet are the innocent victims of the policies of a powerful external force that seeks to completely wipe out the Tibetan national identity. While the world debates the legitimacy and morality of abortions, women in Tibet are subjected to involuntary and forced abortions and sterilizations, designed to reduce the growth of the Tibetan populations. Abortions and sterilizations are conducted without adequate medical facilities or in unhygienic conditions.

Most of the incidents and information are based on National Report on Tibetan Women issued by Women's Issue Desk of Department of Information and International Relations, Central Tibetan Administration and TWA, NGO Post-Beijing Alternative Report on Tibetan Women in 2000. Tibetan women are subjected to wide range of violence as mentioned above and mostly nuns are targeted for gender-based violence. Over 80 per cent of female political prisoners are nuns, which violates both human rights and religious rights.

There were reports in the world community about torture taking place in Tibet, specifically regarding the Tibetan political prisoners. It is evident that tortures are taking place in China since BPFA. According to TWA report (2000), there were 615 Tibetan political prisoners held in Tibet, 162 or 35 per cent of who were women by December 1999. According to Tibet Information Network (TIN), it is estimated that one out of every 22 female political prisoners in Drapchi prison died as a result of abuse under detention.

Tibetan Centre for Human Rights and Democracy (TCHRD) has interviewed a former prisoner who fled to India. Tenzin Choedon, 28 years old, nun, narrated her experience and torture she had to go through while imprisoned:

> We were all hit with rifle butts, then an official set a dog upon me, we were taken to a hall and ordered to remove our clothes, except for our waist coat and petticoat .... I was stripped and told to lie down on the floor as if prostrating. I saw them bringing knotted ropes, electric batons and sticks. First I was hit with

> a stick all over my body. I saw my fellow nuns being abused with electric batons in their anus. When the baton was used on my body, I felt as if a nerve in my heart was being pulled out and my stomach was in pain ... I was told to stand up and lean against the wall. They inserted a stick into my vagina four times with full force, which resulted in pain that lasted for three days and also gave me problems when urinating. Then the stick was rammed into my mouth ... after this incident, I was unable to move and they had to take me to my cell. When I recovered my senses, I saw that my skin had become green and that I had marks on my buttocks.

In a joint report given by LawAsia and Tibet Information Network, 'written and oral accounts by nuns of their experience in prison, particularly in Gurtsa, are strikingly consistent and indicate that nuns have been singled out for special treatment. Especially nuns experienced severe and inhumane torture such as use of dogs to bite prisoners, lighted cigarettes being applied to the torso and face and the use of electric batons in the genitals' (LawAsia and Tibet Information Network, 1991). According to National Report on Tibetan Women issued by Women's Issue Desk of Department of Information and International Relations, Central Tibetan Administration, 'In 1984 China announced a new policy, restricting the number of children per family to possibly one. Orders were issued for the imposition of fines (ranging from 1,500 to 3,000 yuan or US $ 400 to 800) for the birth of a third child. Extra children were denied ration cards, and workers are punished to pay 50 per cent of their salary as a fine for three to six months in some cases'. Officially, one child policy is applied to the Chinese nationalities, minorities are not included. But in reality, this policy is actively carried out in Tibet since 1980s. In July 1990, a team from Shigatse Child and Maternity Hospital visited a remote and poor area of Bhuchung district to carry out examinations. It was found that 387 women in this sparsely populated rural area had been sterilized. Even women well advanced in their pregnancy are forced to undergo abortion, followed by sterilization.

Family Planning Department head, Tsering Dolkar, stated at a meeting:

> There are 1,04,024 women of child-bearing age, of whom 76,220 are married. Of them, 22,634 have already undergone birth-control operations, constituting thirty percent of women of child-bearing age in the TAR'. Thereafter, they can have a child only with a birth permit from the authorities. Then there are various subtle birth-control policies such as restrictions on who may give birth, at what age and where, and fines of up to 2,000 yuan (US $ 400) for 'illegal' children, and also given incentives for one-child families, etc.

Many Tibetan women were tortured by the Chinese authorities and some ran away to exile. A former political prisoner of Chinese Communist regime in Tibet, Dawa Langzom, a nun, was arrested in 1989 in Lhasa, after shouting independence slogans during a demonstration. In the police jeep, when she was being taken to the detention centre, police officers cut off one of her nipples with a scissors, according to nuns who have now fled Tibet. Ngawang Kyizom was arrested for shouting slogans like 'Long live the Dalai Lama' and 'Free Tibet' at the entrance of the Jokhang (the main cathedral in Lhasa). For this outburst, in

September 1990, Chinese secret police kicked and beat her, jabbed her with an electric cattle prod on her tongue, breasts and thighs and then jailed her for three years without a proper trial.

Another Tibetan woman, 26-year-old Sonam Dolkar, was arrested in July 1990 on suspicion of her involvement in independence activities. She went through a fearsome range of torture techniques. She was stripped naked, slapped and punched. She was wrapped in electric wires and given electric shocks until she fainted. She was prodded with electric batons all over her body and on the face. Electric batons were also pushed into her genitals. By early 1991, because of severe health condition, she was eventually transferred to a police hospital from where she managed to escape and fled to India.

They are many more women and nuns in Tibet who have and are still going through such tortures being a suspect member of an independence organization. In fact, on 23 December 2014, Tibetan woman, 19-year-old dies of self-immolation and Chinese police forcibly took away her body to an unknown place and detained her family. Furthermore, Tibetan women suffer disadvantages in areas of education, employment, health and administrative services because of medium of the language is Chinese language. Such incidents led thousands of Tibetans to leave their home and take risk of coming to exile with the hope of better socio-economic opportunities and free from both mental and physical harassment. The fact is that Tibetan refugees left Tibet not as families but individuals and loss of family member affected the kinship stability for most of Tibetan refugees. However, Tibetan women in exile are also not free from these forms of problems.

Tibetan Refugee Women in Exile

India is neither party to the 1951 Convention on Refugees nor the 1967 Protocol. The lack of specific refugee legislation in India has led the government to adopt an ad hoc approach to different refugee influxes. The status of refugees in India is governed mainly by political and administrative decisions rather than any codified model of conduct. The ad hoc nature of the government's approach has led to varying treatment of different refugee groups. Some groups are granted a full range of benefits including legal residence and the ability to be legally employed, whilst others are criminalized and denied access to basic social resources.

The legal status of Tibetan refugees in India is governed mainly by the Foreigners Act 1946 and the Citizenship Act 1955. These Acts do not distinguish refugees fleeing persecution from other foreigners; they apply to all non-citizens equally. Under the Acts, it is a criminal offence to be without valid travel or residence documents. These provisions render refugees liable to deportation and detention. The United Nations High Commissioner for Refugees (UNHCR) is based in New Delhi. Once recognized, Afghan, Burmese, Palestinian and Somali refugees receive protection from the UNHCR. Many refugees receive a small monthly subsistence allowance and all have access to the services provided by the UNHCR's implementing partners in Delhi: the YMCA, Don Bosco and the

Socio-Legal Centre (SLC) (Human Rights Law Network, Report of Refugee Populations in India, 2007: 2).

The largest number of Tibetan refugee stays in India. The problem is that India has not ratified UN Convention on Refugee. So, the Tibetans who are living in India are considered as a foreigner even though they are technically refugees. Therefore, those who fled Tibet to India to seek asylum are considered as foreigners. Yet many Tibetans who arrive recently do not have proper legal document that permits them to stay and makes them stateless. However, the permit Registration Certificate has to be renewed every five years but before the duration was one year. Despite Indian Government having given shelter and education opportunities, they face varied other problems like displacement, dislocation of their normal life, different system, language, etc. making it difficult to approach Indian legal system. It is true that every refugee faced many problems, but women have to face gender specific problem because the burden of building new home is solely on the women in a new environment without proper structure.

Conclusion

Refugees tend to be marginalized in the new societies. They suffer from the feeling of alienation and more often than not, lower status than that they had in their countries of origin. Refugee women find it difficult to adjust to the new and changing circumstances after losing country, community, family, status, property, culture and even a sense of personal identity. Even though there are refugee regimes and numerous Non-Governmental Organizations and Inter-Governmental Organizations who are working for the protection of refugees. UNHCR guidelines for the protection of women's right are less clearly defined and fail to reach them and understand their core problems. Even though countries like China are party to UN Convention such as Convention against Torture and Other Cruel inhuman or Degrading Treatment or Punishment in 1988 and CEDAW-Convention on the Elimination of All forms of Discrimination against Women in 1981, but still they violate such conventions. In this case, it is the state that violates the rights of individual. Hence, UN Conventions and laws are ineffective and challenging.

As a result, refugee women as a whole and Tibetan women formed one of the most vulnerable and marginalized section because they are stateless people without a legal refugee status. Yet those who are in Tibet are refugee in their own land because lack of proper institution to look after them and zero freedom to exercise their basic human rights. In dire situation, international communities should take serious action against violator of human rights and dignity. Moreover, refugee cannot be one who is outside the country but those who are unable to escape from the torture are the one who needs to be taken care of.

References

Buscher, Dale (2011). *Unequal in Exile: Gender Equality, Sexual Identity and Refugee Status*, Amsterdam: Amsterdam Law Forum.

Central Tibetan Administration, Women's Issues Desk, Department of Information and International Relations, 'Tibetan Women Oppression and Description in Occupied Tibet', National Report on Tibetan Women for the Fourth World Conference on Women, Beijing, September 4–5, 1995.

Executive Committee, 1990, Conclusion No. 64 (XLI).

Executive Committee, 1995, Conclusion No. 77 (XLVI).

Foreign Affairs Committee Evidence, Great Britain (2007). *Human Rights Annual Report 2007: Ninth Report of Session 2007–08.*

Geoff, M.C. Goldstein et al. (2005). 'Tibetan Fertility Transitions in China and South Asia', *Population and Development Review*, 31(2): 337–49.

Gyatso, Jannet and Havnevik, Hanna (eds) (2005). *Women in Tibet*, New York: Columbia University Press.

Hans, Asha (2008). 'Gender, Camps and International Norms', *Refugee Watch*, 32, December.

Human Rights Law Network (2007). *Report of Refugee Populations in India*, November.

Kikhang, Yangchen (1992). 'Family Planning Methods in Tibet', *British Medical Journal*, 305(6859).

LawAsia and Tibet Information Network (1991). *Defying the Dragon: China and Human Rights in Tibet*, UK.

Martin, Susan (2010). 'Gender and the Evolving Refugee Regime', *Refugee Survey Quarterly*, 29(2).

Rajput, Madhu (2012). 'Tibetan Women: Past and Present', *Dialogue*, 14(7), October–December.

Sam, Canyon (2009). *Sky Train: Tibetan Women on the Edge of History*, London: University of Washington Press.

Tibetan Women's Association (2000). *NGO Alternative Report on Tibetan Women: The Status of Tibetan Women 1995–2000 for the Beijing +5 Women 2000 Gender Equality, Development and Peace for the 21st Century*, Dharamsala.

UNHCR (1991). *Guidelines on the Protection of Refugee Women*, Geneva.

—— (2005). *Ensuring Gender Sensitivity in the Context of Refugee Status Determination and Resettlement*, Bureau for Europe, Geneva.

8

Gender Stereotyping and Indian Legislation

An Illustrative Analysis

SUVARNA PRAVIN DAMLE

Abstract

'Gender stereotyping' as a way of thinking and attributing gender roles is deeply inculcated in the social psyche. As a result, it has also found a profoundly disturbing position in the Indian legislation. The perspective on gender as a socio-cultural and personalized concept and understanding of the so-called 'gender roles' has crystallized the notion of 'gender-role' and simultaneously made 'gender stereotyping' a strong fracturing concern. Indian legislation has been oscillating between deeply stereotyped and progressive gender neutral provisions. This has had a deep impact on the substance and direction of litigation and the judgments in the Indian Legal System. The primary concern of this paper is to address language used in certain legislation in view of gender stereotyping. It includes general laws as well as certain special legislation drafted on the basis of 'positive discrimination' in favour of women. These are to be seen in the light of Article 14 and 15 of the Constitution of India. An attempt is also made to critically analyse the judgments and the trend of interpretation undertaken by the Indian judiciary, since law also contemplates adjudication and delivery of justice. This paper is an attempt to study and identify provisions that indicate the deeply percolated essence of gender stereotyping in Indian legal system.

Keywords

Gender, Stereotyping, Indian Legislation, Gender-Roles.

Introduction

Law is a social logic which has legislation and custom as its instruments and rectification of wrong as its end. Thus, the end of law is rectification of a wrong. Wrong is any act that denoted law of the land considers being wrong and provides a sanction for it. Customs and legislation are not law per se but they are the instruments of law. Legislation, particularly, may be named as penal, welfare, economic, procedural legislation, etc. The 'Statement of Object and Reason' in a particular legislation may state a specific object/role of that legislation. However, this is a supplementary role, ancillary to the primary role of any legislation, which is 'rectification of a wrong'.

Against this background the paper revolves around two aspects. One is that of drafted law and second is the concept of gender stereotyping. An attempt is made to study, analyse and interpret the language of the provisions of selected four legislations and find out whether they are in any way a product of gender stereotyping. The study shall be restricted to the Indian legislation, the reason being that the phenomena of gender stereotyping should be viewed and understood in a specific socio-economic-cultural-educational-demographic conditions and a social setting which offers the reason to law.

Law: Its Interpretation

Interpretation of any particular draft of law includes aspects like the intention of the legislature, the nature of the legislation, the statement of object and reasons, the definitions, the heading of a particular provision, the content of the provision, the exceptions and proviso and the effect of the legislation. However, this paper proceeds on certain propositions. They are as follows:

1. Law cannot be drafted and applied nor can it be understood in isolation,
2. The objective of law is to undo the wrong and punish the wrong doer,
3. Law generates from a specific social-political-cultural-educational-demographical setting,
4. Gender and law are two interactive phenomena,
5. Often law is viewed in terms of gender-specific norms, and
6. Gender stereotyping can be female gender stereotyping and male gender stereotyping. Both are mutually co-relative and have a directly proportional concretization.

'Sex' and 'gender' are seen as two expressions:

1. Sex: 'I AM A MALE'/'I AM A FEMALE'.
2. Gender: 'I AM A MALE, THEREFORE ...'/'SINCE I AM A FEMALE ...'

These two expressions are vocal enough to locate a basic difference between gender and sex. 'Sex' is a phenomenon which shall remain universal, irrespective of the cultural differences in societies. Gender on the other hand is the attachment of socio-cultural-economic-mythical-emotional/psychological-domestic functional-political attributes to an individual because the person is a male or a female. The concept of gender is subjective and liable to change and may not necessarily be universal. This attribution defines the 'gender roles'.

Gender Roles

'Gender role', on the other hand, can be seen as the functions, responsibilities and legal liabilities arising from such attribution which are typical and could be easily identified. Gender roles are by and large fixed. They get fixed due to a very long unchallenged practice, religious beliefs, social conditions, education system and content, long established customs and traditions, legal compulsions, etc.

Gender Role and Stereotyping

Gender stereotyping is understood as a long, consistent and unchallenged association, attachment or attribution of a particular role, quality, qualification or disqualification, function, right and/or duty to a particular sex resulting into the reinforcement and concretization of that association, attachment or attribution. Thus, the crux of the matter lies not with the mere attachment of a particular attribute to a particular sex, but in the reinforcement and concretization of it. Such reinforcement becomes of a greater concern when it finds an expression through law and is practiced as a standard legal course.

Gender Stereotyping and Indian Legislation

The celebrated concept 'positive discrimination', in which certain legislations in India find their justification, works in a wrongly perceived premise that is of gender stereotyping, which results into superficial equality, reinforcement and concretization of certain gender roles or creation of new labels.

Illustrations

This paper attempts to study and identify provision that indicate the deeply percolated essence of gender stereotyping in Indian legal system. Thus, certain provisions of the Indian legislation have been given as illustrations to prove the gender stereotyping. These are given below:

Provisions Related to 'Offences Relating to Marriage' of the Indian Penal Code, 1860

This should be specifically viewed in the light of the laws related to marriage in India, especially The Hindu Marriage Act, 1955 which, by the specific use of the word 'spouse' affords an equal status to both man and woman in a marital relation and consequentially sets out by and large equal rights and remedies to the husband and the wife (Section 497 of the Indian Penal Code, 1860).

Section 497 defines 'adultery' as 'whoever has sexual intercourse with a person who is and whom he knows or has reason to believe to be the wife of another man, without the consent or connivance of that man, such sexual intercourse not amounting to the offence of rape, is guilty of the offence of adultery.' On correct interpretation, this definition:

1. Links the sanctity of the woman to the sanctity of the marital relation.
2. Stereotypes that breach of sanctity of wife is the breach of marriage.
3. Neglects the consent of the woman and makes consent or connivance of the husband of utmost importance. This resultantly reiterates and reinforces the role of the husband to exercise control and bear the custody of his wife.
4. Stereotypes wife being property of husband and strengthens this attribution.

5. Presumes that the wife will never be an active party in the crime, transgressing the principle of criminal jurisprudence, result being victimization being attached to woman and exploitation attached to the man.
6. Gives the husband the right to prosecute the third man who commits adultery based upon a perception that the husband is deprived of his right over his wife. The wife is deprived of any such locus, the only remedy being divorce.
7. Generates an impression that if the husband consents to the sexual intercourse of his wife with another man, then it will not amount to adultery.

A gender stereotypical drafting like the above illustration produces a bad law. It, however, remains unchanged and supported by the judicial decisions upholding its constitutionality (AIR 1985 SC 1618).

Section 60 of The Code of Civil Procedure, 1908

The Code of Civil Procedure [CPC] is a procedural legislation. Under Section 60 of CPC (Section 60 of The Code of Civil Procedure, 1908), it enumerates what property can be attached. The proviso to the main section essentially prohibits the attachment and sale of certain 'particulars' which includes 'wives and children' as one of the particulars. On correct interpretation of this proviso, it can be observed that:

1. 'Wives and children' are 'particulars', specifically prohibited from being attached and sold for executing a decree,
2. Nevertheless, they are 'property', and
3. It is silent on whether there is a prohibition to attach and sell husband, if the litigant is a woman. In absence of a specific prohibition, question remains whether such an attachment and sale will be tenable in law.

The proviso, though a categorical prohibition fails to remove the stereotyping of woman being a property of a man. Consequently, the provision strengthens the stereotyping that a man will hold his wife as his property. This prohibition also indicates that before the enactment of the CPC, attachment and sale of wives was possible, permissible and legal. This practice also finds reference in the great Indian epic, the *Mahabharat*, wherein the Pandavs used their wife *Draupadi* as bet in the gamble against Duryodhan, their adversary.

CPC is 106 years old legislation and the aforementioned provision remains un-amended till today. It should be noted that neither there is any effort by the legislature nor from the judiciary to amend the provision.

The Sexual Harassment of Women at Work Place Prevention and Protection Act, 2013

The prima facie objection, in case of this legislation, is to the title of the law read in light of the contents of the law, for principles of interpretation guide that any legislation is to be read as a whole.

The Hon'ble Supreme Court of India in Vishakha vs State of Rajasthan (AIR 1997 SC 3011), laid down the guidelines for the protection of women from sexual harassment at workplace following the C-DAW and D-DAW. The aim and objective of the legislation though on the lines of the provisions of the Constitution of India, the argument remains that the drafting of this legislation emerges from a stereotypical view adopted by the judiciary and the legislators. Despite the facts from which the judgment of *Vishakha* has emerged, argument remains that the stereotypical concepts of sexuality of a woman, the extreme sanctity attached to it, and continuous reluctance of considering that there is sanctity to the sexuality of a man, the stereotyped opinion of modesty and its easy breach by any action of a man, the stereotypical view that only a man can be guilty of breaching the modesty and sexuality of a woman and not vice-versa, extreme importance given to the perception of a woman about any act of any man, probably done in good faith, presumption that only a man will always have uncontrollable sexual aspirations, results into such a positively discriminating legislation like the one stated above which grossly fails to carry out the function of law, i.e. to rectify the wrong. This is because the legislation works on a wrong premise. The following observations are made on the correct interpretation of this statute:

1. The legislation is based on the presumption that only women could be sexually harassed. The definition of 'sexual harassment' in the legislation includes such acts which are capable of being done by a man and a woman, for example showing pornography, passing sexually coloured remarks, etc. Despite this, the stereotypical understanding of the legislators does not permit them to foresee otherwise and it is legally established that only a man will undertake such sexually coloured acts.
2. It is presumed that a woman will never have unsatisfied sexual aspirations and that even if she so has, she will never express them in the manner contemplated and condemned by this legislation.
3. The legislation does not provide for easily foreseeable situation where the delinquent is a woman and the victim is a man. The legislation does not provide for a remedy to a man.
4. It places the sanctity of a woman on such a high pedestal that, if stretched a bit far, even a normal compliment could fit squarely into the definition of 'sexual harassment'.
5. The perception of a woman is placed as the standard of proof. Litigation becomes all the more complex in such a situation and the legislation being evidently for women the decisions tend to favour the woman since a woman will not complain of the 'breach of her modesty' without sufficient reason. The sufficient reason is based upon her 'perception' (*Miss Radhabai vs The Union Territory of Pondicherry AIR 1995 SC 1476*).
6. The judicial view is hyper stereotypical about the notions of modesty of a woman (Mrs Rupan Deol Bajaj and Anr vs Kanwar Pal Singh Gill and Anr AIR 1996 SC 309).

The legislation provides for a departmental enquiry for the adjudication of a complaint of sexual harassment. The principle of interpretation and appreciation of evidence in such enquiries is essentially 'preponderance of probabilities' (in *N.K. Suroya vs Union of India 2003*). It is to be noted that the legislation is essentially favourable to women. The adjudication of the complaint works on the stereotypical view as stated above. The preponderance of probability in effect is also viewed in favour of the stereotypical notions stated above. A law, such as this, is expected to rectify and punish a sexually delinquent behaviour at work place. However, this law due to its stereotypical drafting essentially seeks to rectify only 50 per cent of one whole of possibilities of sexually deviant behaviour. The name of the law could have been 'Protection of Persons from Sexual Harassment at Work Place' which would pose to be a gender neutral law and not deny the right of women to work freely at any chosen work place.

Dowry Prohibition Act, 1961

The drafting of Section 4 of The Dowry Prohibition Act, 1961 states about the 'penalty for the demand of dowry'. To quote 'if any person demands dowry directly or indirectly, from the parents or other relatives or guardian of a bride or bridegroom, as the case may be, any dowry, he shall be punishable with imprisonment for a term which shall be less than six months, but which may extend to two years and fine which may extend to rupees ten thousand.'

Certain observations are made on interpretation of this particular section in the light of the practices related to dowry and its consequences:

1. The heading of the section is straight. It is unambiguous as to the aim of the provision. 'Demand of dowry' has been identified as a legal wrong and a sanction has been provided for it, in form of penalty.
2. The heading, read in the light of the contents of the section, make it absolutely clear that the provision does not stereotype that the demand of dowry will be made only by the bride-groom and his family members.
3. It holds both, the bride and her family and the groom and his family criminally liable for the demand of dowry. The use of the word 'person' and 'bride or bridegroom, as the case may be ...' are worth noting in this respect.
4. This provision is a penal provision. Unlike the provisions related to 'offences against marriage' contained in the Indian Penal Code as referred to herein above, this provision affords equal status to both males and females. It does not stereotype the act by attributing it to only one sex. It should be noted that though the practice is largely carried on by the groom's counterparts in a wedding, the legislation is sound enough to foresee a possible demand of dowry by the bride's counterpart in a wedding. This is instrumental in rectifying the ultimate wrong.
5. It does not stereotype women as 'not capable of demanding dowry'.
6. It condemns the practice of demand of dowry and identifies it as an offence.
7. It holds both man and woman guilty for the commission of the said crime. Resultantly, it also provides safeguard from frivolous complaints.

The drafting of this particular law reflects a gender neutral drafting. It is clear as to the wrong that it wants to rectify.

Observations and Conclusion

Legislations are tools of law. Proper drafting is the only way by which law could be effectively implemented. As defined hereinbefore, law is social logic. The essence is that the logic should be reasonably modified as the social phenomena undergo change.

It should be noted that the first three sample legislations that were chosen for interpretation and analysis are studied in the light of the aforementioned propositions. After considering all the four legislations, the following conclusions could be drawn:

1. The law should be such that it is in letter and spirit aimed at correction and rectification of legal wrong/s.
2. It should be based upon sound considerations, logic and reasons.
3. It should not be based upon and/or reflect and/or promote expressly or subtly and/or support and/or reinforce stereotyping of any gender, for stereotyping of one gender results into the stereotyping of the other gender.
4. Law must be gender neutral in order to avoid misuse and/or ineffective application of the law.
5. Though the concept of positive discrimination is cherished, it must not be so nurtured so as to make the so-called beneficiaries dependent, incapable and unequal in the eyes of law. Further the concept must not be engrafted in a way so as to strengthen the long driven stereotypical notions. Stereotyping of a particular gender cannot, at any point of time, be a rationale of any legislation.
6. Law must treat delinquents equally. Further, no law should presume that a person will never be a delinquent since he is of a particular sex.
7. Law must provide equal remedy to an aggrieved, may it be a male or a female.
8. Hyper technical equality is neither expected nor reasonable. However, a law which propagates differential treatment to a particular sex must not promote superficial equality.

True, correct and achievable, equality of sexes in the sphere of law is and shall always be a product of gender neutral law. Gender neutral law can be formulated only when the gender stereotyped notions and rationale behind formulating a law are done away with. This will help to devise sound remedies and reduce the possibility of biased judgments.

References

AIR 1989 SC 1618.

Miss Radhabai vs The Union Territory of Pondicherry AIR 1995 SC 1476.

Mrs Rupan Deol Bajaj and Anr vs Kanwar Pal Singh Gill and Anr AIR 1996 SC 309.

N.K. Suroya vs Union of India 2003(3) SLI 34 CAT.

The Code of Civil Procedure, 1908-Section 60.

The Dowry Prohibition Act, 1961.

The Indian Penal Code, 1860-Section 497.

The Sexual Harassment of Women at Workplace Prevention and Protection Act, 2013-Section 3.

Vishakha vs State of Rajasthan AIR 1997 SC 3011.

Gender and Health

9

Breaking the Magical Spell

An Analysis of the Emancipation of Female Sexuality in Literary Work

SMRITY SHARMA

Abstract

Female sexuality has been repressed, mutilated and distorted in the literary frameworks. Women have been depicted as the marginalized, undermined section of the patriarchal set-up. Their sexuality is feared, not desired in them. Female sexuality is a tabooed area, not to be discussed and analysed. Angela Carter, a self-avowed feminist, iconoclastic in her feministic stance takes up this rebuffed theme and dissects it to its very core. In her seminary, provocative work, The Passion of New Eve, she breaks the mould of conventional female sexuality. She transforms it and catches its monstrous figments and draws a fresh iconography. Carter in her post-apocalyptic work takes a U-turn from the mythical representations and exonerates her Eve from the fretters of conventional sexuality. Carter's magna opus 'The Passion of New Eve' emancipates women (the marginalized, antithetical) from this bondage and highlights the camouflaged and subverted morass of female sexuality. Against this background, the paper analyses the literary framework through Angela Carter's work to argue that sexuality has multifarious dimensions. She also highlights the need to not only redefine female sexuality but the male, as well.

Keywords

Sexuality, Female, Culture, Emancipation, Masculinity, Trans-Sexuality, Mythology, Rewriting.

Introduction

If 'sex' is a biological category then, sexuality is commonly comprehended as an appendage to sex (biological/anatomical identity). How we respond to this so-called 'natural' phenomenon, how we mould and shape our desires establishes and perpetuates our illusion of 'sexuality' as a fixed, intangible position. We do not determine and control our sexuality; rather, it is cultural, social and economical scenarios that govern our perception of it. Keeping in mind the social and historical viability/mutability of sexuality, it is necessary to redefine it; as it is a highly flexible notion. Sexuality is not a concrete fact; it is not 'innate' as we perceive it. One's sexuality may be totally different from one's biological status. To confuse biological instinct with sexuality is a common misunderstanding. Consideration of factors beside biological reality is required to grasp this slippery idea of sexuality. A critical apprehension of difference between sexuality and biology is mandatory. A fresh iconography is needed to substitute this antiquated vocabulary of sexuality. As Laplanche and Pontalis (1973) points out:

> If one sets out with the commonly held view that defines sexuality as instinct, in the sense of a pre-determined behaviour typifying the species and having a relatively fixed object (partner of the opposite sex) and aim (union of the genital organs in coitus), it soon becomes apparent that this approach can only provide a very inadequate account of the facts that emerge as much from direct observation as from analysis.

Foucault (1978) in his seminary work *History of Sexuality* offers similar claims: 'Sexuality is not the most intractable element in power relations, but rather one of those endowed with the greatest instrumentality: useful for the greatest number of manoeuvers and capable of serving as a point of support, as a linchpin, for the most varied strategies'. Cleaning this quagmire of 'sexuality' to excavate and redefine its understanding is very crucial.

Sexuality, for women is a dangerous area; they have been customized to see it (sexuality) as an external fact. An embedded misogyny has been lurking behind the social scene concerning the idea of female sexuality and patriarchal dominance has disciplined the psyche of the female milieu to such an extent that they are scared of acknowledging it. Women have long worn the brunt of such ingrained hatred and violence at the hands of men. As Mother says in a mocking tone, 'Woman has been the antithesis in the dialectic of creation quite long enough' (Foucault, 1978). Bringing women from the periphery to the centre of society may help in redefining and reconstructing the idea of sexuality.

Commenting on the wide reach of sexually-exploitative cultural images, Wolf remarks: 'The woman learns from these images that no matter how assertive she may be in the world, her private submission to control is what makes her desirable' (Wolf, 1991). In order to combat these culturally and historically-spanning images of sexual domination, the debunking of age-old myths is indispensable. Arguing in the same line, feminist critic Juliet Mitchell says:

> Under patriarchal order women are oppressed in their very psychologies of femininity; once this order is retained only in a highly contradictory manner this oppression manifests itself. Women have to organize themselves as a

> group to effect a change in the basic ideology of human society. To be effective, this can be no righteous challenge to the simple domination of men (though this plays a tactical part), but a struggle based on a theory of the social non-necessity at this stage of development of the laws instituted by patriarchy. (Mitchell, 1974)

Female sexuality has always been considered a transgression from the normative codes of literary framework. Representations of sexuality are constrained by masculine and feminine behaviour. In the traditional/conventional line of thought, women have been confined as the sites of compulsory reproduction and as individuals who derive ultimate pleasure from mothering. These patterns of sexuality are choreographed according to the patriarchal will. In the traditional set-up women refuse to acknowledge and exercise their sexuality, considering it a moral perversion and demonic degradation. As men have been privileged over women in patriarchal societies, and women used only for procreation; the concepts of gender and sexuality have emerged as 'natural'. Such seemingly irrefutable position has poisoned the psyches with an atavistic and misogynistic repercussion. Women become complicit in their own subjection and hence, perpetuate patriarchal hold. It can be said that women have been disciplined to be terrified of exploring and enjoying their sexuality, which they have been forced to acknowledge in relation to men, solely. Feminists have been urging to venture into this complex trajectory and embracing of sexuality as an innate part of one's existence. They have been attempting to decipher and contest the popular symbolism of 'delirious sickness of femininity, its passivity, its narcissism' (Mitchell, 1974). The stripping off of cultural and historical artifices is required for grasping the idea of female sexuality.

Feminist critics have tried to depict 'sexuality' as a cultural and a social construct like gender. It is a highly contentious, debatable notion as Jeffrey Weeks (1986) remarks that 'sexuality is a 'fictional unity' that once did not exist, and at some time in the future may not exist again'. Such views deconstruct the established views of such fixed concepts and offers vistas for revisions. Here comes the role of writers as revisionists; rewriting the history to propagate an entirely different picture of the world. We have been 'interpellated', to use Althusser's term, to see sexuality as an alien, different terrain; essentialist to its roots, beyond human grasp. Such seeming fixities of sex and gender have distorted and restricted our understanding of it; since time immemorial. These essentialist notions seem so obvious, so natural that we do not pause to think and question their validity (Althusser, 2014).

Critics like Butler (1990) have argued to rob these notions of 'sexuality' and 'gender' of their essentialist claims. For Butler gender is a 'performance', an 'imitation', that both men and women are subjected to mimic. As she has argued in her ground-breaking study *Gender Trouble*: 'Gender is the repeated stylization of the body, a set of repeated acts within a highly rigid regulatory frame that congeal over time to produce the appearance of substance, of a natural source of being'. Stylization is what Carter does in case of the protagonist of the novel, whose biological identity does not correspond to her sexual identity, both of these categories have been put under constant scrutiny.

Carter's (1982) work appears opaque, bizarre and dystopian, but are equally distilled and punctuated with ideas; and that's too highly intellectual ones. Her literary corpus, keeping in tune with the postmodernist norms offers numerous possibilities of interpretations. By impregnating her feminist concerns with the notions of sadism and masochism, she is not eroticizing sexual exploitation of women, rather is trying to make a seismic shift in the dominant and omnipresent understanding of gender and sexuality, especially that of the female milieu. Carter in a vehement fashion unhinges the female sexuality from its traditional, stultifying moulds; making us shudder at the naked display of power-relations that choreograph and sanction women's sexuality as aberration. In her works, she evades demarcation, classifications, flouting all boundaries of class, gender, sex, etc. There is a constant disdain for all fixities, be it social or biological. Her narratives engage in a quest to formulate new and re-worked identities as they are committed to write down a new iconography, a revived history of all cultural, social and biological deterministic, essentialist notions.

Critic Sally Robinson (2009) argues that in her writings, Carter evolved and promulgated 'her own brand of gender politics, which separate 'woman' as biological entity from 'woman' as cultural category' (qtd. in Gamble, 2009). Carter's works blatantly dismiss mythology and historicizing of both masculinity and femininity. Instilled with a demonic energy, her works do not engage in re-inscribing the patriarchal status quo; rather, they lay threadbare the mechanism that sanctions the subordination and subjugation of female 'Other' as essential. Carter (1979) bluntly and boldly dissects the female paranoia of sexual liberty, in the garb of gothic medium, which uses excess as well as transgression.

In her provocative, post-apocalyptic work, *The Passion of New Eve*, which can be read as a 'feminist tract', there is a continuous dismantling, displacement and deconstruction of age-old patriarchal assumptions. The work offers a critique of gender representations, and portrays these culturally pervading images ranging from biblical to Hollywood manifestations of wounded and innocent female sexuality as a masquerade; imprisoning and tarring the actual essence of both masculinity and femininity. In the figure of Eve/Evelyn, the protagonist of the novel, Carter subverts and demythologizes the traditional, andocentric narrative culture by proclaiming: *'One woman is all women'* (Carter, 1982). She, in asserting this dictum, is not beguiling the readers into believing that 'female experience' is a universal notion as she herself is aware of the heterogeneity of the female experience.

The novel creates an alternate, gender-neutral sphere where both polarities (feminine and masculine) are reconciled, equated. Carter belongs to the tradition of revisionists, who put at stake all the claims made by history as well as mythology to give a concrete, wholesome definition of such elusive concepts as sexuality and gender. Highlighting the vigour and subversiveness of Carter's narrative, critic Merja Makinen (1992) argues: 'Carter's work has consistently dealt with the representations of the physical abuse of women in phallocentric cultures, of women alienated from themselves within the male gaze, and conversely of women who grab their own sexuality and fight back, of women troubled by and even powered by their own violence'. In the present work, Carter identifies 'feminine' with the 'universal'. She discards womb-centred existence for a more meaningful, power-yielding position. The present narrative aims at exposing and expressing female fatigue of suppressed anger and the loss of synchronization with her own inner being. Though it may seem a complex and daunting affair but, redefinition and revitalization of sexual identity is required to gain autonomy and emancipation.

The protagonist Eve/lyn undergoes a contrived metamorphosis when he/she is captured by an army of matriarchs in the desert. The awe-inspiring, grand, all-consuming figure of the Mother; who proclaims herself as the 'Castratrix of the Phallocentric Universe' (Carter, 1982), is relinquished by Carter as mythical. Communion with the Mother is irretrievable as she propounds: 'Mother is a figure of speech and has retired to a cave beyond consciousness'. The persona of Zero 'the avenging phallic fire' has also been evoked so that his inefficacy can be into the context. To lancinate and rebuff these prototypes in order to create a new 'creation myth', Carter denounces both Mother and Father (Carter, 1982).

The sexuality of both Eve/lyn and Tristessa is a contesting matter. Eve/lyn who was formerly a male and after the surgery performed by Mother is transformed into a woman (Eve) is made to imbibe the cultural attitudes of femininity. He/she is lulled to assimilate the attributes that are called 'feminine'; forced to adjust to her newly born sense of sexuality. She/he is forced to garble all the available versions of feminine desires. As he/she recounts when she is put in a womb-like laboratory after surgery: 'I swam in and out of your sickness, your ache of eternal longing, your perpetual reverie, your beautiful lack of being, as if your essence were hung up in a closet like a dress too good to be worn and you were reduced to going out in only your appearance.' If we take biology to be in alliance with sexuality, then Eve/lyn's transformation raises questions that shake the foundation of such seeming fixities. His new self is not in concordance with his/her previous sexuality.

Similarly, the character of Tristessa, the Hollywood-produced version of femininity is also a chimera. Her identity is revealed in the 'The Hall of the Immortals' when Zero grabs her to rape her. Then both Zero and Eve/lyn are stunned to find out that what they have believed for so long was a myth, a complete fabrication. This is how Carter (1982) denounces the concept of sexuality as something 'natural', something which cannot be questioned. The connection between biology and sexuality of both Tristessa and Eve/lyn goes awry. Whereas, Eve/lyn is modelled to swallow the culturally pervasive notions of femininity, Tristessa abhors her/his maleness and fashions her/him as:

> ... the shrine of his own desires had made of himself the only woman he could have loved! If a woman is indeed beautiful only in so far as she incarnates most completely the secret aspirations of man, no wonder Tristessa had been able to

> become the most beautiful woman in the world, an unbegotten woman who made no concessions to humanity. (Carter, 1982)

In the characters of both Tristessa and Eve/lyn, Carter undermines the notion of sexuality as an 'instinct'. These instincts do not run in parallel with their anatomies. In their 'constructedness' Carter underlines the constructed nature of such natural drives. In the forced transformation of Evelyn into Eve, Carter destabilizes 'gendered/sexual' fixities. She demystifies the all-pervasive patriarchal reality and creates a new world order. In this alternative, modified world, women are the emancipated sexual 'subjects', not the 'objects' of sexual whims of men. Carter's women are not only aware of their latent sexuality; instead, they are bold and voluptuous enough to deploy it as a tool to attack the prevalent misogyny. Carter's women are the monstrous, libidinous, liberated counterparts to male.. They are not the mythical representation of virtuosity and chastity personified. Further, they have not been portrayed as raw-materials fuelling men's whims and fancies. Carter engages in a stringent interrogation of asymmetrical power relations that dominate man-woman relationships. Commenting on the nature of Carter's brand of female emancipation, Jago Morrison quotes: 'Across the spread of Carter's oeuvre, there is a commitment to exploring the possibilities for imaginative resistance to the gendered legacies of culture.'

'We must make the oppositional space where our sexuality can be named and represented, where we are sexual subjects – no longer bound and trapped' (Morrison, 2014). Carter vouches for such an 'oppositional space' in her narrative world where there exists no bifurcation on the sexual basis. Her post-apocalyptic America of the present work is where she hopes to arrive at a new beginning, a beginning where the 'subject' has not yet been 'subjected' and subjugated by the omnipresent ideology. Though the denouncing of ideology altogether is not possible, but Carter, here, sitting in her anti-ideologistic position, dreams of a place not marred by ideology. She, like Fevvers (protagonist of Carter's later novel *Nights at the Circus*), walks on a tightrope; always on the verge of falling face down. But she pulls her task till the curtain falls with an expertise.

Angela Carter, who was writing in the second-wave feminist line of thought, felt an urge to topple the conventional hegemony of sexuality and gender. This is what Carter evinces and tries to achieve in *The Passion of New Eve*. She was, in her own words, in the 'demythologizing business'. She breaks these fretters of imposed sexuality and draws her characters with reworked zeal in new colours. In her works, 'sex roles' are not the extensions of the biological or anatomical reality.

The novel plays around with the inherited versions/representations of sexuality (male/female), finding possibilities of transfusions or transformations and engages in constant dissection and subversion of social and sexual orthodoxies. It attempts to expose, analyse and examine various sets of institutionalized patriarchal gender representations where women are ashamed or unaware of their own sexual selves. In an interview given to John Haffenden in 1985, Carter talked about her choice of this trans/hetrosexual protagonist: 'I created this person in order to say some quite specific things about the cultural production of femininity.' This is exactly what she materializes in the textual trajectory of the novel debunking all cultural icons, ideals of masculinity and femininity. In this work, there is an exuberant refusal of entrapment in either mythological framework as Carter calls mythology a 'consolatory nonsense', which has been designed to intoxicate and drowse people with false knowledge of the world they inhabit.

Carter's Eve/Evelyn offers the possibility of reconciliation of both the sexes, the notion of gender-neutrality incarnated in the physical form. Her forced transformation leaves her as a site of sadistic, masochistic fantasies of men themselves (including that of her own former self). The matriarchal comrades of the desert form radical and wildly transgressive subjects, given the history of prescriptive sexual modesty for women. Carter does not camouflage or subvert female sexuality, she rather breaks the accepted codes and invents an all together new language to express and define it. Carter here seems to materialize the idea that refusal and debunking of both archetypal masculinity and femininity is necessary in order to arrive at a 'new beginning'. With a bravado and witchy charm, Carter slashes down the bodies of patriarchal myths concerning women and hangs them as dead carcasses on her fictional stage so that the readers can smell the stench and miasma hovering about these decayed myths.

To conclude the above argument we can say that sexuality, though it has been naturalized through the history of human civilization, offers multifarious dimensions, numerous spots to dig its wreck and construct new structures out of it. Carter in this polemic work shrugs away from all labyrinths of mythological imprisonment. She puts away all the rotten symbolism of the age-old past and begins to starch beneath the surface, throwing away the hieroglyphics that have been obscured. She begins on a fresh path to reach a fresher destination. She defies Father God as well as Mother Goddess. The identities of her radical, androgynous character Eve (lyn) keeps on merging, dissolving and blurring. She not only stresses the need to redefine female sexuality but also implores to restructure the notion of the male sexuality as well. The disposal of sexual archetypes is necessary to ameliorate the sexual inequality that patriarchal history sanctions.

References

Althusser, Louis (2014). *On the Production of Capitalism*, London: Verso Books.

Butler, Judith (1990). *Gender Trouble: Feminism and the Subversion of Identity*, New York: Routledge.

Carter, Angela (1979). *The Sadeian Woman: An Exercise in Cultural History*, London: Virago.

—— (1982). *The Passion of New Eve*, London: Virago.

Foucault, Michel (1978). *The History of Sexuality, Vol. 1: An Introduction*, Trans. Robert Hurley, New York: Random House.

Gamble, Sarah (2009). *Angela Carter: A Literary Life*, New York: Palgrave Macmillan.

Haffenden, John (ed.) (1985). *Novelists in Interview*, London: Methuen, 76–96.

Laplanche, Jean and Pontalis, Jean-Bertrand (1973). *The Language of Psycho-Analysis*, Trans. David Nicholson-Smith, London: Hogarth Press.

Makinen, Merja (1992). 'Angela Carter's The Bloody Chamber and the Decolonization of Feminine Sexuality', *Feminist Review*, 42: 2–15.

Mitchell, Juliet (1974). *Psychoanalysis and Feminism: Freud, Reich, Laing and Women*, London: Allen Lane.

Morrison, Jago (2014). *Contemporary Fiction*, London: Routledge.

Weeks, Jeffrey (1986). *Sexuality*, London: Tavistock.

Wolf, Naomi (1991). *The Beauty Myth: How Images of Beauty are Used Against Women*, London: Vintage.

10

Gender Dynamics and Adherence to Tuberculosis Treatment among Co-Infected Patients in the Greater Accra Region of Ghana

HANNAH BENEDICTA TAYLOR-ABDULAI, PATRICIA AKWEONGO AND PHILIP BABA ADONGO

Abstract

Tuberculosis (TB) and Human Immunodeficiency Virus (HIV) are closely linked. TB is known to be the main opportunistic infection among people living with HIV, and HIV is the leading risk factor for developing TB disease. Gender issues are of extreme importance in health and, for that matter, in TB and HIV treatment. This study explores the gender dynamics of TB treatment adherence, with HIV co-infected patients. The study was mainly qualitative and involved in-depth interviews with 12 participants who were co-infected with TB and HIV and six coordinators of TB Programme. The 12 TB and HIV co-infected persons were made of six males and six females between the ages of 30 and 50 years, on both TB and HIV treatment. They were selected through purposive sampling at selected hospitals in the Greater Accra Region. The in-depth interviews were recorded, transcribed verbatim and analysed by themes using QSR Nvivo 10. Trend analysis and comparative analysis were carried out to compare and contrast the findings by gender. The study revealed gender disparities in all spheres, contributed to adherence to treatment. Perception of TB and HIV led patients of the illness, particular women to conceal their status from their partners, family members and work colleagues as knowledge of their status resulted to being abandoned or stigmatized. Social and behavioural factors played a major role in non-adherence of TB and HIV treatment, with pill burden and cost of transportation to the hospital seen as a barrier to non-adherence for both male respondents. The findings indicated that the emotional burden of TB and HIV contributed significantly to a lower quality of life as patients were stigmatized and discriminated against. Based on the findings, there is the need for TB control programmes to be gender sensitive and attention paid to the different socio-cultural, economic and behavioural factors of both gender assume importance.

Keywords

Gender, Co-Infection, TB, HIV, (Non) Adherence.

Introduction

The World Health Organization declared Tuberculosis (TB) as a global epidemic in 1993. The disease continues to spread, in spite of the fact that there is an internationally recognized Directly Observed Treatment Short Course (DOTS) strategy, which has been acclaimed to be highly efficacious to control the epidemic. This situation has been exacerbated by the HIV epidemic since TB and Human Immunodeficiency Virus (HIV) are closely linked. TB is known to be the main opportunistic infection among people living with HIV, and HIV is the leading risk factor for developing TB disease. According to WHO, people living with HIV are about thirty times more likely to develop TB than those without HIV. TB is the commonest illness among people living with HIV, including those on antiretroviral treatment and it is the main cause of HIV-related deaths. Sub-Saharan Africa bears the highest burden of the dual epidemic, making up for almost 75 per cent of the estimated burden in 2012 (WHO, 2013).

Almost 70 per cent of patients with sputum smear-positive pulmonary TB are HIV positive in majority of sub-Saharan Africa countries, where epidemic of HIV is very high (WHO, 2013). In Ghana, available statistics indicate that HIV is relatively stable with pockets of high prevalence amongst risk groups, whilst 23 per cent of all TB cases are persons living with HIV/AIDS (Ghana Technical Policy and Guidelines for HIV/TB Collaboration, 2007).

TB is reported to kill more women than any other single infectious disease (Diwan and Thorson, 1999) and is strongly associated with poverty, with 95 per cent of all tuberculosis cases occurring in the developing world (Diwan and Thorson, 1999). Seventy per cent of the world's poor are female and these women face the greatest obstacle to seeking healthcare and obtaining successful tuberculosis treatment (Diwan and Thorson, 1999). In 2012, an estimated 2.9 million women fell ill with TB; and 4,10,000 women died from TB in 2012. Of the TB deaths among HIV positive people, 50 per cent (1,60,000) were among women. Almost 90 per cent of the HIV-associated TB deaths among women were in Africa, where TB is estimated to have claimed more female lives than male lives, a typical case of co-infection heavily among women. In 2012, globally more than half of the estimated number of female TB cases went undetected, compared to less than 40 per cent in the total population (WHO, 2013). In view of the above, gender issues have been widely accepted to be of extreme importance in health and for that matter in TB and HIV treatment. This study explores the gender dynamics of TB treatment adherence with HIV co-infected patients. For the purpose of this study, adherence is defined as the continuous uninterrupted taking of prescribed TB medications and non-adherence has been defined as interruption of treatment for five consecutive days.

Methods

Respondents were TB and HIV patients and healthcare workers (12 in numbers) purposively selected to provide in-depth, culturally specific knowledge concerning tuberculosis and gender with reference to adherence/non-adherence. Inclusion criteria for patients were female and male over 18 years of age who had been diagnosed of TB and are HIV and have been on treatment for both infections for a minimum of four months.

Data from the in-depth interviews were transcribed into English by the principal researcher. First, a set of transcripts was reviewed to identify possible concepts and categories. Next, a set of codes was developed based on these categories and all transcripts were subsequently coded. During the coding process, constant comparison was done to compare and review accounts given by male and female patients and healthcare workers. This iterative approach to data analysis was done in order to ensure that the most appropriate categories and themes had been formulated and that all perspectives were included. This method of analysis allowed emergent themes to be inductively derived from the statements made by respondents.

Findings

The mean age of the twelve respondents was 41 years (range 30 to 61 years). Four out of the 12 respondents were married, three were in some form of a relationship, three were married but had been abandoned by their spouses, one was divorced, and one widowed. A large proportion of the respondents (six) had pre-secondary education (made up of three with Middle School Leaving Certificate (MSLC), two Junior High School (JHS) leavers, one primary attendee), one secondary school leaver, two technical school leavers and three respondents had no schooling. Finally, on the occupation of respondents, only five out of the twelve respondents were engaged in some form of employment; majority of the respondents (numbering seven) were not engaged in any gainful employment. With respect to social support, almost all respondents had some form of support from their close associates and family members.

Initial Response to being Diagnosed with TB and HIV

This is a period when most patients are in a state of confusion, when they are first informed of their prognosis. To some, it is the end of the world and they even feel they are better off dying than living, especially those who are diagnosed with HIV, because it is not treatable. For those who have had friends and relations with similar conditions, they are able to manage the situation better. Respondents who were interviewed share their experiences of how they felt when they were first told that they were infected with TB and HIV. This is what some respondents said when they were first diagnosed with the diseases:

> I felt like committing suicide, because at that time there was no free medication for HIV. We had to buy out of our pocket. Stigma was heavy – people looked down on HIV patients and so it was like a death sentence. (A female respondent)
>
> I was so afraid; I felt my world had crumbled. Initially, I didn't tell anybody, but later they got to know, because I could not work and so I lost my job. At that time my wife abandoned me. She left with our son. I am now living with my aged mother. (A male respondent)
>
> I got the HIV before the TB, when my family members got to know about my condition they all abandoned me, now I live in a prayer camp. I know my illness is spiritual, somebody gave me the disease in the spirit – I have since been praying about it. (A male respondent)
>
> I never expected to have this type of disease. It should rather have been diabetic or hypertension, but this is too much. I could lock myself indoors and cry the whole day. But what has happened cannot be changed; we pray that one day there will be a cure just like TB. (A female respondent)

When asked how long it took the respondents to know their status, respondents gave varied responses as to how long they had to live with the diseases, before being diagnosed. Majority of patients did not suspect TB at the onset and were probably unaware of the disease before they presented themselves to the health facilities:

> I had malaria for well over six months, then, I got rashes all over my body including shingles and the doctor advised me to do HIV test and to my utmost shock I was told I had HIV. I was however, diagnosed with TB six months ago, when the coughing became uncontrollable. (A male respondent)
>
> It took the doctors eight months to know that I have HIV. At the time, I was like a ghost. I got TB about five months ago. (A female respondent)
>
> I was diagnosed six months ago with both HIV and TB. I spent so much money in hospitals for about three years before I was tested for both. (A male respondent)

Beliefs about TB, TB Treatment and Co-Infection

A majority of respondents acknowledged the fact that TB could be cured, in spite of their predicament (HIV infection), on the other hand, others thought that it was more difficult to be cured when one had HIV:

> Being HIV positive makes TB treatment difficult. This is because of the many drugs taken. Those without HIV are cured very fast. It takes a long time for you to regain your strength. (A male respondent)

Contrary to the belief of the male respondent, a female respondent was of the view that a patient ought to take the TB medication religiously as prescribed by the TB nurse to be able to regain your strength:

> To me one has to take what the nurse gives you, if you want to survive and take care of your family. You may only survive if you take the medicines correctly.

> With two deadly diseases, they can kill you if you are not careful with your medication and feeding. (A female respondent)

This assertion was corroborated by Health Care Workers (HCWs); this is what one of them had to say:

> It takes a long time for the drugs to work on HIV positive, this is because a lot of them, many are whom are males do not eat well. This has a toll on them. (A TB coordinator)

HWCs acknowledged that once the patient was aware that even if they do not take their medication for one day the probability that they will be put on injection is high and considering the painful ordeal, patients adhered to the treatment. The knowledge of this belief among patients motivated them to take their TB treatment properly because of the fear of getting severe relapse symptoms.

There were conflicting views among patients about which disease they thought was the most severe when comparing TB and HIV. Some mentioned HIV as being the most serious illness that they feared more, while others thought that TB was more dangerous. Patients' views about severity affected the decision about which drugs to discontinue for those patients who decided to take one of the drugs and stop the other. A few (two co-infected), also non-adherent patients made the decision to discontinue with the ART drugs because of adverse effect as a result of not having enough food to eat:

> I was told that HIV does not kill but TB kills if you don't take your medicines properly so I decided not to take the HIV drugs because I become very weak when I take both. I will continue with my HIV drugs when I finish with my TB. I know there will not be any problem because my girlfriend has HIV and does not take ART but she is fine, the people at the fever's clinic say she is ok when they checked on her the first time. (A male respondent)

A factor that most health professionals believed helped patients to gain hope was the improvement they observed in other patients who had previously been critically ill. According to HCWs, that helped patients believe in the efficacy of treatment and hence gave them hope for themselves. A TB coordinator had this to say:

> I think many patients are encouraged to take their medication because they see critically ill patients with co-infection who have improved, some get here looking helpless, but once they start the medication and with proper counseling and constant education, they regain their strength. That gives them lots of encouragement and hope. (A TB coordinator)

TB and HIV Treatment Experiences

TB nurses indicated that there are societal gender discrimination practices that exist within the community and impacted on patients' TB and HIV treatment experiences. The burden, they explained, is heavily borne by women. They expressed the belief that discrimination against women with TB resulted in a lack of support from their families and sometimes led to abandonment and rejection by their spouses and family. They also believed that it was the same for men:

> We have had experiences where husbands have had to neglect their wives because they have HIV and TB. We always invite and counsel the men. We also do so with the wives, but most of the time their partners don't even respond to our invitation. (TB coordinator)

Almost all respondents knew of alternative treatment options for TB. They all mentioned the use of traditional herbal concoctions, which they thought, was equally efficacious and did not also involve long treatment. However, the cost of these herbal medicines was so high that patients sought treatment in the health facility because it is free of charge:

> There are very good herbal medicines that can cure TB and even HIV, but it is so expensive so I cannot afford it. A gallon is about fifteen cedis and one mustn't take it for too long a time, as it is an orthodox medicine. (A male respondent)

> I have heard that there is treatment for HIV. I was told an HIV positive needs a bottle to take for he/she to be cured. I understand a bottle cost one million five hundred cedis, so once I complete the treatment of the TB, I will buy one to relieve me of the HIV disease. (A female respondent)

Gender Roles, Social Support and How they Affect Adherence

All interviewees including HCWs were of the view that men were more vulnerable to TB than women, and that females were more vulnerable to contracting HIV. This is what one of the TB coordinators had to say:

> More men are exposed to TB because of their reckless social exposure such as smoking and drinking. (A TB coordinator)

Most respondents argued that more males than females are infected with TB as they are more likely to be working in more hazardous and dusty environment and also lead reckless lifestyle such as excessive drinking and smoking. Respondents expressed that there was nothing like gender bias in the homes. However, both female and male respondents reported stereotypical gender roles in cultural and social norms. Women are supposed to stay at home to care for the family and at the same time earn a living by working outside the home, whilst men do no household chores or very little household chores and provide economic sustenance to the family:

> The women take care of the burdens of the entire family. They have to multi-task by taking responsibility for the upbringing of the children and the husband, manage the home and apart from that, work to bring money home just like the man. (A TB coordinator)

> Even though I am not well I still have to go out there to look for money. My husband does not care about my condition. I have to look for money to take care of the children or else they will starve to death. (A female respondent)

Studies have shown that not all the factors that influence adherence to treatment exhibit such pronounced gender differences; there are some factors that affect both men and women equally. Getahun and Aragaw (2001), in a community-based study in Ethiopia, identified clinical improvement as the most common reason for treatment discontinuation, followed by the distance of the treatment facility (Getahun and Aragaw, 2001). In their study, family and social supports were found to be a critical element in promoting treatment adherence. These factors were clearly exhibited by respondents. This is what some of them had to say:

> I have the whole family, but they do not care about what happens to me. My friends no longer hang around me. (A male respondent)

> My aunt provides some form of support, I live with my three siblings but they do not know what is wrong with me. I am dating a guy, if I tell him he will leave me. I am waiting for the appropriate time to tell my boyfriend about it. (A female respondent)

> Nobody, there is no point telling people what is wrong with your health, they can't help you but they will gossip about you with other people. (A male respondent)

> My sister is the one who bears the cost of treatment since my husband is not aware of my condition. In fact he has never ever bothered to find out what exactly is wrong with me. I know him too well; if he gets to know about my condition, he will leave me. (A female respondent)

Service/Provider Factors

Respondents praised the TB nurses for having patience for them unlike being at the Out-Patient Department (OPD) where nurses shout at them. However, some of them complained about a few nurses. The following reports were given by respondents on the account of services and attitude of HCWs:

> The health workers were very nice to me and encouraged me to take my medication. But I didn't trust them with my problems. (A female respondent)

> They were ok, but they will let us sit far from them as if to say that they are afraid I might infect them my sickness. A few of them were rude; if you don't come to take your medicines they talk to you anyhow. (A male respondent)

> There is this nurse who does not understand issues, sometimes you want to travel and you need refill, but she won't so it means you have to skip the period. (A female respondent)

> They always call me to remind me a day before my medicines are finished. They are very good. I remember I was not feeling well and there was no one to come for my medicines they visited me in the house. (A male respondent)

An interview with the nurses provided an understanding of what goes on within the chest/TB clinics. According to the TB coordinator, they have recalcitrant patients who do not attend clinics as prescribed and therefore they needed to let them come to the clinic to take their medication even at the continuation phase. These were patients who were non-adherent during the intensive phase so they could not trust them by giving the medication to them without supervision. Again, to the nurses, these patients would have to be called several times to honour their appointment schedules.

Stigma and its Effect on Adherence

The study found out that not only were patients stigmatized, nurses at the TB clinics were equally stigmatized by their own colleagues. A situation found to be very disturbing, in the sense that if health workers who are not infected are stigmatized then, what is the fate of patients. This is what the nurses had to say concerning the way they were stigmatized by their own colleagues:

> It is not easy at all even some of us (TB nurses) are referred to as TB people: our colleagues treat us as if we have TB. A doctor in our hospital refused to use a pen from the DOTs centre because it is from the TB clinic. (A TB coordinator)

> Our colleagues even look down on us because of the nature of patients we handle. We are on a daily basis stigmatized by our own colleagues. (A TB coordinator)

Female respondents perceived being stigmatized as another major challenge of being infected with TB and HIV. Many of the respondents interviewed said that they felt stigmatized even though not directly and so had to withdraw from members of their close social network because they felt ashamed of their condition. Some (male) respondents reported being directly stigmatized within their families, to the extent that they were given different utensils to eat from and different sleeping arrangements were made for them. The majority of respondents (mainly female) indicated that they have resolved not to disclose their TB and/or HIV status for fear of being stigmatized.

> Having the two diseases is very deadly, I was managing with the HIV, but when I got the TB, I became very weak and frail, before the TB, if I don't tell anybody I have HIV they won't know but people started asking questions especially when I started coughing profusely and grew very lean. (A female respondent)

> When my family members got to know about my situation they changed their attitude towards me. I now use different utensils and sleep in the living room. (A male respondent)

> When my wife got to know about my HIV and TB status, she left me. At the moment my brother takes care of me financially. (A male respondent)

Contrary to the experiences of some, other respondents had support of family members. This is what a female respondent had to say about her situation:

> My husband supports me financially but I don't see him often because I live with my mother now. My mum who takes care of me thinks I am a burden on her. (A female respondent)

> My partner has HIV too so she supports me. At the moment she is not on any medication. (A male respondent)

> I never told my husband because he is not concerned about what I do, for the past year that I have been treating these diseases, he has never asked me what's wrong with me. The only person who knows about my health condition is my sister. She takes care of my medical bills. (A female respondent)

Respondents indicated that disclosure of their TB and HIV status might possibly lead to double stigma. Female co-infected patients initially did not open up to me. They only disclosed the TB infection initially, until I probed further and reassured them of confidentiality. HIV patient were perceived negatively, and women were found to be more affected by the socio-cultural consequences of both illnesses, as has been discussed in the proceeding paragraphs. Respondents described negative perceptions of TB and HIV patients on the part of the general population in their various communities. These negative perceptions resulted in rejection for both men and women with the disease. Females, however, reported feeling the burden of TB and HIV stigma more intensely than men. For this reason, most females and some males chose to keep their diagnosis a secret from family members and people outside their close family, due to fear of rejection and stigma. Most females mentioned experiences of stigmatization because of their diagnosis. This was in contrast to males who seemed unconcerned about the attitude of others with regards to their condition.

Discussion

It is a fact that gender in itself is a health determinant, however, gender is influenced in part by biological, psychological and environmental conditions. Gender implication of TB and HIV co-infection in Ghana is one that reflects the African picture and perhaps a global one – more females with HIV compared to males (Long, 2000). However, the reverse is true with TB (Long, 2000).

Gender, as a constrained variable, played out in a different form – males were found to be more vulnerable to non-adherence due to their circumstances. Many studies have found females to be disadvantageous in health and these have been well documented (Allotey and Gyapong, 2008; Bird and Rieker, 2008; WHO, 2013; Connell and Messerschmidt, 2005). However, in this study, males are rather disadvantageous. This is because females have been able to circumvent the challenges they face as the 'endangered species'. For those who are in a coital relationship, disclosure of their status was not part of them. For those who disclosed their status to their partners did so because they knew their partners were also infected with the disease. This led to mutual understanding between the couple in question.

The study found out that two females were non-adherent compared to three males. This show that non-adherence was higher among male respondents. This is consistent with studies comparing adherence among this category of patients (Makombe et al., 2007; Daniel and Alausa, 2006; Rowe et al., 2005).

Findings from the study provided a platform for understanding the numerous factors involved in adhering/non-adhering to TB treatment regimen among patients on concomitant treatment for HIV. More males than females were found to be more likely to have missed their medication. For the respondents, side effects and high pill burden were some of the reasons why they missed their medication for both gender.

On the other hand, lack of finance was the main reason male respondents missed their medication. This is in contradiction of Needham et al. (2001) and Karim et al. (2007) studies that found higher costs for women than for men. Respondents who did not adhere to treatment were of the view that, it was easier taking the TB medication than the ART. Among the male non-adherents, one patient was found to have given up ART treatment and continued TB after weighing the benefits and costs associated with disease severity.

The study found that knowledge about the curability of TB was enough motivation for adherence. This was reflected in the earlier response from respondents who expressed optimism of the curability of TB and again adverse effect of TB, if not treatment properly. Most respondents interviewed knew the fact that TB kills when it is not treated properly especially among people with HIV, therefore traded their HIV treatment for the former.

Pill burden and side effects were major challenges to concomitant treatment, more especially with male respondents. This was found to be consistent with studies by Ingersoll and Cohen (2008) and WHO (2013). Findings show that adherence counselling facilitate adherence among those who saw such side effects as part of the treatment. Some patients expressed zeal that they were effectively counselled on the side effects so it did not affect their medication. Effect of adverse drug was felt more among males than females. Indeed, two male respondents indicated that they had to stop taking the medicines for more than a week as a result of the side effects.

Studies on stigma have suggested that it is a potential barrier to treatment because it makes patients reluctant to attend treatment in clinics located in their neighbourhoods and leads to non-disclosure of illness. Other studies have also found that disclosure can play a positive role because it can help the patient mobilize social support, thereby facilitating adherence; and is also important for public health reasons such as avoidance of further infection transmission. Contrary to many studies on stigma, this study found that stigma was a protective factor, as has been expressed by female respondents. In a situation where consequences of disclosure are uncertain, it may be rational for a patient not to disclose or to have very selective disclosure. Studies have highlighted the negative impacts of HIV-related stigma on TB treatment in co-infected patients (Dodor and Afenyadu, 2005). Female respondents were more comfortable talking about their TB status and not HIV. This is because of the high level of stigma attached to HIV in Ghana. Again, respondents concealing their HIV status are as a result of the fact that TB is curable and HIV is not. Many people associate HIV with promiscuity and so females feel shy disclosing their status. Among the six female co-infected patients, three of them earlier denied having HIV. These three did not also disclose their status to their partners for fear of being stigmatized or abandoned. On the other hand, male respondents who divulged their condition to their wives had them abandoning them to their fate. The situation was aggravated when the males had to stop working because of the adverse effect of the medications. This study is consistent with similar study in Thailand (Ngamvithayapong et al., 1997). As a result of the stigma, co-infected patients accessed care very far away from where they lived. This was found to be characteristic of both female and male respondents, as they avoided meeting people they may know. This finding supports a study from Nigeria where patients defaulted because their treatment centre was relocated to a neighbourhood, which was closer to their homes (Daniel and Alausa, 2006). While TB and HIV are not exclusively a disease of the poor, the association between poverty and TB/HIV co-infection rates is well documented and these are well known, co-infected patients were more likely to be unemployed and male respondents were found to be poorer, leading to inconsistency in appointment schedules. Interviews with HCWs corroborated the findings. Evidence (Baker et al., 2008) has shown that there is a link between poverty and vulnerability to TB. TB can make patients more vulnerable to poverty; in the case of most of the respondents who had to quit their jobs to concentrate on their treatment. There were gender differences with regards to the level of support that respondents received from their partners, family and friends depending on disclosure. Male respondents who disclosed their condition to close family members had some form of support. This level of support was not adequate as revealed by a couple of them. Again, disclosure by some male co-infected respondents led to their partners abandoning them. This group was those who did not adhere to treatment. On the other hand, two female respondents did not adhere because of the work and family responsibilities. They explained that they missed her medication because of attending funerals and work commitments. Majority of the females interviewed said there had very close confidant whom they confided in and they have been of tremendous support to them.

The study found that there was a good relationship between HCWs and patients, leading to high clinic attendance among adherent patients. This study is consistent with a similar one conducted in Ghana by Dodor and Afenyadu (2005), which showed that a good relationship between patients and health staff was the main facilitator of adherence.

Conclusion

The study concludes that a lot more needs to be done that the social needs of women are taking care of with respect to health. Education has to be intensified to demystify TB and HIV infection so as to give room for disclosure and consequently support to affected persons to avert possibly reinfection and spread of the diseases, especially TB among families and households. The NTP in collaboration with the Ministry for Gender and Social Protective should team up to provide meaningful support in the form of daily/weekly stipends to the poor and vulnerable TB and HIV patients.

References

Allotey, Pascale and Gyapong, Margaret (2008). 'Gender in Tuberculosis Research', *International Journal of Tuberculosis and Lung Disease*, 12: 831–36.

Baker, M., Das, D., Vengopal, K. and Howden-Chapman, P. (2008). Tuberculosis associated with household crowding in a developed country. *Journal of Epidemiological and Community Health*, 62, 715–21.

Bird, E. Chloe and Rieker, P. Patricia (2008). *Gender and Health: Effects of Constrained Choices and Social Policies*, New York: Cambridge University Press.

Chesney, M. (2003). 'Adherence to HAART Regimens', *AIDS Patient Care STDS*, 17: 169–77.

Connell, R.W. and Messerschmidt, W. James (2005). 'Hegemonic Masculinity: Rethinking the Concept', *Gender and Society*, 19: 829–59.

Daniel, O.J. and Alausa, O.K. (2006). 'Treatment Outcome of TB/HIV Positive and TB/HIV Negative Patients on Directly Observed Treatment, Short Course (DOTS) in Sagamu, Nigeria', *Nigeria Journal of Medicine*, 15(3): 222–26.

Diwan, V.K. and Thorson, A. (1999). 'Sex, Gender, and Tuberculosis', *Lancet*, 353: 1000–01.

Dodor, E.A. and Afenyandu, G.Y. (2005). 'Factors Associated with Tuberculosis Treatment Default and Completion at Effia-Nkwanta Regional Hospital in Ghana', *Transnational Royal Society of Tropical Medical Hygiene*, 99(11): 827–32.

Getahun, H. and Aragaw, D. (2001). 'Tuberculosis in Rural Northwest Ethiopia: Community Perspective', *Ethiopian Medical Journal*, 39: 283–91.

Ingersoll, K.S. and Cohen, J. (2008). 'The Impact of Medication Regimen Factors on Adherence to Chronic Treatment: A Review of Literature', *Journal of Behavioural Medicine*, 31(3): 213–24.

Karim, F., Islam, A., Chowdhury, A.M.R., Johansson, E. and Diwan, V.K. (2007). 'Gender Differences in Delays in Diagnosis and Treatment of Tuberculosis', *Health Policy and Planning*, 22: 329–34.

Long, N.H. (2000). 'Gender Specific Epidemiology of Tuberculosis in Vietnam', Unpublished dissertation, Stockholm: Karolinska Institute.

Makombe, S.D., Harries, A.D., Yu, J.K., Hochgesang, M., Mhango, E., Weigel, R., Pasulani, O., Fitzgerald, M., Schouten, E.J. and Libambia, E. (2007). 'Outcomes of Tuberculosis Patients Who Start Antiretroviral Therapy under Routine Programme Conditions in Malawi', *International Journal of Tuberculosis and Lung Disease*, 11(4): 412–16.

Needham, D.M., Foster, S.D., Tomlinson, G. and Godfrey-Faussett, P. (2001). 'Socio-economic, Gender and Health Services Factors Affecting Diagnostic Delay for Tuberculosis Patients in Urban Zambia', *Tropical Medicine and International Health*, 6: 256–59.

Ngamvithayapong, J., Uthaivoravit, W., Yanai, H., Akarasewi, P. and Sawanpanyalert, P. (1997). 'Adherence to Tuberculosis Preventive Therapy among HIV-infected Persons in Chiang Rai, Thailand', *AIDS*, 11(1): 107–12.

Rowe, K.A., Makhubele, B., Hargreaves, J.R., Porter, J.D., Hausler, H.P. and Pronyk, P.M. (2005). 'Adherence to TB Preventive Therapy for HIV-positive Patients in Rural South Africa: Implications for Antiretroviral Delivery in Resource-poor Settings?', *International Journal of Tuberculosis and Lung Disease*, 9(3): 263–69.

Somma, Daryl B., Auer, Chirstian, Abouihia, Abdallah and G. Weiss, Mitchell (2005). *Gender in Tuberculosis Research*, Gender and Health Research Series, Department of Gender, Women and Health, Family and Community Health, WHO.

World Health Organization (2003). *Adherence to Long-term Therapies: Evidence for Action*, Chapter 5, Geneva, 11–18, 145–52.

—— (2013). *Global TB Report*, Geneva. Retrieved from www.who.int/tb/data.

11

Gender Differences in Perceived Health Status of Family Care-Givers of Frail Elderly

A Study in Japan and South Korea

JUNG NIM KIM

Abstract

The gender differences in the perceived health states of family care-givers in Japan and South Korea are very well known. However, these are important to improve the high levels of care of frail elderly and quality of life for family care-givers at home. The paper investigates whether the difference in family care-givers' gender affected their perceived health states and socio-economic status (SES) in Japan and South Korea. The current socio-economic models to explain the gender differences in health were considered in the study. The data was collected in the 2010 using the survey conducted by the research team, which covered the situations of frail elderly and their family care-givers in Japan and South Korea. Data was analysed using multiple linear regression. The dependent variable included the perceived health states of family care-givers while the independent variables included SES. The result of multivariate linear regression analysis showed that in gender differences of family care-givers, female care-givers with white-collar jobs in both countries were positively associated with perceived health states, whereas the annual household income of female family care-givers were positively associated with perceived health states only in Japan. However, SES of male family care-givers were not significantly associated with health states in both countries. Further the study evidenced that care-givers, those with white-collar jobs and higher levels of annual household income were positively associated with perceived health states in both countries. Implications for research were discussed at the end.

Keywords

Family Care-Givers, Perceived Health States, Gender Differences, Socio-economic Status, Japan and South Korea.

Introduction

Life expectancy at birth, on an average, has increased greatly over the past few decades in Japan and South Korea. According to OECD, in 2012, it was 82.7 and 81.1 years, respectively. The proportion of people aged 65 years or older in Japan and South Korea was 23.3 per cent and 11.4 per cent in 2011 (OECD, 2013) and the rapid aging process of the elderly in both countries has led to an increase in the frail elderly adults. In these contexts, the public long-term care insurance system has been established in both countries and it has an important role for frail elderly and their families. However, long-term care services cannot sufficiently support every frail elderly due to insufficient funds and care workers.

In fact, gender differences are well documented for multiple health related outcomes, such as women live longer, have higher morbidity rates, and self-report worse health compared to men (Kim, 2013). In contrast to the paradoxical gender differences in physical health, men's and women's overall mental health is similar, but specific conditions differ by gender (Rieker and Bird, 2005). Women experience substantially higher rates of depression and anxiety disorders than men, whereas men have higher rates of substance abuse, antisocial behaviour, and suicide (Kessler et al., 2003). However, even though more women, than men, are likely to become informal family care-givers at home in both countries and to support their spouses, parents and parents-in-law compared to their elderly parents, the number of men providing care for aging family members is increasing. Yet research on male care-givers is limited and more is needed to understand the issues of men and health states.

The paper investigates whether the difference in family care-givers' gender affected their perceived health states and socio-economic status in Japan and South Korea. The current socio-economic models to explain the gender differences in health were considered in the study. These are important to improve the high levels of care of frail elderly and the quality of life of family care-givers at home.

Among several factors, socio-economic status (SES) is most frequently implicated as a contributor to the disparities in health (Andresen and Miler, 2005). Adler and Newman (2002) presented that SES impacts health including that it is associated with health care, environmental exposure, and health behaviour and lifestyle. The study concluded that the differences in SES are the cause of differences in health states and outcomes between population groups. Furthermore, higher levels of education may provide additional health knowledge by various social networks, and an opportunity for better employment conditions and higher income levels. People with higher incomes are more likely to have the means to pay for healthcare and to afford better nutrition, housing, schools and recreation (Adler and Newman, 2002), thus they make the effort to maintain good health.

Gender issues are significant in promoting healthy care-giving (Kim, 2012) and gender differences in SES offer considerable insight into women's greater morbidity and the gendered patterns of health disorders. Thus, gender differences in income may result from a variety of factors over the course of life, including social role-related expectations and activities, occupational choice, opportunities for employment and advancement, work-related skills and experience, as well as access to job benefits including health, pensions, and other retirement income (Rieker and Bird, 2005; Shavers, 2007). Therefore, because women receive lower payment and have a longer average life span than men, they make choices for less payment for their self-health, and have the ability to meet basic needs that may be associated with a wide range of deleterious health consequences. Therefore, SES inequality contributes to differences in men's and women's exposure to stressors and impact of coping resources (Rieker and Bird, 2005). Watson (2013) argued that males have lower care-giver burden than females, but they receive less social support. However, these differences do not all have the same effect, such as the specific aspects of male and female family care-givers on health behaviours and coping style. For this reason, the gender differences in the health states of family care-givers are lesser known.

Against this background, the study hypothesizes that SES might differentially affect male and female care-givers' health states, and lower SES in female compared to male care-givers are associated with poorer health states (for the positive and negative health behaviours, exposure to stressors, coping styles, help from others) in both countries.

Method

Data Collection

The data was collected from family care-givers who provided care to frail elderly while living in the same home in both Japan and South Korea in 2010. Frail elderly included only those who received care needs certification in the public long-term care insurance system (LTCIS) in both countries.

The data was collected using a cross-sectional survey conducted by the research team, which covered ADL of frail elderly, SES (education, employment states, and household annual income), and subjective health status of family care-givers.

The samples included 500 cases (95%) in Japan and 930 cases (91%) in South Korea. The data was collected using the placement method and face-to-face interviews with paper questionnaires in October and November in Japan and South Korea, respectively.

Table 1 shows public LTCIS in Japan and Korea. Japan and Korea introduced a new social insurance scheme for long-term care in 2000 and in 2008, respectively. LTCIS was planned by the Ministry of Health and Welfare and executed by the municipalities, and National Health Insurance Corporation. Eligibility for the recipients is dependent on the certification of LTCIS. The LTCIS recipients can be classified into seven classes in Japan, and four classes in Korea, with those in the seventh class and first class having the most severe disabilities in Japan and Korea, respectively. LTCIS system provides institutional care and in-home service. The LTCIS system has been funded by contributions from people over 40 years old and over in Japan, however, all participants are members of the NHI in Korea. The family care-givers who have a home care worker's license can give home care service to their parents and can be paid for their services by NHI in Korea but not in Japan. In Japan, charges are 10 per cent for in-home services and residential care, however, in Korea, charges are 15 per cent for in-home services and 20 per cent for residential care. In 2014, the number of people that needed long-term care was 58,03,000 and 3,30,000 in Japan and Korea, respectively.

Table 1

The Long-term Care Insurance System (LTCIS) in Japan and South Korea

	Japan	*South Korea*
Implementation	April 2000	July 2008
Premiums	Each municipality	National Health Insurance Corporation
Insured persons	Persons aged 65 or over, persons aged 40 to 64	Persons aged 20 or over
Eligible persons	Persons aged 65 or over and aged 40 to 64 with certain disability	Persons aged 65 or over and under age 65 with certain disabilities
Long-term care requirement certification	Support required 1–2, care level 1–5	Care level 1–4
Using care services	Contract with the policy-holder, long-term care service planning by care manager	Contract with the policy-holder, no long-term care service planning
Insurance benefits	In-home service, services at facilities, community-based service small multi-functional satellite home-care services	In-home service at facilities
Careworks of family care-givers	Unpaid careworks for family care-givers	Paid care works for family care-givers
Out-of-pocket payment	10 per cent of the cost of the insured services in home services and facilities	15per cent of the cost of the insured services in home services and 20 per cent of services at facilities
The number of LTCIS requirement certifications	5,803 thousand people (17.8% of among the elderly, 2014)	330 thousand people (5.7% of among the elderly, 2014)
Assess to in-home services	More than 3 million frail elderly, 2011	More than 30,000 frail elderly, 2011

Note: The table was written by the author.

Measurement

Dependent Variable

Respondents were asked their perceived health states and the question was: 'How do you rate your current health state?' The scale was based on five possible responses: excellent, good, fair, poor, and very poor. It was so coded that a higher score indicates better health. Despite the subjective nature of this question, indicators of perceived general health have been found to be a good predictor of mortality and functional ability (DeSalvo et al., 2005; Bond et al., 2006).

Independent Variables

SES included current employment status, the annual household income of family care-givers, and education levels of family care-givers and their spouses, respectively. The education level was coded such that a higher score indicates a higher level of education attainment. The annual household income of family care-givers was coded so that higher score indicates a higher annual household income. The current employment status was coded as a dummy variable (white-collar workers=1, blue-collar workers=1, and unemployment=reference category).

Control Variables

Respondent characteristic items as control variables included the sex and age of frail elderly, and age of care-givers. The analysis is restricted to male and female family care-givers in both countries. I have used a multiple linear regression analysis because of the limitations of traditional SES measures and the belief that the context in which one lives is as important as the influence of individual SES factors. Multi-level approaches combine compositional and contextual measures each that each measures a different aspect of SES (Shavers, 2007). The software of analysis was performed in SPSS 21.0.

Results

Table 2 shows descriptive statistics for all study variables for the overall samples and both genders of family care-givers in both countries. There were more female than male frail elderly in both countries, but more than half of the frail elderly were 85 years or over in Japan while about half of the frail elderly were 75 to 84 years of age in Korea. Over half of the frail elderly was level 1 or 2 of care needs in Japan, and level 3 of care needs in Korea. Almost 60 per cent of care-givers were over 60 years old in Japan while only 24 per cent were over 60 in Korea. Almost 60 per cent of family care-givers were daughters and daughters-in-law of frail elderly in both countries.

In SES factors, about three quarters of both genders of family care-givers reported an education level of post-secondary or above in both countries. Among both genders of family care-givers, approximately 30 per cent were white-collar workers, with male family care-givers reporting a slightly higher percentage compared to women in both countries. A higher number of female family care-givers had an annual household income of over four million yen in Japan, while a slightly higher percentage of male family care-givers than female had an annual household income of over 3.5 million won in Korea.

Table 2

Profiles of the Subjects

(Men and Women N=30,71,190 in Japan; Men and Women N-1,49,837 in Korea, %)

		Frail Elderly				Family Care-Givers	
		Japan	Korea			Japan	Korea
Sex	Male	35.4	33.3	Sex	Male	20.5	15.1
	Female	64.4	66.7		Female	79.5	84.9
Age	74 years or under	15.3	31.0	Age	79 years or under	12.6	36.2
	75–84	32.5	45.8		50–59	29.0	39.5
	85 years or over	52.2	23.2		60–69	34.4	13.8
					70 years or over	24.0	10.5
Levels of care needs	Level 1	25.0	22.1	Relationship to the frail elderly	Spouse	27.9	17.7
	Level 2	25.4	51.8		Daughter-in-law	29.7	30.4
	Level 3	19.1	17.4		Daughter	26.0	29.6
	Level 4	17.3	8.4		Son	12.0	8.1
	Level 5	13.3					

Family Care-Givers

		Japan		Korea	
		Men	Women	Men	Women
Education levels	<High school	35.8	23.4	22.9	24.7
	>High school	64.2	76.6	77.1	75.3
Current employment status	White-collar workers	30.9	25	36.2	30.2
	Blue-collar workers	17.6	18.7	29.5	22.1
	Unemployment	47.2	53.8	32.2	42.9
Annual household income	<4 million yen	48.3	34.2		
	>4 Million yen	54.7	65.8		
	<25 million won			48.3	52.5
	>35 million won			51.7	47.5

Figure 1 shows perceived health states of men and women family care-givers in both countries. Half of both genders were in good health states in Japan while about 35 per cent of men and almost 28 per cent of women family care-givers were in very good health states in Korea. Slightly more male family care-givers compared to females were in good health and more of both genders of family care-givers were in good or very good health states than poor or very poor health states in both countries. On the other hand, according to OECD (2013), less than half of the adults in Japan and Korea rate their health as good or very good; however, there is a little gap between OECD and our data, because the family care-givers may be older than those in OECD data. Nevertheless, similarly, men were more likely than women to report being in good health and there are large disparities in self-reported health states in the OECD data and with our family care-givers.

Figure 1

Perceived Health States of Family Care-Givers

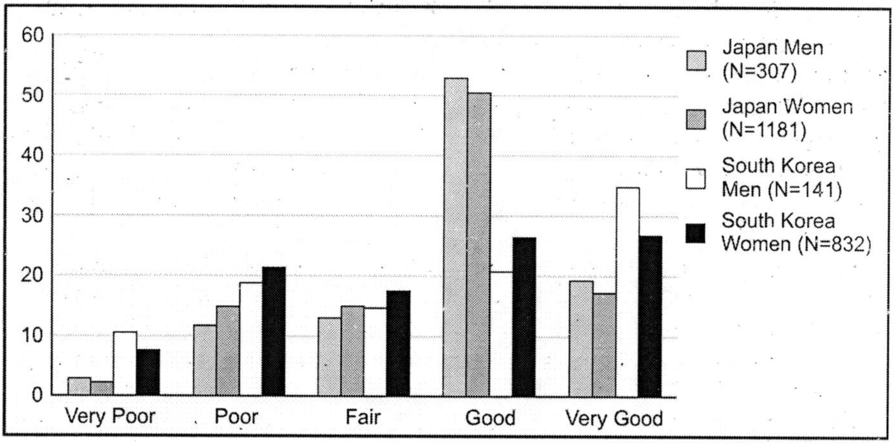

Multilevel Analyses

Table 3 indicated multivariate regression results of the overall sample and in observed perceived health states among men and women family care-givers in Japan and Korea. In gender differences of family care-givers, female family care-givers with white-collar jobs in both countries were positively associated with perceived health states, whereas female family care-givers with blue-collar jobs only had positive association with health states in Korea. This means that female family care-givers with white-collar jobs in both countries, and blue-collar jobs in Korea were in better health than unemployed female family care-givers. An annual household income of female family care-givers were positively associated with perceived health states only in Japan. Thus, it is seen that female family care-givers with higher annual incomes had better health states. However, the level of education attained by male and female family care-givers and family care-givers' spouses had no significant differences in perceived health states in both countries. Therefore, SES of male family care-givers had no statistical significance on health states in both countries.

According to the overall sample, family care-givers with white-collar jobs were significantly related to perceived health states in both countries. This means that family care-givers with white-collar jobs were in better health than unemployed family care-givers. Moreover, the annual household incomes of family care-givers were significantly related to health states in both countries. Thus, it is seen that family care-givers with higher annual household incomes were in better health. Therefore, education attainment of family care-givers was significantly associated with health states only in Japan. This means that family care-givers who attained higher education were in good health. It could be hypothesized that low educational attainment means low literacy, which might have an impact on the family care-givers' ability to read and comprehend written instructions in Japan compared to Korea.

In this controlled model, elderly family care-givers were negatively associated with health states in only female family care-givers in both countries.

However, education attainment of family care-givers had statistical significance on health states only in Japan.

Table 3

Regression Analysis for Perceived Health States and SES of Family Care-Givers

	Japan		*Korea*		*Japan*				*Korea*			
	Total Samples				*Men*		*Women*		*Men*		*Women*	
	B	*p*	*B*	*p*	*B*	*p*	*B*	*p*	*B*	*p*	*B*	*p*
Sex of frail elderly women=1	.137		.014		.517		.018		-.456		.092	
Age of frail elderly	-.008		-.002		-.018		-.002		-.015		-.002	
Family care-givers sex women=1	-.165		-.135									
Age of family care-givers	-.015	**	-.015	*	-.004		-.020	**	.005		-.019	*
Educational attainment of FC	.098	*	.123		.207		.061		.246		.096	
Educational attainment of FC spouse	-.062		.032		-.032		-.057		.002		.044	
Employment: Blue collar workers dummy	.121		.0318	*	-.049		.149		.529		.274	*
White-collar workers dummy	.292	**	.440	**	.304		.281	*	.643		.392	*
Annual household income of FC	.088	*	.039	*	.089		.085	**	.084		.024	
R	.317	**	.324	**	.418	**	.317	**	.513	**	.296	**
R2	.101		.105		.175		.101		.264		.087	
N	1497		986		307		1190		149		837	

Note: *p<.05, **p<.01

FC means family care-givers.

Current employment status was using of dummy variable (blue-collar workers=1, white-collar workers=1, unemployment=0)

Conclusion and Limitations of the Study

This study is the first to examine the association between SES and perceived health states in both genders of family care-givers in Japan and South Korea. In the study, most gender differences of family care-givers decreased across perceived health states in both countries. Overall, the findings are consistent with the hypothesis that higher levels of SES had a positive correlation with perceived health states of family care-givers in both countries. Regarding gender differences, female family care-givers supported the hypothesized between with current employment status and perceived health states in both countries. Historically and culturally, women are expected to take on the role of main support or assistance to frail elderly as family care-givers at home and in community (Kim, 2013) in both countries, as a consequence, genders of family care-givers were largely ignored and rarely viewed as a public issue. Almost half of family care-givers are employed either full-time or part-time, balancing work with their care-giving role in both countries; however, for unemployed female family care-givers it becomes too stressful to juggle care-giving activities with other family responsibilities, or have to concentrate to provide care, especially without breaks or hobbies for the most intensive level of care-giving. With regards to female family care-givers, Pinquart and Sorensen (2003) showed that providing care to a chronically ill family member or close friend can have profound negative effects on the care-giver's own physical and psychological health, increase social isolation, and adversely impact their quality of life and well-being.

The impact of annual household incomes of family care-givers had a positive effect on perceived health states of female family care-givers only in Japan. Therefore family care-givers with the lowest incomes might have reduced or stopped spending money on their own health and begun spending more of their annual income on care-giving expenses. However, the great majority of Japanese elderly receive a national pension and they can have efficient care services out-of-pocket for 10 per cent payment when they are using long-term care services compared to Korea. Female family care-givers with higher incomes are more likely to afford better nutrition (e.g. better quality and variety of fresh fruits and vegetables), housing, schools and recreation (Adler and Newman, 2002), and to have the means to pay for private care workers and by using long-term care services in Japan. This result suggests that the most common use of SES in health disparities research has been as a variable that explains differences in outcomes among racial/ethnic and other population subgroups (van de Mheen et al., 1998).

In addition, only for male compared with female family care-givers have not yet demonstrated that such SES are directly linked to perceived health states in both countries. These results show that health inequality exists only for female and not for male family care-givers in both countries, even though both countries guarantee public health care services for all their citizens. It is likely that education, occupation and income disparities might be eliminated in the near future in men; however, there is some evidence that SES inequalities in both countries are increasing, especially in South Korea compared to Japan.

Family support for elderly is a key driver in remaining in one's own home and in the community, but it comes at a substantial cost to the care-givers themselves, to their families, and to society (Feinberg et al., 2011). If females could not support their elderly families any longer, males who work outside the home would have to quit their jobs and support their family. Then the household income and GDP would decrease, however the economic cost to the public health care and the long-term care would increase astronomically in both countries.

The study is not free from limitations. It is based on cross-sectional analyses for both genders in Japan and South Korea. Longitudinal research is needed in such surveys. The study focussed on the levels of SES and perceived health states of family care-givers in genders. However, emerging evidence suggests that other factors such as frequent use of public in-home care services, the needs of level of frail elderly might effect the health status of family care-givers. Similarly, certain factors such as an effective linking of clinical check evaluation of health states as a dependent variable with community-based factors would require further study in the future. In conclusion, providing help significantly addresses the needs and desires of male and female care-givers of frail elderly and contributes to positive health effects. Thus, the government and future researchers need to develop and test interventions designed to maintain and enhance the health of care-givers.

Acknowledgement

The authors wish to thank the Japan Society for the Promotion of Science KAKENHI Grant Numbers 21330121 for funding the study.

References

Adler, N.E. and Newman, K. (2002). 'Socioeconomic Disparities in Health: Pathways and Policies', *Health Aff*, 21: 60–76.

Andresen, F.M. and Miler, D.K. (2005). 'The Future (History) of Socioeconomic Measurement and Implications for Improving Health Outcome among African Americans', *The Journals of Gerontology: Series A*. 60. 1345–50.

Bond, J., Dickinson, H.O., Matthews, F., Jagger, C. and Brayne, C. (2006). 'Self-rated Health Status as a Predictor of Death, Functional and Cognitive Impairments: A Longitudinal Cohort Study', *European Journal of Ageing*, 3: 193–206.

DeSalvo, K.B., Fan, V.S., McDonell, M.B. and Fihn, S.D. (2005). 'Predicting Mortality and Healthcare Utilization with a Single Question', *Health Services Research*, 40: 1234–246.

Feinberg, L., Reinhard, S.C., Houser, A. and Choula, R. (2011). *The Growing Contributions and Costs of Family Caregiving*, AARP Public Policy Institute, 1–28.

Ishihara, K. and Tabuchi, R. (2012). *Changing Families in Northeast Asia*, Tokyo: Sophia University Press, 89–110.

Kessler, R.C., Berglund, P., Demler, O. et al. (2003). 'The Epidemiology of Major Depressive Disorder: Results from the National Comorbidity Survey Replication', *Journal of the American Medical Association*, 289: 3095–105.

Kim, J.N. (2012). *Financial Support to Parents and Parents-in-law: How the Social Status of Married Women Affects Financial Support for Parents in Korea, Japan, and China*.

—— (2013). 'The Study of Socioeconomic Status and Health Disparities in Japanese Elderly', *The Science of Health (Hoken no Kagaku)*, 55(3): 173–79.

OECD (2013). *Health at a Glance 2013: OECD Indicators*.

Pinquart, P. and Sorensen, S. (2003). 'Differences between Caregivers and Non-caregivers in Psychological Health and Physical Health: A Meta-analysis', *Psychology and Aging*, 18: 250–67.

Rieker, P.P. and Bird, C.E. (2005). 'Rethinking Gender Differences in Health: Why We Need to Integrate Social and Biological Perspectives', *The Gerontological Society of America*, 60B: 40–47.

Shavers, V.L. (2007). 'Measurement of Socioeconomic Status in Health Disparities Research', *Journal of the National Medical Association*, 99(9): 1013–023.

van de Mheen, H., Stonks, K., Looman, C.W.N. et al. (1998). 'Does Childhood Socioeconomic Status Influence Adult Health through Behavioral Factors?', *International Journal of Epidemiology*, 27: 431–37.

Watson, L.N. (2013). *Men as Caregivers of Frail Elderly: Gender Differences in the Caregiving Experience*, Tennessee: Middle Tennessee State University (para 61).

12

Gender-Based Sexual and Reproductive Health among Urban Adolescent Students

A Study in Hyderabad, India

VARALAKSHMI MANCHANA

Abstract

Adolescence is stated as the period of transition from childhood to adulthood, which starts with the onset of puberty. It comprises the individuals between the ages of 10–19 years. It is a stage of behavioural and attitude formation. Sensitization and appropriate guidance helps them to take right decisions and develop healthy behaviours. Adolescent health needs are unique. If they are not well guided, they are likely to experiment with risky behaviours that could harm them and others. Against this background, the paper attempts to assess the knowledge on sexual and reproductive health (SRH) and gender perceptions among school going adolescents. 150 adolescent students between age group of 13–18 years were chosen by random sampling. Single group pre-test post-test design was used. A structured questionnaire on identification data, gender attributes and attitudes and sexual and reproductive health was administered before and after the educational programme. The study concludes that gender balanced adolescent friendly health care approach is the need of the hour. Parents, teachers and health care providers need to be sensitized about gender balanced adolescent reproductive and sexual health.

Keywords

Adolescents, Reproductive Health, Sexual Health, Gender Attributes, Gender-Based Violence.

Introduction

Adolescence is stated as the period of transition from childhood to adulthood, which starts with the onset of puberty. It comprises the individuals between the ages of 10 to 19 years. During this vital period, a child undergoes biological transition, which is characterized by puberty, related changes in physical appearance and attainment of the reproductive capability, psychological or cognitive transition, which reflects an individual's thinking and social transition, which is related to rights, privileges and responsibilities of an individual (Steinberg, 1990). Rapid physical, physiological and psychosocial development of this age may lead to the experience of varying situations of risk. Adolescent health needs are unique. Adolescents prefer to develop relations beyond the family and may get attracted towards the opposite gender. They are more inventing and exploring in attitude and behaviours. If they are not well guided, they are likely to experiment with risky behaviour that could harm them and others. It is a stage of behavioural and attitude formation. Attitudes formed in this stage are difficult to change. Attitudes and behaviours are formed at this stage towards gender role; influence their understanding of 'man-women role' responsibilities, relation in the society. Gender socialization begins early in life. It is very essential to initiate measures to shape their attitudes and transform behaviours. Biologically determined gender characteristics are universal, social difference and gender roles are learned and acquired. To reduce gender-based violence and improve gender equality, the behavioural change must start with adolescents.

Background

Adolescence represents a window of opportunity to prepare for a healthy adult life. The world's adolescent population – 1,200 million persons, 10–19 years of age, or about 19 per cent of the total population-faces a series of serious challenges not only affecting their growth and development but also their livelihood as adults (NHS-3). Despite 35 per cent of the population constituting adolescent age group, the health needs of adolescents remain a largely neglected. In the past few years, the growing evidence around gender attitudes and reproductive and sexual behaviour patterns of the younger generation reveals the persistence of gender bias worldwide and inadequate addressing of RSH issues of the adolescents (Barker, 2000). As much as 30 per cent of India's population (327 million) is in the age group of 10–24 years (WHO, 2011); 30 per cent of women in the age group of 15–19 years have had a live birth by 19 years (NFHS-3); 60 per cent of girls in the age group of 15–19 years were anaemic (NFHS-3). Anaemia is a contributing factor for age specific female mortality. Fifty per cent of children in India have reported some form of sexual abuse (Ministry of Health and Family Welfare, 2007) out of which 53 per cent victims were boys. A majority of non-consensual sexual experiences go unreported. The shift towards globalization, urbanization and opportunities for education, increased independent social interactions are some of the reasons for such a situation. Lack of confidential communication, correct information may delay sexual initiation. Information on issues related to gender norms, sexual and reproductive health remains inadequate to young peoples' needs. Adolescent health services remain inaccessible, unaffordable, judgmental and of indifferent quality. Transforming the attitudes of adolescents towards developing healthy behaviours will be having an inter-generational impact. The association between menstrual hygiene maintenance and education, socio-economic status, knowledge prior to menarche, accessibility to water and bathroom facilities and menstrual disorders are also issues in reproductive health. Watsa (1994), in a study of 4,709 respondents, showed that adolescents received sex information usually from mass media and friends but it was not reliable.

Inadequate knowledge on reproductive and sexual health may lead to indulgence in pre-marital sex at an early age, increasing the incidence of teenage and unwanted pregnancies, unsafe abortions, contracting sexually transmitted infections, HIV and so on. Against this background, the study attempts to explore the knowledge on RSH and gender perceptions among urban adolescent students of Hyderabad.

The Study

This study has the following objectives:

1. To assess the knowledge on sexual and reproductive health among adolescent students between the age group of 13 to 18 years.
2. To measure the perceived gender attributes attitudes on gender equality.
3. Development and administration of gender-based adolescent sexual and reproductive health education programme.
4. Evaluating the education programme.

Methodology

Tool

A quasi experimental, pre-post test single group design was chosen for the study to assess the knowledge on gender-based sexual and reproductive health and the effectiveness of the ARSH (Adolescent Reproductive and Sexual Health) educational programme on knowledge regarding gender-based sexual and reproductive health among school-going adolescents. As many as 150 students (79 girls and 71 boys) from grade 8th to 12th standard, between the age-group of 13–18 yrs, studying in a government school in Hyderabad, who were willing to participate in the study were selected by simple random sampling after securing institutional approval. An interviewer assisted structured questionnaire was used to measure:

1. Reproductive and sexual health
2. Gender attributes, role and responsibilities
3. Gender-based violence

Based on the students' learning needs, structured education programme was developed and validated. The tool was validated by the subject experts and the reliability of the tool was obtained by the test-retest method. The subject's first and repeated scores were compared by coefficient of correlation method. A value of r = 0.96 was obtained, indicating the reliability of the tool. Single group pre-test post-test design was used.

O1 X O2

The pre-test and post-test scores were compared to evaluate the effectiveness of the ARSH educational programme. Girls showed gender equality scores at baseline and 28 per cent boys gained gender equality scores.

Inclusion Criteria

The inclusion criteria was as follows:

1. Adolescent students from 8th to 12th standard between the age group of 13 to 18 years
2. Adolescent students who are willing to participate in the study.

Exclusion Criteria

The exclusion criteria included:

1. Adolescent students who are not available during the data collection period
2. Adolescent students who are with difficulty to understand and mentally challenged

Ethical approval was secured from the institution. Assent from the students and written informed consent from the parent/guardian was secured.

Instrument

The instrument used in the study included the following:

1. Interviewer assisted, structured questionnaire on reproductive and sexual health; which contained 40 questions. The right answer was given a scored of 1 and the wrong answer was given 0.
2. The structured questionnaire on perceptions related to gender attributes, gender role and relations; contained 20 questions.
3. The structured questionnaire on perceptions related to gender-based violence, which contained 15 questions.
4. Gender equality related attitudes were measured by the following scoring:
   (a) Agreed '0' (gender biased response)
   (b) Not sure '1' (neutral)
   (c) Disagree '2' (gender balanced responses)

Analysis

Majority of the students are aware of the puberty changes in self and in the opposite sex such as increase in height, change in voice, breast development, and growth of facial hair, growth of hair in private parts, onset of menstruation in girls, etc. Adolescent students feel hesitant to seek information from teachers and parents. They are willing to take help from teachers but teachers were not adequately equipped with knowledge nor do they feel comfortable to discuss issues related to reproductive and sexual health.

The present study reveals that 52 per cent of the boys and 63 per cent of the girls have reported some or the other reproductive health issues, among them

41 per cent of the girls and only five per cent of the boys have reported the issue to the closed family member for support. Though they were ready to seek the support from the teachers, teachers were not adequately equipped with the knowledge and attitude to discuss the RSH issues with the children.

Overall, 13 per cent students were highly gender equitable; 52 per cent had moderate gender equality scores and 25 per cent were with overall low gender equitable scores. Students were asked about their experience of physical/verbal/emotional/sexual abuse or violence at home or school or any other place, both as victims/and cause; and their response was measured.

Knowledge scores were raised from minimum of 11 per cent to 92 per cent in the post-test scores.

Table 1

Frequency and Percentage Distribution of Subjects Pre and Post-Test Knowledge Levels (N=150)

Knowledge Levels in RSH	*Pre-Test*				*Post-Test*			
	Girls		*Boys*		*Girls*		*Boys*	
	n	*%*	*n*	*%*	*n*	*%*	*n*	*%*
Below average	32	40.5	36	50.7	7	8.9	11	15.5
Average	29	36.7	20	28.2	23	29.1	24	33.8
Above average	18	22.8	15	21.1	49	62.0	36	50.7
Total	79	100	71	100	79	100	71	100

The knowledge about RSH was measured among the students. A majority of them (51.90% of girls and 61.90% of boys) reported that they did not learn the information on RSH before (Table 2).

Table 2

Knowledge about RSH before

Item		*Girls*		*Boys*	
		N	*%*	*N*	*%*
Did you learn the information on RSH before	Yes	38	48.10	27	38
	No	41	51.90	44	61.9
Total	79	100%	71	100%	

Table 3

Frequency and Percentage Distribution of Students' Pre-Test and Post-Test Knowledge Level (N=150)

Area of Knowledge	*Level of Knowledge*											
	Pre-Test						*Post-Test*					
	B.Av		*Av*		*Ab.av*		*B.Av*		*Av*		*Ab.av*	
	n	*%*	*n*	*%*	*n*	*%*	*n*	*%*	*n*	*%*	*n*	*%*
Area 1: Reproductive system and function related	20	29.4	20	40.8	16	48.5	2	11.1	15	32	28	33
Area 2: Reproductive hygiene, right practices and common RT infections	31	45.6	13	26.5	11	33.3	4	22.2	22	46.8	32	37.6
Area 3: Sexual health and common problems and prevention	17	25	16	32.7	6	18.2	12	66.7	10	21.3	25	29

The area-wise scores in the RSH knowledge in terms of the reproductive system and function, hygiene and practices, health and prevention was also measured. It can be understood from the table that the levels have increased and were above average after the educational programme (Table 3).

The gender equality scores were also measured. The pre and post-test scores range from a minimum of 13 (8.66%) to 114 (75.99%) (Table 4).

Table 4

Students' Distribution according to Gender Equality Scores

Scores	*Total*		*Girls*		*Boys*	
	Pre	*Post*	*Pre*	*Post*	*Pre*	*Post*
Higher	13	114	9	58	5	48
Moderate	52	28	30	18	21	17
Low	85	8	40	3	45	6

An attempt was also made to know whether the students' experience of violence was physical, verbal, emotional and sexual from the students. According to Table 5, girls experienced sexual violence in a majority of cases followed by emotional abuse (60%), verbal abuse (50%) and physical abuse (40%) compared to boys. It is also interesting to note that only 48 per cent reported the acts of violence and 12 per cent students reported that they did not experience any form of violence.

Table 5

Percentage of Students' who Experienced Violence

	Total %	*Girls %*	*Boys %*
Physical	15	40	60
Verbal	30	50	50
Emotional	15	60	40
Sexual	20	70	30

Table 6 reveals that there is a remarkable improvement in the gender balanced responses, which is comparatively more in the boys after the education.

Table 6

Frequency and Percentage Distribution of Students' Gender Attributes Score in Pre- and Post-Test

Item	*Pre-Test*				*Post-Test*			
	Girls		*Boys*		*Girls*		*Boys*	
	n	*%*	*n*	*%*	*n*	*%*	*n*	*%*
Gender biased	21	26.6	29	40.8	8	10.1	3	4.2
Gender balanced	52	65.8	39	54.9	64	81	65	91.5
Uncertain	6	7.6	3	4.2	7	8.86	3	4.2

Discussion

Lack of communication with parents and trusted adults keeps young people ill-informed and unlikely to receive parental support in relation to sexual matters, information on issues related to growing up remains inadequate and irrelevant to young people's needs. Adolescent health services remain inaccessible, unaffordable, judgmental and indifferent in quality and unfriendly (UNICEF, 2007). Despite 35 per cent of the population being in the 10–24 age group, the health needs of adolescents have not been addressed adequately; particularly the reproductive health needs are often misunderstood, unrecognized or underestimated. Karim et al. (2003), in a study for improving reproductive health among rural college youth, states that boys had more liberal attitudes towards premarital sex as compared to the girls. In the study about 11 per cent of boys and 1 per cent of girls reported to have experienced pre-marital sex. A multi country study found that between one-fifth and one-half of women of reproductive age have experienced physical violence by a male partner (Heise et al., 1999). Violence against women is on the rise. The quality of life and liberty ought to be similar for a human being irrespective of the persons' sex-identity.

Conclusion

Adolescence is the right age of attitude formation. Education and counselling on RSH and gender concepts helps them to develop gender balanced attitudes and adapt healthy behaviours. The findings of the study support the need for school based education and counselling for the right development of adolescent friendly and gender-based sexual and reproductive health education. Though reproductive system and reproduction were part of the syllabus in classes 9, 10, and 11 in the old course, these topics were never taken up in the classroom, as teachers themselves hesitated and were uncomfortable in teaching these topics. They either made a passing reference to these topics or assigned them to their students for self-study. Teachers felt ill equipped to discuss reproductive health topics with their students. Teachers reported being insulted by the parents of the students when they taught the topic in school.

Teachers acknowledge the need for reproductive health information, but not all are in favour of providing sex education to school children at least in rural areas. According to them the community in the rural areas would not be comfortable with such education being imparted to students in the schools and they also feared that increased knowledge might encourage adolescents to indulge in experiments.

Sexuality is a natural and intrinsic part of an individual's personality and needs to be nurtured and developed like all other facts of life. This fact is completely ignored by parents and teachers in our society, because they themselves do not feel comfortable in discussing their issues with the youngsters. They have inhibition about discussing and expressing themselves on sex-related issues. They rather discourage the children from any form of sexual expression and encourage them to hide their sexuality. In the Indian socio-cultural setting sex is a taboo, and hence the society does not provide them with channels for being appropriately educated in this area. The adolescents generally do not get adequate advice and guidance regarding, various aspects like puberty, menarche, reproductive health, from their parents and teachers or any other groups of professionals.

Inadequate knowledge about understanding of reproductive system and reproductive health were found among students and teachers. Most of them expressed a desire to know more about reproductive health as part of the school curriculum. Boys and girls felt attraction towards the opposite sex. Relatively less social support was provided to boys as compared to girls, in terms of reproductive changes occurring in body. Majority of the adolescents expressed their willingness to avail the services of adolescent friendly school health services.

Family being the first social unit, adolescents accepts the prescribed gender roles at home. Directly or indirectly parents influence their attitude formation towards gender norms and reproductive health behaviour. India is a country with values and culture greatly influencing the family system, the patriarchic system with a male child preference may grew in the mindsets of children with glorification of man and subordination of the woman. To minimize the gender inequality and gender-based violence, creating an environment in which the boys and girls with equitable contribution in the society with proper gender norms should begin early in adolescence so that they contribute to the healthy development of the society.

Acknowledgement

The author wishes to acknowledge the support of the school principal for his support in conducting the study and the junior faculty who assisted in data collection. Special appreciation is extended to all the student participants of the study.

References

Agampodi, B. Suneth, Thilini, C. Agampodi and Piyaseeli, U.K.D. (2008). 'Adolescent Perception of Reproductive Health Care Services in Sri Lanka', *BMC Health Services Research*, 8: 98.

Andre, Tylee, Halier, D.M., Graham, Tanya, Churchill, Rachel and Sanci, Lena A. (2007). 'Youth-friendly Primary-care Services: How are We Doing and What More Needs to be Done?', *Lancet*, 1565–573.

Barker, G. (2000). 'Gender Equitable Boys in a Gender Inequitable World: Reflections from Qualitative Research and Programme Development in Rio de Janeiro', *Sexual and Relationship Therapy*, 15: 263–82.

Britto, M.T., Klostermann, B.K., Bonny, A.E., Altum, S.A. and Hornung, R.W. (2001). 'Impact of a School-based Intervention on Access to Healthcare for Underserved Youth', *Journal of Adolescent Health*, 29: 116–25.

Dunkle, K.L., Jewkes, R.K., Brown, H.C., Gray, G.E., McIntryre, J.A. and Harlow, S.D. (2004). 'Gender-based Violence, Relationship Power, and Risk of HIV Infection in Women Attending Antenatal Clinics in South Africa', *Lancet*, 363: 1415–421.

Haberland, N. and Rogow, D. (2007). *Promoting Healthy, Safe, and Productive Transitions to Adulthood*. Brief No. 22, New York: Population Council.

Heise, Lori, Ellsberg, M. and Gottemoeller, M. (1999). 'Ending Violence Against Women', Population Reports, Vol. XXVII, No. 4, Series L, No. 11. Available at: http://www.infoforhealth.org/pr/l11/violence.pdf

Karim, A.M., Magnani, R., Morgan, G. and Bond, K. (2003). 'Reproductive Health Risk and Protective Factors among Unmarried Youth in Ghana', *International Family Planning Perspectives*, 29(1): 14–24.

Koyama, A., Corliss, H.L. and Santelli, J.S. (2007). 'Global Lessons on Healthy Adolescent Sexual Development', *Curr Opin Pediatr*, 21: 444–49.

Lundgren, R., Beckman, M., Prasad, Chaurasiya, S., Subhedi, B. and Kerner, B. (2013). 'Whose Turn to Do the Dishes? Transforming Gender Attitudes and Behaviours among Very Young Adolescents in Nepal', *Gender Development*, 21: 127–45.

Ministry of Health and Family Welfare, Annual Report 2007–08, mohfw.nic.in/reports/.%5cindex.html.

National Family Health Survey-3, www.nfhsindia.org.

Pulerwitz, J., Barker, G., Segundo, M. and Nascimento, M. (2006). *Promoting More Gender-equitable Norms and Behaviors among Young Men as an HIV/AIDS Prevention Strategy*, Horizons Final Report, Washington, DC: Population Council.

Saramma, Royee (2005). 'Stress Experienced by Homemakers with Young Children', *Social Welfare*, 51(12).

Steinberg, L. (1990). 'Autonomy, Conflict and Harmony in the Family Relationship', in S. Feldman and G. Elliot (eds), *At the Threshold: The Developing Adolescent*, Cambridge: Harvard University Press, 255–76.

Tolman, D.L., Striepe, M.I. and Harmon, T. (2003). 'Gender Matters: Constructing a Model of Adolescent Sexual Health', *Journal of Sex Research*, 40(4): 12.

UNICEF (2007). *State of the World's Children Report: The Double Dividend of Gender Inequality*, www.unicef.org/sowc/index_37436.html.

Verma, R., Pulerwitz, J., Mahendra, V., Khandekar, S., Singh, A.K., Das, S. et al. (2008). *Promoting Gender Equity as a Strategy to Reduce HIV Risk and Gender-based Violence among Young Men in India*, Washington, DC: Population Council.

Vlassoff, C. and Moreno, C. García (2002). 'Placing Gender at the Centre of Health Programming: Challenges and Limitations', *Social Science and Medicine*, 54: 1713–723.

Watsa, M.C. (1994). *Youth Sexuality*, Mumbai (SECERT) Family Planning Association of India.

WHO (2011). *The Sexual and Reproductive Health of Younger Adolescents: Research Issues in Developing Countries*, Geneva.

13

Stress Amongst Destitute Women and its Impact on Their health

A Study in Guwahati, Assam

SABIHA ALAM CHOUDHURY

Abstract

In Guwahati, homeless widows or divorced women live with severe stress because of their terrible circumstances. Their independent living is hampered owing to several stressors such as poverty, unemployment, lack of shelter and abuse. These stressors contribute to higher rates of mental illness, substance abuse and health problems among them. It is important for them to cope with persisting stress to prevent harmful impact of stress on health. Stress is exceedingly prevalent and affects individuals in a variety of ways; therefore developing skills to combat stress is imperative. Homeless women report greater stress levels than homeless men and may significantly benefit from a stress management group. The position of women in Assam is not different from that of women in other regions of the country. Against this background, the paper attempts to depict a picture of the level of stress faced by the destitute women in Guwahati city of Assam, India and its overall impact on their health using various indicators based on primary and secondary data. The study reveals the condition or feelings experienced when a destitute women perceives that demands exceeds the personal and social resources and how it affects one's physical and mental health. The study concludes that a structured stress management programme and appropriate counselling techniques offers better coping strategies through raising self-awareness about stress and helps to reduce perceived stress and brings improvement in the overall health for destitute women.

Keywords

Stress, Stress in Women, Health, Mental Health, Destitute Women, India

Introduction

The term 'stress ', as it is currently used, was coined by Hans Selye in 1936, who defined it as 'the non-specific response of the body to any demand for change'. Thus, we can say that stress is a state of physiological and psychological imbalance where there is a discrepancy between the situational demand and the individual's capacities to meet those demands. While it is argued that the term 'stress' is so ubiquitous that it has been entirely cut adrift from both professional discourse and real life experience, it still retains a profoundly serious currency.

The wider the usage of the term 'stress', the more elusive its meaning. Modern definitions of stress recognize that it is a personal experience caused by pressure or demands on an individual, and impacts upon the individual's ability to cope or rather, his/her perception of that ability. Stress, it seems, is everywhere – across the language of our everyday lives, in scientific and social scientific inquiry and as an increasingly important focus within a diverse range of policy environments. It is a relatively new phenomenon, is hard to define and explain and is extraordinarily costly. 'Stress arises when individuals perceive that they cannot adequately cope with the demands being made on them or with threats to their well-being', as per Blaug, Kenyon and Lekhi (2007).

It is the experience of a perceived threat (real or imagined) to one's mental, physical or spiritual well-being resulting from a series of physiological responses and adaptations. Stress is a very important and inevitable part of life in the modern world. It is an important issue and is growing rapidly in every facet of life. The words *stress* and *change* have become synonymous to a great extent. Changes in the economy, technology, communication, information retrieval, health care etc. are some of the forces one encounters every now and then. But it is quite evident that an average person does not prefer these or other changes, because it tends to disrupt one's comfort zone. However, the rate of change has become so fast and daunting, without an adequate reference point to anchor oneself, that stress holds a potential to create a perpetual sense of uneasiness in the hearts and minds of nearly everyone. At one time, getting married, changing jobs, buying a house, raising children, going back to school, dealing with the death of a friend or close relative, and suffering from a chronic illness were all considered to be major life events that might shake the foundations of anyone's life. Stress has been linked to all the leading causes of death including heart disease, cancer, lung ailments, accidents and suicide. Some health experts even speculate that as much as 70 to 85 per cent of all diseases and illnesses are stress related. But not all kinds of stress is bad for an individual.

There are three kinds of stress – eustress, neustress and distress. Eustress is good stress and arises in any situation or circumstance that a person finds motivating or inspiring. Neustress describes sensory stimuli that has no consequential effect and is considered neither good nor bad. Distress is considered as bad and can be of two types again, i.e. acute stress which surfaces is quite intense, and disappears quickly, and chronic stress, may not appear quite so intense, yet seems to linger for prolonged periods of time (Seaward, 2012).

The causes of stress in an individual's life can be many and might range from being unhappy in a job, death of a dear one, having poor managerial skills, marital conflict, working under risky or dangerous situation, etc. The life stresses as mentioned in The Life Events Stress Scale, such as the death of a loved one, divorce, getting married, traumatic event, etc. can also have a big and inexplicable impact on the life of an individual and cause stress. Sometimes stress is the result of internal factor's, i.e. there might not appear to be a probable explicable cause, but still stress is caused. This stress might thereafter result in health related problems.

Stress in Women

Even though women are biologically equipped to do many things simultaneously, they never seem to have enough time to do all that they want to. The human brains are hardwired to enable us to do multitasking, therefore most of the women push the envelope and try to do more, thinking that they can handle one more additional thing. But whenever they try to do much they end up creating a nagging sense of urgency and the feeling that they will never catch up. They race from one activity to another or one chore to another, stretching themselves to the limit, rarely taking time to relax. Women are also conditioned to be responsive to others' well-being and to try to please. This nurturing tendency make women susceptible to higher stress levels when they take on too much and find themselves overloaded. In women of all ages, whether or not they are aware of it, stress disrupts their bodies' intricate balance and create illness. Thus, it is quite evident that stress is at the root of many of the physical and psychological problems. Health care for women is especially inadequate and they deserve the attention of the health care community as individuals and as the foundations of families. Strong healthy women make strong healthy society (McClellan and Hamilton, 2010).

Mental Health

Mental health is defined as a state of well-being in which every individual realizes his or her own potential, can cope with the normal stresses of life, can work productively and fruitfully, and is able to make a contribution to her or his community. Mental disorders are significant contributors to the global burden of disease. Worldwide it is estimated that approximately 450 million people suffer from a mental disorder. Although mental disorders have a potential impact upon all individuals, it is important to recognize gender differences in the rates, experience and course of mental disorders. Women and mental disorders not only have higher morbidity and mortality rates, but are also more at risk for the under diagnosis of major physical illnesses. Despite an increase in life expectancy and a variety of new medications for more effective treatment of mental disorders, women continue to face increased vulnerability and gender-based risks for major depression, PTSD, and anxiety disorders. In addition, women with mental disorders, continue to face significant social stigma and discrimination. Since mental and substance use disorders begin in childhood and adolescence, successful efforts in prevention and early intervention should be initiated during this critical time period (Levin and Becker, 2010).

Indian society has been extremely complex and its social and economic structures are significantly different. Going by Indian traditions, the role of women is that of housewife. However, during post-Independence, it has been realized that the nation cannot progress without the active participation and cooperation of women. Therefore efforts had been made to provide equal opportunities to women – be it in the field of education or occupation. These efforts have increasingly brought a great change in the life of women, influencing their attitudes, values and participations in different walks of life. In our society – each woman has a social role which appears to have its own demands and requires adjustment on the part of women to successfully deal with it. A large body of empirical work shows that women's involvement affects their physical and psychological health or well-being. It is concerned with her feelings about her daily life experiences. All such events result in stress in women. Such stressful events produce serious adverse effects on the health and psychological well-being of women. Researches have been undertaken regarding the relation between stress producing events and illness. But not all women respond to major life changes. The stressful life events for women are causally expressed in a variety of undesirable effects on the performance – household or at job and in worst circumstance on the health (Mansuri, 2012).

Destitution in Women

Destitution is popularly understood as a state of poverty so severe that the individual concerned is dependent for their survival on the goodwill of others, including charity from the public or welfare support from the state or non-governmental agencies. 'Destitute' in relation to a woman and a widow means any female who has no independent source of livelihood or is not being looked after by any family member or relative. There is accumulating evidence that links mental disorders with poverty, powerlessness and alienation, conditions most frequently experienced by women. Very large number of destitute women and widows in our country are leading a miserable life. They do not have any means for their own subsistence and for their dependent children. They work as maids and perform various domestic chores such as cleaning utensils, washing clothes, dusting, etc. for very small wages. They can do such a work only when they are physically healthy. But many widows are not so fortunate. Homelessness has been well known consequence as well as cause of the mental illness and disability. For many women, homelessness follows years of violence and abuse which undermines their self-esteem, contributes to the pain of powerlessness and reinforces the social invisibility of their lives. The multiple implications and the magnitude of the problem, calls for an urgent attention, of all the service provider and policy-makers (Jemina, 2009).

In a report of ASHADEEP, which is a mental health society in Guwahati, Assam, 2007, they have mentioned that there is a sizeable population of those who are homeless and live on the streets in our country. It is also reported that there are homeless who are in the shelter homes. A number of such people suffer from mental disorders. Some of them are on the streets because of their mental disorder while some have developed such disorders because of their homelessness. They are perhaps the most vulnerable group amongst the homeless. In addition to various risks that homeless people face – poor living conditions, infections, inaccessibility to basic health services, premature death and so on, the mentally ill, because of their affected condition, are not only shunned but also receive no support or sympathy of any kind.

The position of women in Assam is not different from that of women in other regions of the country. In fact in some respects, especially health, women in Assam are more disadvantaged. Anjuman Ara Begum (2011) reported that according to a survey by sSTEP (Society for Social Transformation and Environment Protection) in 2009, the total homeless people in Guwahati were 980 out of this male were 530, female 390, children 63, mentally challenged nine and physically handicapped 15. Out of the total homeless, 46 were mentally ill and 40 were physically challenged. In mentally ill category, 19 were female and 27 were male. In Guwahati city, homeless people are mostly from the underdeveloped districts like Kamrup, Barpeta, Goalpara, Dhuburi, Sonitpur, Nagaon and Golaghat. The concentration of homeless population in Guwahati can be witnessed almost all over the city area though the highest number of concentration is in the Sukreswar Mandir near Panbazar, Paltanbazar, Railway Station and Lakhtakia. It was found that there are about 100 people living in and around Sukleshwar temple and about 30 of them were women.

The study attempts to identify and illustrate the stress level and its impact on the health of destitute women who are given shelter in the destitute homes of Guwahati city of Assam. These women might have varied skills to manage in extremely adverse situations and under more favourable conditions they might manage to be self-sufficient. But this does not indicate that destitute women do not have health problems as a result of the stress they encounter.

Methodology

Objectives

1. To observe the level of stress experienced by destitute women of selected destitute homes of Guwahati city,
2. To observe the health of destitute women of selected destitute homes of Guwahati city,
3. To correlate the level of stress and health of destitute women, and
4. To find out the significance of difference between the destitute women abandoned by their family members and destitute women who had undergone marital separation on stress and health levels.

Hypotheses

1. There will be a significant difference between the destitute women abandoned by their family members and destitute women who had undergone marital separation on their stress level, and

2. There will be a significant difference between the destitute women abandoned by their family members and destitute women who had undergone marital separation on their health level

Sample

The sample for this study consisted of 60 destitute females (30 abandoned by family and 30 marital separation) around the age group of 21–70 years. The sample was selected through incidental sampling from Guwahati city of Assam from three randomly selected destitute homes viz. SENEH, which is situated in Nizara path, Kahilipara, Guwahati, Missionaries of Charity, Baralumukh, Guwahati; and Missionaries of Charity, Lankeswar, Guwahati.

Formal permission was obtained from the head of the institution. After obtaining the informed consent from the sample and assuring about confidentiality of the information obtained, the data collection process was executed.

Tools

General Health Questionnaire-12

The General Health Questionnaire originally introduced by Goldberg in 1972, was used in the present study to assess the mental health of the destitute women. It is a very successful tool to assess mental health. The GHQ-12 was standardized on a sample of women of ethnic Indian origin living in the United Kingdom. The Cronbach's alpha was 0.89 and the split half reliability was 0.91. Principal component analysis revealed two significant components which accounted for 75.2 per cent of variance. The psychometric properties and factor structure of the Hindi and English versions were similar. The GHQ has been validated in India in Kannada by Shamsunder et al. in 1986 and in Hindi by Gautam et al. in 1987. It has also been validated among women of ethnic Indian origin living in the United Kingdom (Jacob et al., 1997). It has a total of 12 items and the scoring is on a Likert scale. Low scores indicate less health related issues, whereas high scores on the scale indicate symptoms of severe health and psychological distress.

Holmes and Rahe Stress Scale

The Holmes and Rahe stress scale which gives an account of the life events stress of an individual was used to find the stress level of the destitute women. It includes 43 items. This scale, was developed in 1967 by Thomas Holmes and Richard Rahe, shows the kind of life pressure that one is facing. Here low scores indicate low susceptibility to stress and stress related illness and high scores indicate high susceptibility to stress and stress related illness. Their results were published as the Social Readjustment Rating Scale (SRRS), known more commonly as the Holmes and Rahe Stress Scale. Rahe carried out a study in 1970 testing the reliability (statistics) of the stress scale as a predictor of illness. There was a +0.118 correlation between stress scale scores and illness, which was sufficient to support the hypothesis of a link between life events and illness. The scale was also tested cross-culturally, comparing Japanese and Malaysian groups with American populations.

Procedure

General Health Questionnaire-12 was translated in Assamese and was administered on the participants selected for the study, i.e. sixty destitute females (thirty abandoned by family and thirty marital separation) to assess their health status and was thereafter scored using the scoring manual.

The Holmes and Rahe stress scale which was translated in Assamese was used to assess the level of stress leading to health problems on the same sample i.e 30 destitute women abandoned by family and 30 destitute women who had undergone marital separation and was thereafter scored using the scoring manual.

A Non-Experimental-Descriptive Correlational Design was used in the study. A descriptive method is used when the researcher wants to describe a specific behaviour as it occurs in the environment. A correlational method was followed as it was intended to find a correlation between the two main variables, i.e. Stress and Health. A correlational study is a quantitative method of research in which there are two or more quantitative variables from the same group of subjects. Since that study determined whether a relationship between the two variables exists or not and if it is significant, a correlation study was conducted. The data collected was tested statistically using t test and Pearson's Product Moment Correlation in the IBM SPSS (Statistical Package for the Social Sciences). In addition, descriptive statistics like Mean and SD were also calculated.

Results and Discussion

The data collected was analysed in terms of the stress level and the health along with the correlational analysis of stress and health of destitute women and presented in table format wherever necessary.

Table 1

Stress Level of the Destitute Women

Stress Level	*Frequency*	*Per cent (%)*
Low Stress	3	5.0
Medium Stress	20	33.3
High Stress	37	61.7
Total	60	100.0

Table 1 shows that 5 per cent of the destitute women in the shelter homes had low stress, 33.3 per cent had medium stress and 61.7 per cent had high stress; which indicates that homelessness is a cause of stress. Studies have shown a higher occurrence of stressful life events in females without homes than in those with homes. Some studies have considered homelessness itself as a stressor (Goodman, Saxe and Harvey, 1991).

Table 2

Health of the Destitute Women

Health	Frequency	Per cent (%)
Typical	5	8.3
Evidence of distress	23	38.3
Severe health and psychological problems	32	53.3
Total	60	100

Table 2 shows that 8.3 per cent of destitute women had typical and lesser health related problems, 38.3 per cent showed evidence of distress and 53.3 per cent showed severe health and psychological problems; which shows that homelessness results in greater health related issues. In a study by Zima et al. (1996), it was found that 72 per cent of homeless mothers had a probable lifetime substance use disorder, mental disorder, or both.

Table 3

Pearson Correlation between Stress and Mental Health Correlations

		Stress	Health
Stress	Pearson Correlation	1	.736**
	Sig. (1-tailed)		.000
	N	60	60
Health	Pearson Correlation	.736**	1
	Sig. (1-tailed)	.000	

**. Correlation is significant at the 0.01 level (1-tailed).

As seen in Table 3, correlation between stress and mental health is 0.736 and significant at level 0.01. This means that increase of stress can increase health related and psychological problems in destitute women. A study by Stead, et al. (2010) found that higher levels of procrastination and stress were predicted to correlate with poorer mental health status and fewer mental help-seeking behaviours.

Table 4

t-test Analysis on Stress and Health Levels for Destitute Women Abandoned by their Family Members and Destitute Women who had Undergone Marital Separation

Items	Destitute Women Abandoned by Family	Destitute Women who had Undergone Marital Separation	t-ratio	Not Significant
Stress	Mean = 2.63 SD = 0.615	Mean = 2.50 SD = 0.572	0.8478	0.01 level
Health	Mean = 2.53 SD = 0.615	Mean = 2.37 SD = 0.681	0.9551	0.01 level
p> 0.01**				

Table 4 shows that there is no significant difference between the destitute women abandoned by their family members and destitute women who had undergone marital separation on stress and health levels. Thus, it seems that destitute women whether abandoned by their family or who had undergone marital separation, probably experience a feeling of rejection and feel they are alone, having no close family member supporting them in all respects. In a study by Bogard et al. (1999), it was found that mental health services had little impact on the stress and depression levels of homeless women; it was isolation from the social network and a feeling of being alone which caused their stress.

Thus, it is demonstrated by the study stress levels of destitute women is high whether the reason is abandonment by family or marital separation. It appears that it has similar level of impact on their health. Destitution for a woman is a condition where she has to be completely by herself, without any support emotionally. It is an offshoot of a majority of family problems in India. She is always at the receiving end of the broken families, and this tends to appear not only in the economically low families, but also in the financially well-off and high-class families. As a result, few women tend to be rejected by their spouse and few other face the brutal atrocities of their family members, whether it be of the family of origin or the family of procreation. This results in homelessness of many women and they end up seeking shelter from the destitute homes, even which has limited resources. Such a woman has no independent source of livelihood or is not being looked after by any family member, which could be a cause of major stress and the resultant health problems.

Thus, stress and health of destitute women are correlated positively and significantly. When a destitute woman perceives that demands exceeds the personal and social resources it affects her physical and mental health.

Conclusion

It can thus be concluded that:

1. There is no significant difference between the destitute women abandoned by their family members and destitute women who had undergone marital separation on their stress level, i.e. the stress level of destitute women abandoned by family and destitute women who had undergone marital separation is almost similar.
2. There is no significant difference between the destitute women abandoned by their family members and destitute women who had undergone marital separation on their health level.

Limitations of the Study

1. The sample size was small and as a result it is difficult to generalize the findings to all the destitute women in the shelter homes of Guwahati city.
2. The inmates of the destitute home were distracted at times.
3. Time restraint is another limitation in the data collection process, as majority of the inmates of the destitute homes were illiterate, and hence each participant had to be approached individually and all the items to be explained to them, or to the caretakers.

The study concludes that a structured stress management programme and appropriate counselling techniques could offer better coping strategies through raising self-awareness about stress and could help to reduce perceived stress and thereby probably bring improvement in the overall health for destitute women. The women in the shelter homes could be given training in certain areas where they could explore their expertise. They should be given occupational therapy and strategies should be employed by the shelter homes to approach the various Governmental and Non-Governmental Organization for the collection of funds, so that a proper psychiatric, psychological and physical treatment could be provided to them on a regular basis. In addition, efforts should be made to educate the destitute women, majority of whom are illiterate, and an attempt should be made to keep them engaged in various creative activities which would give them satisfaction and contentment.

References

Begum, A.A. (2011). *The Homeless in Guwahati: An Observation*. Retrieved from http://twocircles.net/2011feb28/homeless_guwahati_observation.html#.vhp7wiuufka.

Blaug, R., Kenyon, A. and Lekhi, R. (2007). *Stress at Work: A Report Prepared for the Work Foundation's Principal Partners*, London: The Work Foundation.

Bogard, C.J., McConnell, J.J., Gerstel, N. and Schwartz, M. (1999). 'Homeless Mothers and Depression: Misdirected Policy', *J Health Soc Behav*, 40(1): 46–62.

Goodman, L., Saxe, L. and Harvey, M. (1991). 'Homelessness as Psychological Trauma: Broadening Perspectives', *Am Psychol*, 46(11): 1219–225.

Jacob, K.S., Bhugra, D. and Mann, A.H. (1997). 'General Health Questionnaire-12: Psychometric Properties and Factor Structure among Indian Women Living in the United Kingdom', *Indian J Psychiat*, 39(3): 196–99.

Jemina, V. (2009). *Assessment of the Level of Stress and Coping Strategies among Destitute Women*, Bangalore: Rajiv Gandhi University of Health Sciences.

Levin, B.L. and Becker, M.A. (2010). *A Public Health Perspective of Women's Mental Health*, New York: Springer Science and Business Media.

Mansuri, A.J. (2012). *A Study of the Effects of Social Support, Life Event Stress, and Certain Personal Variables on Physical and Psychological Health of the Employed and Unemployed Women*. Retrieved from http://shodhganga.inflibnet.ac.in/bitstream/10603/4636/8/08_chapter1.pdf.

McClellan, S. and Hamilton, B. (2010). *The Ultimate Stress: Relief Plan for Women*, New York: Free Press.

Seaward, S.L. (2012). *Managing Stress: Principles and Strategies for Health and Well-being*, 7th edition, Burlington: Jones and Bartlett Learning.

Sharma, A. (2014). 'Stress and Depression in Destitute and Normal Females', *International Journal of Academic Research in Psychology*, 1(1). Retrieved from http://hrmars.com/hrmars_papers/stress_and_depression_in_destitute_and_normal_females1.pdf.

Stead, R., Shanahan, M.J. and Neufeld, R.W.J. (2010). 'I'll Go to Therapy, Eventually: Procrastination, Stress and Mental Health', *Personality and Individual Differences*, 49: 175–80. Retrieved from http://www.psychologytoday.com/files/attachments/41207/ill-go-therapy-eventually-stead-shanahan-neufeld-2010.pdf.

Zima, B.T., Wells, K.B., Benjamin, B. and Duan, N. (1996). 'Mental Health Problems among Homeless Mothers: Relationship to Service Use and Child Mental Health Problems', *Arch Gen Psychiatry*, 53: 332–38.

14

Social Life of AIDS Affected (HIV Positive) Women in Kashmir

An Empirical Analysis in India

KHALIDA GULL

Abstract

The HIV prevalence is considerable low in Kashmir as compared to other states of India. The factors responsible for such low prevalence to HIV/AIDS are not known but definitely this is being attributed to strong socio-religious factors prevalent in Kashmir society. In such a situation, it is very important to know how Kashmiri women infected with HIV/AIDS are coping with their lives in a society strongly guided by socio-religious norms. This paper empirically analyses the social life of AIDS affected women in Kashmir, India. The socio-economic background of these women, level of awareness they have about the disease and social stigma attached are also analysed in the paper.

Keywords

Social Life, AIDS, Women, Kashmir.

Introduction

AIDS is an acronym of 'acquired immune deficiency syndrome' which is a fatal disease described variously as modern plague, modern scourge, devastating disease, insidious microbiological bomb, biological disaster and so on. It has emerged as an unprecedented pandemic cutting across all boundaries – international, socio-economic, age, sex and race. AIDS is already established in several countries of the world. Its exponential progress and tremendous impact on the mankind is still frightening. HIV (human immune deficiency virus) catches person in their prime youth (20–39 years), opening avenues for opportunistic diseases – both infectious and cancerous leading on to exceedingly complex clinical science and symptoms with high fatality. It's a world health problem of extraordinary scale and urgency. AIDS emerge as one of the most important public health issues of late 20th and early 21st centuries and is now one of the leading causes of global morbidity and mortality (Wallace and Maxcy et al., 2008).

Young women and girls are more susceptible to HIV than men and boys. Their vulnerability is primarily due to inadequate knowledge about AIDS, insufficient access to HIV prevention services, inability to negotiate safer sex and lack of female controlled HIV prevention methods; about half of all people living with HIV in world are female (NACO, 2013). In India, 35 per cent of all reported AIDS cases are among the age group of 15–24 years, indicating the vulnerability of younger population to the epidemic (Verma, 2008). The epidemic is moving from high risk groups, such as sex workers to the general population (Park, 2007). There were five million new HIV infections in the world during 2002, of these two million were women as per National AIDS Control Organization (NACO) reports (NACO, 2013). It is estimated that about 24,00,000 people in India are living with HIV/AIDS (www.photius.com). According to National AIDS Control Organization (NACO) in India, the prevalence of AIDS in India in 2013 was 0.27, which is down from 0.41 in 2002 (www.ndtv.com). India yet discussions about women's vulnerability to HIV often focus on individual factors which increase risk; there is generally less focus on the underlying causes of poverty, violence and gender inequality (Verma, 2008). The younger women when they first have sex, the more likely it is to have been forced sex, forced sex is correlated to HIV risk (Watts, 2009).

At the Vienna 2010 International AIDS Conference, Charlotte Watts presented the results of a study which draws on data from 96 countries, which shows conclusively that intimate partner violence doubles women's risk of contracting HIV (Hale and Vazquez, 2011). During the conflict and post conflict periods, women become defenseless against HIV infection due to break down of law and order and the interweaved prospects of sexual abuse by military personnels, forced flight from home, loss of their families, livelihood and a little or no access to health care. Women can also be subjected to repeated assaults, such as gang rape, where the exposure to multiple partners increases their risk of infection (Welbourn, 2010).

There is much larger body of work on stigma and discrimination against people – including women living with HIV. A key gap is the lack of systemic mechanism for mutual learning between women's organizations and HIV organizations (Nayar, 2010). Prosecution has also been reported against people living with HIV who use condoms during sexual relations (CWGLH, 2006). Numerous studies have linked HIV-related stigma with delayed HIV testing, non-disclosure to partners and poor engagement with HIV services (Eyawo et al., 2010). Anti-stigma programmers are most effective when they simultaneously address individual, organizational and public policy factors that enable stigma and discrimination (Cohen et al., 2011). Evidence indicates that anti-stigma programming reduces social isolation and improves HIV treatment adherences (West et al., 2013).

The structural impacts of gender inequality on women and girls as it relates to HIV/AIDS, and particularly on access to HIV care, treatment and support services has been the subject of a number of reports and pre-reviewed scientific literature over the past few years. Consistent themes regarding the potential impact of gender inequality on women and girls include differential access to ART and other health services compared with men; HIV related stigma and discrimination (both an individual and community levels), fear of losing their partners, of domestic violence as a result of HIV disclose or taking antiretroviral medications, financial insecurity (Baird et al., 2012).

Jammu and Kashmir has 3,492 people living with HIV. As per J&K AIDS Prevention and Control Society (JKAPCS), Jammu division tops in HIV positive with 90 per cent cases, while Kashmir with only 13 per cent of HIV positive cases being detected so far. This puts the total number of HIV positive cases in J&K at 452 in 2011–12 (International AIDS Society, 2010). According to IANS/Daily India.com there are 745 HIV cases in Kashmir. However unofficial estimates put the number at 2,500. The influx of migrant workers, security personnel, truck drivers, tourist in Kashmir, commercial sex industry, low literacy rate and socio-cultural diversity had made fighting HIV/AIDS difficult (Greater Kashmir, 2012). In J&K one of the major prevalence group among women was found to be wives and associated partners of truck drivers. The fact that HIV infection is more likely to be found in women with lower education status is an additional challenge to HIV information and education programmers, signifies the high vulnerability of women in the state of Jammu and Kashmir. The main age group affected is that of 31–40 years and the male: female ratio of 4.2: 1 was observed (Indo-Asia News Services, 2006). In a study done by M.A. Mir et al. (2010) in Kashmir reported that the clinical and demographic profile of HIV/AIDS patients in Kashmir is largely similar to the rest of India. In another study done by Bashir Gaash in Srinagar reported that 76 per cent of the participants were aware of HIV/AIDS (Mir et al., 2010).

According to the latest figures of Jammu and Kashmir AIDS Prevention and Control Society (JKAPCS), J&K, has 2,406 HIV patients registered while Kashmir has 373 such patients as on 31 August 2013. Data revealed by the JKACS earlier in December 2012 stated 3,492 cases of HIV in Kashmir from 2005–11, 223 patients died of HIV in the state and in 2011, 3,066 HIV positive cases were registered in the state. In 2010, there were 2,649 HIV patients in J&K (76 in Kashmir and 582 in Jammu) which numbered at 2,222 in 2009. Currently 1,101 patients are registered at Anti Retroviral Therapy (ART) clinic in Jammu and 141 in ART centre Kashmir. According to Jammu and Kashmir AIDS Prevention and Control Society, the state is a low prevalence state where the mean prevalence rate of HIV infection among high risk groups (STD) is 0.3 per cent and low risk groups (ANC) is 0.04 per cent as per various setline surveillance rounds conducted during last eight years (Bashir et al., 2003). The HIV/AIDS is 2–3 times more common in males than females peaks in the persons dyed between 15–50 years. There may be a chance of secondary infections in HIV patients like infection of mycobacterium tuberculosis which was prevalent in 70 per cent of patients (*Kashmir Times*, 2013). The trend of HIV prevalence among the populations of remote area in southern Indian state of Tamil Nadu was found to be declining irrespective of dye, residence and literacy, indicating the effectiveness of NACP-III interventional programmes. The state HIV prevalence in female population and decrease in male population indicates that present interventions must be strengthened to control HIV prevalence with a special focus on females (Ramalingam et al., 2012). Against this background the study analyses the social life of AIDS affected women in the Kashmir region of India.

Objectives

The objectives of the study are:

1. To know the socio-economic background of infected women,
2. To analyse how infected women are coping with their lives in a religious bound society of Kashmir,
3. To known the level of social stigma attached to being a HIV positive, and
4. To ascertain the amount of awareness they have about HIV/AIDS.

The Study

The study was conducted in an ART centre in SKIMS, Srinagar (Kashmir). A total number of twenty AIDS epidemic women from both the rural and urban areas were selected randomly from different areas of Kashmir. The study was descriptive in nature and utilized cross-sectional interview method of gathering information, about the problems, socio-economic conditions, social stigma attached to HIV positive women and the level of awareness they have about HIV/AIDS. All the respondents were Muslims and majority were illiterate. A semi-structured pre-tested questionnaire was administrated to the AIDS epidemic women to gather information about their socio-economic condition, knowledge about means of transmission of the infection, modes of prevention, attitudes towards them being HIV positive, counselling and testing social stigma and level of awareness they have about HIV/AIDS.

Findings

It was interesting to note that 70 per cent of the HIV positive women had never heard of HIV/AIDS before they come into contact with this disease. Among those who were aware only few were having the accurate knowledge about HIV/AIDS, the rest were, however, ignorant.

Economic status of the respondents was comparatively low; they were in critical financial condition. Husbands of the married respondents (85%) were all labourers, and the respondents whose husband were also positive (75%), their economic condition was worst, as their husbands were not in the position to work much due to their repeated illness.

Knowledge about the modes of transmission was scanty among those who were not aware of the disease before they come into its contact. A little less than half of the respondents (30%) had no idea about the possible modes of transmission majority of the respondents were married (85%), so they blamed it to sexual contact with an infected person, only 8 per cent to infected blood, 5 per cent to use of infected needles and syringes, only about 3 per cent were aware of the fact that HIV/AIDS can be transmitted from mother to child, and only few (20%) were using condoms during sexual intercourse. Most of the respondents believed that HIV/AIDS could also spread through eating with victim, sharing clothes, sleeping with victim (Table 1). While a sizeable portion didn't commit at all.

Among those 85 per cent of infected respondents, 15 per cent of the respondents were unmarried, one girl from 9th standard was infected by parents, and another girl from class first year was infected by her boyfriend. Majority of the respondents (75%) were infected through their husbands.

Table 1

Awareness about the Modes of Transmission

1.	Sexual contact with infected person	75%
2.	Infected blood	8%
3.	Use of infected needles and syringes	5%
4.	Mother to child transmission	3%

Asked whether respondents ever discussed HIV/AIDS with someone, 45 per cent admitted that they never had enough courage to discuss the topic with anyone. About 60 per cent who admitted having discussed about HIV/AIDS at some time with their husbands but only after coming into contact with the disease.

About 75 per cent of the respondents face different problems when their HIV positive status was revealed. Married respondents whose husbands were negative (10%) were violated and ill-treated and even beaten by their husbands.

About 30 per cent were facing violence by their in-laws and about 20 per cent had kept their HIV (+ve) status hidden. Even a little portion (1%) of the respondents were facing violence by their own kids (Table 2).

Table 2

Social Stigma attached to HIV/AIDS Epidemic Women

1.	Problems faced when HIV positive status was revealed	75%
2.	Discrimination by family and relatives (in-laws)	30%
3.	Violence faced by husbands	10%
4.	Violence faced by kids	1%

The chief source of information about HIV/AIDS to vast majority of respondents were doctors who treated them (80%), friends/relatives and family (15%), radio/TV (5%) and print media (1%). About 30 per cent of the respondents had no access to TV/radio (Table 3).

Table 3

Source of Information

1.	Doctors	80%
2.	Friends/relatives/family	15%
3.	Radio/TV	5%
4.	Print media	1%

Those with the correct knowledge of various preventive measures were 60 per cent, a great majority named sterilization of needles before infection (25%) followed by safer sex (20%) and ensuring safe blood practices (15%).

Availability of ICTCS (integrated counselling and testing centres) centres was in fewer regions of the residing places of respondents. Majority of respondents (70%) didn't visit their nearby testing centre with the fear that their HIV positive status might be disclosed. Respondents visit the ART centre in SKIMS (Srinagar) the only ART centre in Kashmir, where they feel that their HIV positive status is kept hidden. A very vast majority of respondents (98%) were satisfied with the treatment and medicines they got in this ART centre.

Discussion

The HIV prevalence is considerably low in Kashmir as compared to other states of India. The factors responsible for such low prevalence to HIV/AIDS are not known but it can be attributed to strong socio-religious factors prevalent in Kashmir society. In such a situation it is very important to know how Kashmiri women infected with HIV/AIDS are able to cope with their lives in a society strongly guided by strong socio-religious norms. The socio-economic background of these women, level of awareness they have about the disease and social stigma attached also assumes significance.

The study has shown that a majority of women were economically weak. There is a lot of social stigma attached and most of the women were facing violence by their in-laws, relatives and family too. Some of the women were also facing violence by their husbands. Women also faced violence by their kids in some cases. The main source of the information about HIV/AIDS affected women were doctors who treated them followed by family/relatives/friends and then media. Less awareness through the media was due to inaccessibility to radio/TV.

Conclusion

The study shows a dismal picture of HIV/AIDS related stigma and discrimination and the awareness, which indirectly points out to the worse discrimination among AIDS affected women. In view of the fact that every hour 50 young women are newly infected with HIV globally, the widespread and ignorance about HIV/AIDS among women in Kashmir is a serious concern and needs to be addressed appropriately, through intensive HIV/AIDS awareness campaigns in both rural and urban areas. Media can be an important tool to spread the information and awareness about the deadly disease.

The high rates of stigma and discrimination towards HIV/AIDS appear to be driven primarily by negative feelings towards PLHIV, lack of experience as well as misconceptions and fear of casual transmission. Stigma reduction interventions are, thus, urgently needed to target transmission misconception and to increase interactions with these AIDS affected women. Such programmers need to be designed and implemented in collaboration with PLHIV and the use of gender sensitive approach.

References

Baird, S., Melntosh, C. and Ozler, B. (2012). 'Effect of a Cash Transfer Programme for Schooling on Prevalence of HIV and Herpes Simplex Type 2 in Malawi: A Cluster Randomized Trial', *Lancet*, 379(9823): 1320–29.

Bashir, Gassh, Ahmad, M., Kausar, Rehana and Bashir, Shabnam (2003). 'Knowledge, Attitude and Belief on HIV/AIDS among Female Senior Secondary Students in Srinagar District of Kashmir', *Health and Population Perspectives*, 26(3): 101–09.

Centre for Women's Global Leadership and Health (2006). *Meeting Report: Action on Gender-based Research*, Policy Programming and Advocacy, Toronto, http://www.cwgl.rutgers.edu/globalcentre/policy/hiv/aids/toronto.pdf.

Cohen, M. et al. (2011). 'Prevention of HIV-1 Infection with Early Antiretroviral Therapy', *New England Journal of Medicine*, 365: 493–505.

Eyawo, O. et al. (2010). 'HIV Status in Discordant Couples in Sub-Saharan Africa: A Systemic Review and Meta-Analysis', *Lancet Infection Diseases*, 10: 770–77.

Hale, Fand and Vazquez, Marijo (2011). *Violence against Women Living with HIV/AIDS: A Background Paper*, Washington, D.C.

HIV/AIDS – People Living with HIV/AIDS (2012). http://www.photius.com/ranbings/population/hiv-aids-people-living-with-hiv-aids-2012-o.html.

Indo-Asia News Services (July 2006). HIV/AIDS – Spreading in Jammu and Kashmir. http://www.ndtv.com/video/player/news/world-aids-day-india-records-sharp-drops-in-number-of-cases/299798.

International AIDS Society (July 2010). *Environmental Scan: Mapping HIV Research Priorities for Women and Children*, Switzerland: International AIDS Society.

J&K State AIDS Prevention and Control Society (2012). http://jksacs.org/prevalencephp

Kashmir Times (30 September 2013). *37500 HIV Patients in Jammu and Kashmir 39 Died in Valley since 1999*.

Mir, M.A. et al. (2010). 'Clinical and Demographic Profile of HIV/AIDS Patients Diagnosed at Tertiary Care Centre in Kashmir', *JPMA*, 60(6).

NACO (2013). India: Annual Report.

National AIDS Control Organization (2005). *India Resolves to Defeat HIV/AIDS*, Ministry of Health and Family Welfare, Government of India, New Delhi.

Nayar, Sudha (2010). *Violence against Women in South Asian Communities: Issues for Policy and Practice*, New Delhi: Navyug Books.

Nyqvist, M.B., Corno, L., de Walque, Damien and Svensson, J. (2013). 'Evaluating the Impact of Short-term Financial Incentives on HIV and STI Incidence among Youth in Losotho: A Randomized Trail', TUPDC0106 Poster Discussion Session, IAS 7th International AIDS Conference on HIV Pathogenesis, Treatment and Prevention, Kaulalumpur.

Park, K. (2007). *AIDS: Textbook of Preventive and Social Medicine*, 19th edition, Jabalpur: Banarsidas Bhanot.

Ramalingam, Sekar, Murugesan, Amudhan, Moorthy, Sivashankar and Manoharan, Mythreyee (2012). Recent Trends in HIV Prevalence in Remote Setting of Southern India: Insights into Arranging HIV Control Policies.

Trivedis, Boraste A., Vamsi, K.K., Jahadav, A., Khairnary, Guftan, Patil, P., Gufta, G., Gulta, M., Mujapara, A.K. and Joshi, B. (2009). 'Biostatical Analysis of HIV-AIDS Patients with Reference to Various Factors', *International Journal of Parasitological Research*, 1(3).

Verma, Salwalia Bihiri (2008). 'Rural Infrastructure Sensation Housing Health Care', in S. Prasad and L. Panda (eds), *The Social Dimensions Emphasis to Women and Girls*, New Delhi: Sarup and Sons.

Wallace, R.B., Maxcy, K.F. and Rosenau, M.J. (2008). *Public Health and Preventive Medicine*, 15th edition, New York: McGraw Hill.

Watts, C. (2009). *Violence against Women and HIV: Dimensions and Responses*, London Department of Public Health and Policy, London School of Hygiene and Tropical Medicine.

Welbourn, A. (2010). Absence of Evidence Does Not Mean Evidence of Absence: Open Democracy, www.opendemocracy.net/5050/alice-welburn/we-hear-thunder-but-we-see-no-rain (Accessed on 1 September 2010).

West, P.A., Scarb, L., Horwrtz, J., Klein, F., Nuffenzweig, M.C. and Bjorkman, P.J. (2013). Computational Analysis of Anti-HIV-I Antibody Neutralisation Panel Data to Identify Potential Functional Epito Residues. Proceeding of National Academy of Sciences of the USA, Vol. 110(26), pp. 10598–603.

15

Political Violence

It's Impact on Women's Mental Health in India

MOUSUMI MAHANTA

Abstract

Violence is a common situation that one comes across in India. The inhuman brutalities of violence can lead to homelessness, deprivation of dignity and privacy, poverty and struggle for existence and survival. Violence, as a result of political conflicts, usually have a long term impact on the overall well-being of people. Most of the violent acts that occur in India are internal, between two groups of different communities. Assam, a state of North-East India usually undergoes certain political disturbances that create serious threat to the people's life directly. Women are more prone to such violence in the state. Women facing these cruelty and inhumanity usually come under trauma and lose their mental as well as physical well-being. This paper, discusses the impact of political violence on women's mental health of Assam. The study is based on the fieldwork conducted in different areas of Sonitpur District of Assam, India.

Keywords

Political Violence, Mental Health, Women, Assam, India

Introduction

Political violence is a means that is used by people and government around the world to achieve political goals. 'A key element of modern political violence is that it penetrates the entire fabric of social relations as means of social control' (Subbian et al., 2010). Political conflicts squash social control, disturb the social, economic and cultural configuration and identity of a particular area. It also has a negative impact on individual mental health and total physical well-being. Mob violence is a common form of political violence that one comes across in India. The inhuman brutalities of mob violence can lead to homelessness, deprivation of dignity and privacy, poverty, disease and struggle for existence and survival.

'In this flight worst affected, are often women' (Subbian, 2010: 277). Political conflicts usually have a long term impact on the overall well-being of people's life. Most of the violent conflicts that occur in our country are internal, between two groups of different communities. Most of those under attack come from the economically weak groups and ethnic minorities.

Trauma

Post-Traumatic Stress Disorder was previously known as shell shocks, combat stress, delayed stress syndrome and traumatic neuroses. Although there is considerable variation depending on gender, race, and the type of trauma, it has been estimated that 5–11 per cent of trauma victims will develop Post-Traumatic Stress Disorder (PTSD) (Sigmund, 2003).

In psychiatry, rape, child abuse and a number of other violent occurrences have been understood in terms of Post-Traumatic Stress Disorder and diagnoses of some dissociative disorder also have been switched to that of trauma (Caruth, 1995). Trauma is a 'temporal delay' that leads a person 'beyond the shock of first moment' (Caruth, 1995). Post-Traumatic Stress Disorder is the state of harassment created by 'compulsive repetition of traumatic scenes' of past and by which 'future is blocked' of the victim (LaCapra, 2001). 'PTSD is an anxiety disorder including three symptom clusters: re-experiencing the trauma through nightmares, flashbacks, or intrusive memories; autonomic hyperactivity, such as exaggerated startle response, night sweats, and irritability; and avoidance symptoms, including social isolation, restricted range of emotion, and absence of intimacy in relationships' (Sigmund, 2003). Post-Traumatic Stress Disorder occur in a person due to major social disturbances such as riots, revolutions, economic or political breakdowns and affect a large segment of people.

Women as Victims of Political Violence

In mob attack or other ethnic clashes, women and children are easy victims and often the first ones to be killed. Even when they manage to survive from direct physical violence, they have to bear heavy economic and psychological responsibility. After conflict it is seen that the women headed household increases at large. Sexual violence is used as a means of inflicting terror upon the population at large and it has usually been used as a tool of war. Rape and sexual assault have been used as a tactic by one ethnic group to attack the honour' of another group and to force people to flee their homes and communities in fear. Women usually suffer from emotional loss and trauma after experiencing such violence. Urvashi Butalia is a pioneer in the fields of conflict studies and women studies who explored the effect of communal violence on women. Women's *izzat* is equated with that of the community and a woman is seen as the face of a community in times of heightened communal tension. Outsiders pollute the purity of the community and the religion, first by violating the women and then by hybridizing the next generation (Butalia, 1998). She argues that women during communal strife and violence are 'non-violent' and they always become victim of violence (Butalia, 1993). Quoting from the report brought out by women against fundamentalism, she says, 'Violence is almost instigated by men, out its greatest impact is felt by women. In violent conflict, it is women who are raped, women who are widowed, women whose children and husbands are sacrificed in the name of national integrity and unity'. But these stories remain unheard. Butalia (1993), describing the process of recovering women from history of partition, says, '... women must have been part of the whole process, but we heard so little about them because history, like other disciplines, a patriarchal in nature, and had thus marginalized women'.

Methodology

The texts for study constitute the narratives collected from the field centring Lokopriya Gopinath Bordoloi Regional Institute of Mental Health (LGBRIMH), Tezpur Assam. It is the only government mental health institute in entire North-East India. The British had set up the 'Tezpur Lunatic Asylum' in the year 1876. The concept of mental hospital and psychiatric care, day care centre, and outdoor patient's facilities changed after Independence. In 1919, Tezpur Lunatic Asylum was rechristened as Tezpur Mental Hospital and in 1978 it was renamed as 'Lokopriya Gopinath Bordoloi Mental Health Institute'. Later in 1999, it was designated as 'Lokopriya Gopinath Bordoloi Regional Institute of Mental Health'.

In this study, the population consists of family members of the selected patients with major mental disorders who accompanied their relatives to the outpatient services of the selected hospital during the period of data collection. Mental health professionals providing treatment to the patients have also been included. Purposive sampling technique was used in this research. Direct observation and face-to-face interaction and qualitative analyses of narratives collected from the field constitute the methods of this work. Informants have been purposely selected on the basis of their willingness to cooperate.

The methodology specially draws on feminist theory. My fieldwork has drawn on feminist assumptions regarding women's situation, with special interest in mentally ill women's situation in a patriarchal society.

Addlakha describes that 'disease is the medical formulation of problem in terms of pathology' and in opposition to this biomedical version 'illness is the subjective experience and understanding of the same problem from the perspectives of patients and care-givers' (Addlakha, 2008). This study has used illness and the term mental illness instead of mental disorder or mental disease to describe any form of severe mental health problems (in biomedical term), including schizophrenia.

Case Studies

Mitali is a 40-year-old educated lady suffering from schizophrenia since the age of 20. She lives with her brother and sister-in-law and their two children in Tezpur town. Her brother is a teacher while her sister-in-law is a housewife. They are well off. Mitali's parents died during the period of her illness. Mitali was a good singer and she was very sharp in her studies. She had passed Higher Secondary examination with good marks during her illness. Many a time she came and left the mental health institute on her own.

Mitali's brother recounts the days of the Assam movement (1983) as he was actively involved in the movement. He was also arrested by the police during this movement. Mitali underwent a lot of stress and anxiety during that time and had lost control over her mental ability. He said, 'You know how busy people are these days. I have a job, I offer private tuitions. If you admit her in the mental hospital within one month they (hospital authority) call me for her discharge. The procedure of discharge and admission takes a whole day. How can I waste two days in a month? How will I get leave from school? I have two kids and their future is at stake; we have lost discipline in our house. There is a lot of disturbance in their study. We are doing a lot for Mitali. These days even parents do not take care of such a person in the way we are doing.'

Her sister-in-law said: 'Mitali's behaviour has been strange since her early age. She has been treated in the mental hospital for the last fifteen years. But there is no improvement. The treatment at the mental hospital was good earlier. They used to keep the patient for a long period; these days they release the patients after a very short interval. Who will go again and again to bring her home? Her madness is growing every day and after being discharged from the hospital she thinks we are her enemies. They could not cure her in the hospital even after a prolonged period of treatment and they now blame us that we (family members) do not take good care of her. She is not at home right now. She must be roaming around in the whole town and telling people that we punish her. She will come back home late in the night. We are ashamed of her. We cannot go anywhere leaving her alone in the house; none of our relatives ever invite her. When she was being admitted in the hospital, we planned to go for an outing. She is very dirty, we are ashamed of her... does not take bath and swears at me ... .'

Treating nurse says: 'Mitali was in love with a boy, but she was betrayed. As a result she became mentally ill. Mitali talks a lot about marriage. She blames her brother and sister-in-law for not getting her married. Mitali mentioned in the hospital that she was not being properly treated by her family. She said that her family members used to physically abuse her. She usually gets herself admitted and self-discharges from the hospital. Sometimes she comes to hospital in a very untidy condition with very dirty clothes and long hair.'

Psychiatrist's narrative: 'Mitali's medication is very irregular. She completed her graduation in music and sings well. But she lives in delusion that a boy will marry her and she will spend a better life. But now her delusion has turned to psychosis.' Mitali was admitted in LGBRIMH several times and her experience in the institute was very unpleasant. Mitali, in her narratives, says, '*We were beaten in the hospital for not doing the task properly... people shouted at me as pagali* (mad)... *food is not served for me at home'*. Mitali roams here and there though she belongs from a very well-to-do family and leads a very pitiable life.

One of the neighbours says: 'Mitali had some family clashes. She was a brilliant singer. But now she sings roaming here and there in a very rude voice. Sometimes early in the morning she collects plastics from dustbins'

Biju is a 30-year-old girl from the Bodo community from a village about 40 kms away from Tezpur. She had been suffering from mental illness for a long period but was admitted in LGBRIMH when I was doing my fieldwork there. For the first time she went to the hospital with her father.

Her father said: 'We are a simple family. Biju is my eldest daughter and I have one more daughter and a son. We are economically not so sound. We live on agriculture. Biju's *mama* (maternal uncle) lives in Guwahati. She studied till the tenth class and could not study further. She has been helping her mother in household work and also in the paddy field for a long time. One day Biju left with her *mama* for Guwahati to look for work. She worked as a telephone operator in a PCO in a place called Beltola Tiniali, in Guwahati city. One day when there was mob violence in Beltola, she was there in the PCO. There she had witnessed the fight between some local people and people from outside Guwahati. She felt terribly scared and fell unconscious. She was then brought to her *Mama*'s house, where she lived. After that she became mad. She was sent back to our house. She showed some abnormality. She started to release herself wherever she wanted to and threw things here and there. She kept murmuring to herself and threw water on the floor. Then we brought an *ojha*. Everybody said she was possessed by ghosts; some said that she was possessed by Kali Maa. Everybody advised me that she should be married off for her good health. So, I married her to a boy near my village. They did not know about her disease. But after 15 days of her marriage, the groom's family left her in my house after beating and harassing her. The people of the village now throw stones at her and beat her. One day, her uncle and some other neighbours hit her and tied her to a tree. From that day she became even more mad. Now she is uncontrollable. We had to tie her for many days to control her. I brought a *bej* from a long distance away and spent a lot of money. But she was still not cured. I lost nearly all my money in the process. After that I took her to Guwahati Medical College. There she was admitted for 14 days. But nothing changed. Then one of my friends advised me to bring her to the *pagala phatek* (mental asylum). Then I brought and admitted her here.'

The LGBRIMH diagnosed Biju as schizophrenic with violent nature.

Biju in her medical health practioner's narratives:

The nurse of LGBRIMH who was taking care of Biju said: 'Biju's situation was very bad when she was admitted. She was very weak and dirty; her clothes were stinking. Her hair was dull and rough. We always checked if there were any cut marks or scratches on the patient's body before admission. On finding them, we report it to the doctors. We notice these marks in many patients. We see wounds on their bodies and hands. She was aggressive and it was very tough to control her. Such patients are directly treated by ECT and after that they are treated with drugs. Biju was also treated in that way. But recently she has been diagnosed as pregnant.'

Biju's neighbour said: 'We could not tolerate the girl. She became fully mad. Do not know what happened in Guwahati. Parents should not send her to such place. For us it is not easy to survive in Guwahati. Someone must have exploited her there due to her poor economic condition. She is very violent now. The children of our village are afraid of her. We can't trust a mad person. In our village she is the first dangerously mad person. There is a mad boy in our village but he is not dangerous like her. He just lives in his house silently. Now, it is good for us that she is in *pagala phatek*.'

Analysis

North-East Indian region has witnessed an ongoing political conflict including insurgent movement, ethnic conflicts, and violent counter insurgency movement for almost three to five decades now. In early 1983, the whole of Assam burnt when violent clashes broke out between different communities during the Assam Agitation (Mazumdar, 1980). People were massacred, displaced; many were rendered homeless. This is the major political movement against illegal migrants from neighbouring Bangladesh. Two groups of agitators – the All Assam Students' Union and the All Assam Gana Sangram Parisad were actively involved in the movement. Everyone felt the impact of the air of uncertainty and insecurity that was prevalent then. Violent mobs attacked each other's villages. Women and children were the worst victims. They set fire to the villages (Weiner, 1983). Many people lost their lives. Most of the people who had a first-hand experience of violent activities were afraid. Moreover, there was a lot of rumour and gossip about the thirst for vengeance of other communities. This added to a general atmosphere of panic and deep mistrust among people (Mazumdar, 1980). Mitali could see the brutal picture of the movement with her own eyes. Mitali underwent a trauma because of the political movement; the fight, the bloodshed whatever she faced in her life during that period. She, under that severe stress, suffered from a Post-Traumatic Stress Disorder. She was neglected and discriminated in the family as well as by the neighbours due to her mental illness. In 19th century women's experiences were very pathetic inside the asylum in the West. Elaine Showalter describes that women living in mixed asylum (where both male and female patients were kept) had to suffer from discrimination as they were served less food than man. Though female patients were kept under strict surveillance, 'careful watching' and confinement, they were raped and seduced by male keepers and male patients (Showalter, 1980: 166). Mitali's narratives reflected that LGBRIMH is also not different from the Victorian asylums even after advent of 'modern' medical practices. Providing a separate cell in LGBRIMH with more special care in strict confinement for women in the name of security shows the tendency of hospital plans and policies to segregate women patients from rest of the patients and represent them as the more vulgar, dangerous group from whom society must be protected.

Mitali's brother and sister-in-law's narratives clearly reflected the LGBRIMH has become an easy alternate place for home, leaving them free to pursue their own interests. LGBRIMH is used by family to 'rescue' themselves from the burden of the patient as she is an unwanted material in the family. On the other hand, LGBRIMH became a secure place for the patients providing basic amenities such as food and shelter. On 24 November 2007, at mid-day, a huge procession of around a thousand *Adivasis* including males and females with bows and arrows in their hands marched towards Dispur through Beltola, Guwahati. It was a weekly market day and Beltola was overcrowded as usual. Suddenly there was violence. The demonstrators started damaging vehicles parked on the roadside, shops and even private properties. Pedestrians were also attacked by them. After a few hours they were counter-attacked in turn by the local youths. The place turned into a battlefield with bloodshed, molestation; many were wounded and killed. Biju was present there during the event and she witnessed the incident. She felt the threat of violence and underwent a trauma. Any type of violence in society, riot, war or movement faced by a person may traumatize and she may suffer from Post-Traumatic Stress Disorder and severe disability. Biju faced the violence in Beltola and was traumatized and thus became mentally disabled.

The stereotypical notions of mental illness affect not only the caste Hindus of Assam but also the tribes. Biju, including her neighbours, belong to the Bodo tribe of Assam. This is a very prominent plain tribe of Assam which has made great contribution to the social and cultural construction of greater Assamese society. The stereotype of mentally ill as bizarre, strange and dangerous has made Biju's life more pathetic. Another notion of mental illness is that a mentally ill can be cured after their marriage. Biju was married off but marriage made her life even more difficult and she was sent back home. Other stereotypical notion on mental illness is that by beating or punishing a mentally ill he/she can be controlled or cured. Biju was brutally beaten up by the neighbours and family members in order to control her abnormality. Not only Biju, most of the mentally ill are beaten in our society. Like castes, tribes of Assam are also seen involved in socio-religious practices such as magical and occult practices. Biju was treated by shamans, and other magical treatments that delayed her treatment in the hospital. In my interview psychiatrists argued that the illness became severe as most of the patients were usually brought for treatment after a long gap. First they were treated by magical men, shamans, and faith healers and when they failed to deliver, they were brought to the hospital.

Stigma is a serious obstruction for the well-being of the person who faces such an experience. Goffman illustrated that the ancient Greeks came up with the term stigma to refer to bodily signs designed to expose something unusual and bad about the moral status of the signifier (Goffman, 1963). Stigma is a form of deviance that leads others to judge an individual as ineligible to participate in social interaction (Goffman, 1963). This is because of the perception of lack of proficiency to interact with society which is influenced by the person's dangerousness and unpredictability. Stigma is a 'collection of negative attitudes, beliefs, thoughts, and behaviours that influence the individual, or the general public, to fear, reject, avoid, be prejudiced and discriminate people' (Gary, 2005).

Stigma is a social construct and it seriously impacts patients and families alike. Stigmatized persons are regarded as people who have lost social value and are 'spoiled' forever. It could be described as a construct which changes depending on time and society. Stigma is a serious problem and a barrier for achieving life-goals for those with mental illness or sexually transmitted disease.

Stigma is a phenomenon associated with many chronic health conditions, including leprosy, HIV/AIDS/STD, mental illness, epilepsy, disability and tuberculosis. As history has unfolded, mental illness has become one of the most stigmatized diseases; the person suffering from mental illness is regarded as threatening and dangerous as well as 'most deviant'. Biju and Mitali become dirt of the society with the deep root of stigma towards mental illness and that has made their lives miserable.

Conclusion

Women living under the conflict situations have suffered acute mental health problems. The psychological trauma associated with sexual violation and with the loss or disappearance of family members lasts long after peace returns. Women have had to cope with these situations without any support from either the state or the society. In situations where armed conflict persists there are increased patriarchal controls on women, so women groups face problem to work in these areas. Women are unable to lead a healthy life due to lack of rehabilitation policies and psychological counselling.

The mentally ill usually lose all their rights as human being. All the constitutional rights of the citizens of a democratic country are unavailable for the mentally ill. They lose the right of life and liberty, right of property, marriage, lawsuit, and political participation. They are not provided insurance facilities in India. Ironically those who are in the greatest need of support and love of their family are forced to lead a life of isolation and stigma.

References

Butalia, Urvashi (1993). 'Community, State and Gender: On Women's Agency during Partition', *Economic and Political Weekly*, 28(17): 12–24, Web 25 August 2014, http://www.jestore.org/stable/4399641.

—— (1998). *The Other Side of Silence: Voices from the Partition of India*, New Delhi: Viking.

Caruth, Cathy (ed.) (1995). *Trauma Explorations in Memory*, Baltimore and London: The John Hopkins University Press.

Gary, F.A. (2005). Stigma: Barrier to Mental Health Care among Ethnic Minorities. *Mental Health*, Vol. 26(10), pp. 979–99.

LaCapra, Dominick (2001). *Writing History, Writing Trauma*, Baltimore: The John Hopkins University Press.

Mazumdar, Prasanta (1980). 'Assam Movement', *Economic and Political Weekly*, 15(30): 1246, Web 8 November 2012, http://www.jstor.org/stable/4368884.

Showalter, Elaine (1980). 'Victorian Women and Insanity', *Victorian Studies*, 23(2): 157–81, Web 31 March 2012, http://www.jstor.org/stable/3827084.

Sigmund, A. Judith (2003). 'Spirituality and Trauma: The Role of Clergy in the Treatment of Posttraumatic Stress Disorder', *Journal of Religion and Health*, 42(3): 221–29, Web 29 October 2012, http://www.jstor.org/stable/27511689.

Subbian, Rajaram et al. (2010). 'War Impact on Women and Post-War Psycho Social Interventions', in K. Sekhar, Prakashi Rajaram, Rameela Sekhar and Mubarak Ali (eds), *Women and Mental Health*, Bangalore: NIMHANS.

Weiner, Myron (1983). 'The Political Demography of Assam's Anti-Immigrant Movement', *Population and Development Review*, 9(2): 279–92, Web 8 November 2012, http://www.jstor.org/stable/1973053.

16

Parenting Cross-Cultural and Mixed Race Children

A Perspective

ANTOINETTE ZLOTY

Abstract

The purpose of this paper is to demonstrate through personal experience and parental views, as to why parents of cross-cultural mixed race children need to provide opportunities for cultural and racial experiences through parental caring and support, readings, educational programmes, travel and open unbiased discussion. These are examples which may assist in addressing the cultural and racial needs of children. This subject may be of interest to parents, future parents, relatives, students, policy consultants, social workers, nurses, educators, trainers, spiritual care workers, and recreation workers, to name few. These professionals, paraprofessionals or lay people will see the value of being more aware of their own attitudes and behaviours within their own families, workplace and social networks. Improved awareness of their communication with others can be of benefit. Compassion, respect, and responsiveness to others' needs can be fostered and practiced, regardless of gender, age, culture, race, religion, disability, or sexual orientation.

Keywords

Cross-Cultural, Mixed Race, Parenting, Microaggression, Communication.

Introduction

This paper applies to parenting cross-cultural mixed children worldwide because it is a reality for many families. The author's personal approach to parenting her cross-cultural mixed race children which may or may not be similar to other parents also provided a perspective for the paper. The parenting approach presented includes providing opportunities to assist children in developing into responsible adults with positive cultural and gender identities. Some clarification of terms and statistical information on multiracial families in Canada and the United States is included as changes are occurring where more people are entering multiracial, multicultural families. There is an explanation of how concepts such as microaggression can negatively affect communication within parent to child interactions, across genders, cultures and religions. The concept of microaggressive communication was defined and discussed as they can affect children's health and perpetuate negative interactions into future generations.

Communication whether verbal or non-verbal, is a powerful way to affect people. Sexism and racial discrimination, although commonly considered to occur within work and other environments can also occur within the family. Such behaviours need to be monitored and ceased for the betterment of children. Appropriate communication within families is critical to development of children with healthy cultural identities. Exposure to inappropriate, insensitive communication is discussed as a barrier to the development of children into responsible adults, needed for non-sexist and non-racist communities.

Cross-cultural Children

Ruth Van Reken and Paulette M. Bethel (2012) have described children cross culturally indicating that a Cross-Cultural Kid (CCK) is a person who has lived in – or meaningfully interacted with – two or more cultural environments for a significant period of time during developmental years. She adds that this group (CCKs) includes first, traditional cross-cultural children or children who move into another culture with parents due to a parent's career choice. Second, bi/multicultural and/or bi/multi-racial children who are children born to parents from at least two cultures or races. Third, there are children of immigrants or children whose parents have made a permanent move to a new country where they were not originally citizens. It is important to note that in today's ever changing world, people move not only because of career choice but other reasons such as interest in experiencing other countries and cultures. Multiracial is defined as made up of or relating to people of many races. In the United States, the 2000 census was the first in the history of the country to offer respondents the option of identifying themselves as belonging to more than one race. This multiracial option was considered a necessary adaptation to the demographic and cultural changes that the United States has been experiencing (Wikipedia, 2014). Our personal, work, recreational, religious, career and other experiences affect our parenting. Due to global travel, many people have had personal or other experiences with multiracial, cross-cultural families. People may have doubts about marriages or other situations which led to multiracial families. Some support may have been rendered to such unions, despite apprehensions by relatives and friends. In some cases, parent, or other relatives have deserted their own family members out of feelings of shame, loss, and emotions. Some of these feelings are rooted in racism, sexism and other learned behaviours. When relationships end for whatever reasons, the losses may be immeasurable and unrecoverable. Therefore, adults' attitudes and behaviours have far reaching consequences for children as they may never get to know their own relatives.

Quoting her own case, the author states that 'I was just a teenager when I immigrated to Canada in 1968. I am of African, European, and Caribbean ancestry. I am a black woman, born in Barbados, to Barbadian parents. My husband is white. He was born in Canada to Canadian born parents of Ukrainian and Polish heritage. We married in 1988. I am also the mother of a daughter and a son who are both mixed race, cross-cultural young adults attending university. In any society, our experiences influence our parenting and care of others whether or not they are children. We are expected to care for and nurture our children as they represent the future'.

In a multicultural society such as in Canada, 'I have had experiences with different races, cultures and religions. My personal friends, associates and colleagues have been Canadian, Aboriginal/First Nations, Chinese, Finish, Italian, Polish, African, European, Ukrainian, Barbadian, Jamaican, American, Welsh and Indian, to name a few, plus a number of people who practice different religions. My education in Canada commenced in grade eight, in rural Manitoba and includes a bachelor's and a master's degree in social work, from the University of Manitoba, Canada. I have been fortunate to live in rural, northern and urban areas of Manitoba where I acquired experience in health and social serve provision, policy and programme analysis within government and Non-Government Organizations. In addition I have had opportunities to acquire knowledge through participation and/or development of workshops, task forces, conferences, volunteer/board positions, etc'.

The collective experiences will have an affect on the approach to parenting. As a parent, the somewhat unique approaches become apparent. The elders do not always agree on the parenting methods and may disapprove of the choice of spouses since they were parented in a different time when diversity and openness to others, who look, speak, dress etc. differently, and may have been frowned upon. The world is changing. There is a need for people to become more inclusive and less divisive.

Parenting together with a person of a different race or even the same race means that understanding, cooperation, communication and collaboration are required as these individuals have had no time to rehearse being a parent. Almost after two-and-a-half decades, the approach has included first, a desire to educate the kids at home, in good schools, through community events and opportunities like summer camps, cultural festivals and other such events.

Second, the need to keep them well fed, clothed and sheltered. Even though the children are adults, they rely for these basics as they pursue higher education. Supportive parenting includes helping the children to achieve an education. Education is one of the core values for a family. While the children are being educated, that time can become extended beyond their childhood years, until they can assume full responsibility for their own food, clothing and shelter. Should unpreventable circumstances prevent them from acquiring or keeping the skills learned, e.g. loss of ability, the children may need your assistance and support of parents temporarily or indefinitely. The attitudes and behaviours toward the children are determined through cultural background and the additional experiences and education one acquire. As the children live responsibly into adulthood, respecting others and themselves, continual support through provision of food, clothing and shelter is not unreasonable until they can undertake total responsibility for themselves.

Third, there is a desire to keep the children safe. There are common worries which the parents have about their children regardless of how old they are. It does not matter which culture they belong to. Safety is, thus, a major consideration for most parents. The resources parents have, however, to keep their children safe, vary widely from family to family, community to community, country to country. In society, not all people are treated equitably nor have the resources necessary for their children. Some people are therefore not able to provide safe interactions and safe homes for their children. Sometimes parents of cross-cultural mixed race children try to shelter their children from harsh words from others. However, harsh words or behaviours cannot always be prevented even if parents have financial and other resources. This is why it is never too early to make sure they have inner strength to deal with a sometimes cruel world.

In addition to safety there is a need to love them and have them feel loved. No one can take this away from a parent unless there is rejection by the child himself/herself. Love is not determined by material possessions but by true emotions. Again, some people will make the child feel different or unloved. Having open discussions with the children about race is important and awareness that even if they were not mixed race, not everyone will love them.

Moreover, there is a wish to instill pride in the children regardless of their gender or place of birth. It is important not to treat the children differently because they are a male or a female. Expectations to help around the house should extend to both sexes. Both need to learn skills which were traditionally assigned to one or the other sex. In a changing world, each needs to learn to function and demonstrate independent living skills without dependency on the other sex. As mixed race cross-cultural kids, an effort is needed to familiarize them with their multicultural heritage and multiracial identities. This can be challenging as some relatives may be racist or present barriers to knowing and accepting other people and cultures. It is also possible that, some relatives will reject the children for reasons which they claim to be non-racist but are still unconscionable. Despite any internal conflict within the family, the children should be helped to become the best they can be. They can be encouraged to take pride in who they are despite challenges within or outside the family. This is possible with a lot of personal support and encouragement to help them be themselves. There is a need to keep the communication channels open in order to be kept informed and aware of the challenges and the opportunities coming their way. Beyond the family, it is important as parents to be available to speak frankly about topics of interest including worldwide issues.

Finally, there is a desire to have the children like who they are. Although parents have no guarantees that their children will like themselves, efforts should be made to show them that they are liked and make the right choices which will make them feel positive about who they are. Friends and partners, the media and other sources of messages will impact the children. There is only so much that parents can do as parents. The parenting method may have been more intense because the children are mixed race and cross-cultural. It is fair to say that the parenting approach would have been the same in some respects had our kids not been mixed race and cross-cultural. Interracial marriages are on the rise in Canada; therefore, this may mean that young people in the country do not perceive parenting these children as problematic.

According to Cheryl Chan (2013), interracial marriages still stir prejudice among many Canadians. Information from an interview with a mixed race couple and comments from the groom's father, an immigrant from India, are featured in her article. There is reference made to Statistics Canada which indicates that mixed race unions grew a dramatic 33 per cent between 2001 and 2006, more than five times the growth of all couples, due, in part, to the growing number of visible minorities in Canada. In Metro Vancouver, 8.5 per cent of couples are in mixed unions, more than double the national figure of 3.9 per cent. In the article, University of British Columbia sociologist, Wendy Roth, states that the growing number of mixed-race unions indicates a steady erosion of social and racial barriers between different groups.

People are forming unions across genders, within genders, across cultures and within cultures, creating non-traditional partnerships. Children are then born or adopted into these unions. A study was released by Statistics Canada (2011 a, b) on mixed unions in Canada which indicates that:

> As Canada's population is becoming increasingly diverse; more people are forming a conjugal union with someone from a different ethno-cultural background. Data from the 2011 National Household Survey evidences that about 3,60,045 couples were in mixed unions, that is, relationships where one spouse or partner is a member of a visible minority while the other is not, or where the spouses or partners are from different visible minority groups. The proportion of couples in mixed unions increased over a 20-year period, from 2.6 per cent of all couples in 1991 to 3.1 per cent in 2001 and 4.6 per cent a decade later in 2011. Most mixed unions involved partners who were born in different countries, with one spouse or partner born in Canada and the other born outside Canada (49.2%). About one in five (19.4%) were mixed unions where both were foreign-born, but from different countries. (Statistics Canada, 2011 a, b)

Statistics Canada added that compared to persons in couples who were not in mixed unions, persons in mixed unions were younger, did better socio-economically and were more likely to live in large CMAs (census metropolitan areas). For the visible minority population, there were more spouses or partners in mixed unions who were Canadian-born compared to those who were foreign-born, and the proportion increased with generation status. There were proportionally more couples in common-law relationships in mixed unions than couples who were legally married, and a higher proportion of same-sex couples were in mixed unions than couples who were in opposite-sex couples.

More couples with at least one child present in the home were mixed compared to couples who did not have children, reflecting the fact that mixed union couples were generally younger and more likely to be at their life cycle stage of having young children. In addition to the number of children whose parents were in mixed unions, the concept of mixed families, like those comprising of a child belonging to a visible minority but not the parents, further broadens the implications of ethno-cultural identity.

The impact of mixed unions could be far-reaching in changing the dynamic and nature of Canada's ethno-cultural diversity in future generations. These consequences may impact the language transfer that takes place within mixed union households, as well as the experiences of children in mixed families and the way in which children of mixed unions report their ethnocultural origins and identify with visible minority groups (Statistics Canada, 2011 a, b).

A mixed race cross-cultural family, makes time to discover the roots through visits to maternal place of birth with plans to also explore paternal heritage in the future. Other mixed race families include the president of the United States, Barack Obama and celebrities. Some people are electing through adoption, to have mixed race families while others have had their children through giving birth to mixed race children. Regardless of how famous or wealthy a family is, parents, guardians and care-givers need to demonstrate a number of behaviours which are conducive to positive self-esteem in their children which will build sound cultural identities.

Whether or not adults are themselves in one of the unions noted above by Statistics Canada, all adults need to be more culturally sensitive and be more aware of their own behaviours and attitudes and how they affect children. They need to be role models for the younger generation and develop more inclusiveness and tolerance of others who are different from themselves whether there is a difference of ability, race or sexual orientation. People need to deal with multicultural, multiracial and other characteristics which define them in ways which foster compassion for others.

The Declaration of Human Rights of the Child, 1959 (2014) is a document familiar to all.

The Declaration of the Rights of the Child lays down ten principles:

1. The right to equality, without distinction on account of race, religion or national origin,
2. The right to special protection for the child's physical, mental and social development,
3. The right to a name and a nationality,
4. The right to adequate nutrition, housing and medical services,
5. The right to special education and treatment when a child is physically or mentally handicapped,

6. The right to understanding and love by parents and society,
7. The right to recreational activities and free education,
8. The right to be among the first to receive relief in all circumstances,
9. The right to protection against all forms of neglect, cruelty and exploitation, and
10. The right to be brought up in a spirit of understanding, tolerance, friendship among peoples, and universal brotherhood.

In addition to following the principles, children need exposure to positive cultural and racial experiences through parental caring and support demonstrated by reading to them, accessing educational programmes, opportunities to travel and open discussions. Modelling good attitudes and behaviours, parents may communicate compassion, respect, and responsiveness to others, regardless of their gender, age, culture, race, religion, disability, and sexual orientation.

In Ontario, a Canadian province, Steven and Wendy Walton established 'The Positive Parenting Centre' to make parenting information available to the public. They indicate that communication is the first step in developing a positive family culture. The second is perpetually practicing strategies to improve it (The positive Parenting Centre, 2014; Walton, 2013).

However, there are racial and gender barriers which affect communication. Barriers include microaggressions. Microaggression theory is a social theory that describes social exchanges in which a person says or does something, often accidentally, and without intended malice, that belittles and alienates a member of a marginalized group.

In 1970, Chester M. Pierce, Psychiatrist and Harvard University Professor, coined the word microaggression to describe insults and dismissals. He said he had regularly witnessed non-Black Americans inflict on Black people. Then in 1973, Mary Rowe, an economist at Massachusetts Institute of Technology, extended the term to include similar aggressions directed at women. Eventually, the term came to encompass the casual degradation of any socially marginalized group, such as poor people, disabled people and sexual minorities (Wikipedia, 2014).

Parents need to be cognizant of these barriers and express concern regarding their use. Sue et al. (2007) indicated that microaggressions seem to appear in four forms:

1. *Microassault*: an explicit racial derogation; verbal/nonverbal; eg: name-calling, avoidant behaviour, purposeful discriminatory actions.
2. *Microinsult*: communications that convey rudeness and insensitivity and demean a person's racial heritage or identity; subtle snubs; unknown to the perpetrator; hidden insulting message to the recipient of colour.
3. *Microinvalidation*: communications that exclude, negate, or nullify the psychological thoughts, feelings, or experiential reality of a person belonging to a particular group.

Sexism or gender discrimination is prejudice or discrimination based on a person's sex or gender. Sexist attitudes may stem from traditional stereotypes of gender roles and may include the belief that a person of one sex is intrinsically superior to a person of the other. Several studies have found that women earn a smaller average wage than men. Many economists and feminist scholars have argued that this is the result of systemic gender-based discrimination in the workplace. Extreme sexism may foster sexual harassment and other forms of sexual violence.

Communications which support racism, sexism and gender discrimination need to be addressed in the family, workforce, social networks, etc. Discriminatory hiring practices, unequal compensation or treatment between the sexes will continue to be perpetuated if the behaviours which support such practices continue in the family.

Questions like – Are these future parents want for the children and children to come in the future? Do they not want to live in peace and harmony with others regardless of differences in race, gender, ability, ethnicity and religion?

Parents must take action and be aware of how their own verbal and non-verbal communication affects on their children and others. Parents need to correct these behaviours. These behaviours when modelled for children carry over into their later relationships and workplaces and lead to undesirable outcomes for all genders.

Some good parenting and care-giving practices include but are not limited to not laughing at racist or sexist jokes. Children should not be teased or made to feel strange or different because they have a dominant trait from one or more racial group. Children should be treated the same regardless of their sex, ability or gender to prevent sexism, gender discrimination and abuse. Children need to be aware of their ancestors even if they were from a different culture or race. Supporting policies which foster inclusion of all people in education and research so that their voices are heard assumes significance.

The author has had the opportunity to speak with people regarding their views on the topic of raising cross-cultural mixed race children. Some comments from parents of mixed race cross-cultural children were noted as well as comments from others who are not parents. A working professional woman, who is not a member of a visible minority, suggested that parents should instill self-confidence in their children as some people are racist and will be unkind to them. She added that females need to be aware that privileges are still extended to males. Therefore, women need to speak up when they are passed over for promotions or other opportunities in favour of men. Another person, a retired married man, indicated that he never thought about his kids as being mixed race and cross-cultural. He just thought of them as his kids. A working professional married male stated that one should encourage one's kids to be what they want to be, not what the parents want them to be. Lastly, an adult single male who is a university student commented that parents should encourage their kids to be the best that they can be.

In conclusion, whether or not parents are in mixed race, cross-cultural families, the need to be aware of what is being said and done within the families, work places, schools, community places/centres, etc. and how these behaviours and attitudes are affecting others are important. Proper communication, encouraging compassion, respect, and responsiveness to others' needs, regardless of their age, gender, culture, race, religion, disability, or sexual orientation is the need of the hour.

References

Chan, Cheryl (2013). 'Interracial Marriages Still Stir Prejudice among Many Canadians', *The Province*, canada.com, 9 January 2014, Web 29 March 2014. http://www.theprovince.com/life/Interracial+marriages+still+stir+prejudice+among +many+canadians/9053783/story.html.

'Declaration of Human Rights of the Child, 1959'. Web 29 March 2014. http://www.humanium.org/en/childrens-rights-history/references-on-childrights/declaration-rights-child/.

'Microaggression Theory'. Wikipedia 21 November 2014, Web 29 March 2014. http://en.wikipedia.org/wiki/microaggression_theory.

'Multiracial'. Wikipedia 21 November 2014, Web 25 November 2014. http://en.wikipedia.org/wiki/multiracial.

'Sexism'. Wikipedia 26 November 2014, Web 17 January 2014. http://en.wikipedia.org/wiki/sexism.

Statistics Canada (2011a). *A Portrait of Couples in Mixed Unions* by Anne Milan, Hélène Maheux and Tina Chui, Statistics Canada Catalogue No. 11-008-x2010001. http://www.statcan.gc.ca/pub/11-008-x/2010001/article/11143eng.htm#a12.

—— (2011b). *Mixed Unions in Canada* in National Household Survey in Brief Series, Statistics Canada Catalogue No. 99-010-x2011003. http://www.statcan.gc.ca/daily-quotidien/140617/dq140617b-eng.htm.

Sue, Derald Wing et al. (2007). 'Racial Microaggressions in Everyday Life: Implications for Clinical Practice', *American Psychologist*, 62(4): 271–86. Wikipedia 26 November 2014, Web 17 January 2014. http://en.wikipedia.org /wiki/microaggression_theory.

Van Reken, Ruth and Paulette M. Bethel (2012). 'What are Cross Cultural Kids? Third Culture Kids: Prototypes for Understanding Other Cross-Cultural Kids', *Cross Cultural Kids Blog*, Word Press, Web 6 December 2013. http://blog.crossculturalkid.org/what-are-cross-cultural-kids/.

Walton, Stephen (2013). 'The Importance of Communication in Building a Positive Family Culture', in Stephen Walton (ed.), *The Positive Parenting Centre*, Positive Parenting Centre. Web 8 February 2014. http://www.the-positive-parenting-centre.com.

17

Female Body in Every Day Life

A Perspective on the Respect and Control for Women in Society

MADHABI MAITY

Abstract

Soil and female body are synonymous in Indian culture, since both are productive. History proves that women, the primary producer of crops, dug the soil and sowed the seed by making a sowing shaft, which could be compared to a phallus. Women knew the technology of birth by their own body mechanism. Child birth was and still is totally a women centric affair, visually proven and directly engaged whereas the role of men in this process is hypothetic. Old Indian sculpture 'Salabhanjika' shows intertwining figure of woman and tree. An inscribed seal of Mahenjodaro had shown a woman who gave birth to a tree. Sowing seed, particularly pumpkin seed by the pregnant women is a common ritual in some parts of West Bengal. Women themselves are like plants. They are as beautiful and soft as flowers or creepers. Their finger, foot, breast, eye, nose, hand, thigh, all are compared with different types of flower, bud, leaf, fruit, stem of the tree or plant. Earth, plant and woman, all are fertile, hence they personify a mother. Thus, the female body gained respect out of both fear and amazement. Use of conch-shell, cowrie-shell, betel-nut, betel-leaf, vermilion, turmeric, lac-dye, durba grass completes a hindu ritual. The shape of these elements are similar to that of vagina. The red colour of vermilion and lac-dye recollect the memory of menstruation. This paper examines the cause of cultural taboo on women during menstruation and child birth. Is it a technique to curb the power of women as a producer of humankind in this patriarchal society? This paper examines how the female body and body parts are represented and respected in the everyday life, and how it is related with the Mother Earth. The paper also delves on how the patriarchal society recognizes it and controls it.

Keywords

Ploughshare, Sowing Seed, Pregnancy, Tree, Plant, Soil, Body, Birth, Menstruation.

Introduction

Historically it is proved that the first plough-man was not a man, but a woman or a group of women. Capable of being a productive body they knew the technology of birth from their own body experiences. So they made a ploughshare like phallus and began to plough the soil. The primitive hunter and food-gather nomads began to settle down with the knowledge of farming and the teachers were the women. Our dear Earth became habitable and growing more beautiful because of women. The word 'linga' of Sanskrit and 'langal' of Bengali were derived from the same word which means phallus. Phallus like plough is very common in the different parts of the World (Bhandari, 2009).

Prehistoric Indian sculpture 'salabhanjika' is an intertwining body of a woman and a tree. One seal of Ma-hen-jo-da-ro is inscribed with the figure of pregnant woman, giving birth to a tree (Sharma, 1999). Women in their pregnancy stage are considered most worthy to sow the seed of a plant generally. It is a regular custom in different parts of the world. In the district of Midnapore of West Bengal, it was a common practice in some villages at least twenty years ago that the seed of pumpkin or bottle-gourd should be sown by the pregnant women. On the contrary, Arundhati Roy wrote that there is a taboo in Dandakaranya of Madhya Pradesh whereby women are restricted from sowing any kind of seed on the soil of tribal land.

Some communities believe that the tree does not bloom until a virgin hugs it (Choudhury, 2002). The paddy plant in its flowering state is treated like pregnant woman in different areas of West Bengal. 'Sadh' is a very common ritual in Bengal where a pregnant lady is blessed in an occasion by the other elderly ladies giving her desired articles of food. Farmers do the same to their pregnant paddy plants on the last day of the autumnal month *Ashwin* with some other insecticidal plants specially in the district of Midnapore and Birbhum. In the district of Midnapore, particularly in the border area Odisha, a little girl is frequently called as bottle gourd. In the same area, women in their menstrual cycle, are often called to be in blossom. The placenta is also considered as flower in Bengali language.

In literature as well as in our everyday life the girls are as beautiful and soft as flower. Families name them Mallika, Maloti, Tagar, Juth, Bakul, Parul, hena, Jaba (varieties of jasmine, hibiscus, creeper) even garland, bouquet etc. The eye, nose, lip, breast, finger, feet, thigh even whole body of the woman are compared with the different types of flower, vegetables or plants. Wide and beautiful eyes are shaped like one kind of kitchen vegetable (patol), nose is so sharp like the flower of sesame, lip is as beautifully red as the bimba fruit. The face is a lotus itself. Breasts are like pomegranate, young woman's thigh is like a banana plant. The slim body of a woman is also compared with the cane plant. The name of the kitchen vegetable lady's finger is obviously related with the shape of lady's finger. The feet are also be treated as lotus.

In ancient Assyrian civilization, tree-trunk was worshipped as a symbol of phallus. In Harappan civilization, the symbols of vagina and penis both are adored (Sharma, 2009). The incarnations traced from different parts of India proved that the goddess 'Yoni' (vagina) was worshipped in Maharashtra, Uttar Pradesh and Andhra Pradesh in India in BC and as well as in AD. In Bengal, the worship of Durga idol, includes a circular painting drawn at the back of the idol containing 13 lotus with a dot in the middle. Lotus and dot symbolizes the vagina and penis respectively (Bhandari, 2009). In the folk culture of Bengal many trees are worshipped as the god of fertilization, e.g. Banyan, Arjun, Ashoka etc.

Women are as productive as soil. As the Mother Earth gives birth to the trees and plants by splitting her body, women did the same. It is a direct productive activity which men lack. Primitive people wandered for their productive power. The existence of the tribe fully depends on the increasing number of the groups. Pre-historic economy fully depended on the mother who gave birth to the members of their group, which is the main strength of the tribe. The structure of the body of a woman proves that they can give birth; the breasts, vagina, menstruation cycle, the expanded abdomen at the time of pregnancy and at last child birth. Men knew about their contribution to this process at least at the age of rearing the livestock. But there was no direct proof that men can give birth. Like germination of plant from the soil, a female body gives birth to her baby by splitting her own body which men cannot. It is totally a women centric affair, visually proven and directly engaged whereas the role of men in this process is hypothetic. Until a woman recognizes her partner as her child's father he is nothing. Even there was a time when the woman herself did not know who is the actual father of her child before the introduction of marriage system. So the Mother Earth and the woman as mother both are very important for the continuity of life cycle. The Earth is habitable and beautiful for this kind of procreation. Thus, they enjoyed the power and obviously gained superiority.

The image of Mother God in pre-historian age with wide vagina, more developed breasts and expanded thighs was significantly the body of a child producer. The cave paintings of Kathotia, Bhimbetka and Kharvai expressed the women's existence assimilated with their sexuality. The psychological bonding of mother and child was the first expression of religion (Chakravarty, 2006).

Act of child birth was itself a mysterious, miraculous and marvellous incidence at least to rest of the people of the primitive society. They were amazed and also got scared. A big question mark they faced was – she, who gives birth can take back life again? The worshipping of Mother God was started at a larger scale from this fear, which was admitted by researchers. Primitive people could not understand the mystery of life and nature. The tree, stone, mother all are mysterious, yet so adorable.

The very different type of female body from their male counterpart, still carrying the legacy of adoration, in our everyday life has various signs of representation. Every auspicious ceremony of Bengal, including India, be it religious or otherwise the representation of female body or the part of their body is essential. The conch-shell, cowrie-shell, betel-leaf, betel-nut, betel-nut cracker, vessel for preparing collyrium all are vagina in structure and are essentially used in every marriage ceremony or *puja* (offering) in Bengal. Lac-die (alta) especially used by the Hindu women to paint their feet, vermillion on the parting of hair on the head of Hindu married women, red sarees or red bordered sarees, red bangles, even *mehandi*, all are auspicious and essentially used in the marriage ceremonies because of shear similarity in colour with menstruation. The colour of blood is essentially significant of birth. No birth occurs without bleeding. Blood is the symbol of Elan vital. Married women wear different types of red symbols from their head to toe. It expresses her capability of power to produce. Sexuality is controlled in case of widows by not allowing her to bear any type of red symbol. Newly married wife sets her firststep in her in-law's house upon a plate full of milk and lac-dye. Her every red footstep assures the family that she can bear a child. The scientists of old and middle age like Aristotle believed that accumulated blood of menstruation turned to be the foetus. The human bones which were traced from the graveyards of stone age were coated with red colour – the colour of life (Chattopadhyay, 1998) and even the sign of any kind of taboo is always red, not blue or green.

Hindu marriage ceremony does not occur without besmearing of the bride and bridegroom with the paste of turmeric in bath on the eve of their wedding. In the villages of Midnapore district, a ritual where turmeric painted bettle-nut were used as an invitation, exists even now. When the modern invitation cards replace them it is also stained with turmeric paste in the corner. The dresses of bride and bridegroom are also stained by the turmeric paste. They wear red and yellow cord in their wrist. The bride's saree is essentially red in Bengal. We know spring is the mating season. The Goddess Saraswati is worshipped in this season as Basanta Panchami, the dress code of this ceremony is yellow and red. All signifies the act of procreation.

Placing of a consecrated pitcher or pot full of holy water, usually round in shape and have a narrow neck, made by clay or brass or copper in Indian Hindu family is considered sacred and essential in every auspicious ceremony. It looks like a women in her period of gestation. A small banana tree is also placed at the back of the pitcher dressed like a married woman with long veil. It proves that woman's womb is to be considered as the most sacred thing in life. It provides the members to the society and continuing the life cycle gives inheritors to the family. Thus, it is respected in every auspicious occasion. What is called 'gouna' in the other parts of India, Bengal celebrates it as 'Dwiragaman', which is the coming back of a newly wed bride second time to her in-laws house. Actually it is the celebration of procreation. The virgin female body first menstruates and is then ready to be fertile.

It is believed that in the different parts of India, the mother earth also menstruates. The occasion 'Ambubachi' in Bengal and Assam, 'Rajasankrati' of Odisha are observed. In Bengal three consecutive days usually of the month of 'Ashara', on the eve of the rainy season, Hindu widows observe fast. The farmers obey the taboo of not plouging the paddy field for those very days. After 'Ambubachi', they started plouging and sowing the seed. In the state of Assam, it is observed by the women in their state of menstrual cycle (Choudhury, 2002). In Odisha the last two days of the month of 'Jaishtha' and the first day of 'Ashara', the virgin girls do not do any work and take bath with turmeric water. The cultivator society shows respect to the women's fertility power. Bengal restricts their widows by keeping fast in those days to control their sexuality as well as their fertilization power.

The patriarchal society with Brahmanical value system outcastes the women in menstrual cycle by levelling them 'unclean' and untouchable. It is a long practiced taboo that women in menstrual cycle cannot participate in any auspicious work, like *puja* (offerings) or *brata* (keeping fast). In some village she is not allowed to touch even rice pot especially made by clay. She is highly restricted to enter in temples or any kind of offering place, even in kitchen. Times before the women were confined in a darkroom of the house during this period. Arundhati Roy wrote that the tribal women of Dandakaranya in Madhya Pradesh have to live alone in a small mud house in their menstrual state.

Uncleanliness is a state of mind. It sabotages the women's level of confidence. It is a way of control of the patriarchal and Brahmonical value system. They rule the people of lower rung of the society and marginalize them by labelling as untouchable. When a woman menstruates, she should get the highest honour in family and society. It is the most sacred physical state of woman because her body becomes ready to be fertile. On the contrary, they are treated as untouchable. It is a technique to curb the power of women as a producer of human kind in the patriarchal society. In conclusion, it can be said that women deserve their due respect at every stage of their life cycle as not only producers of the human kind but also as citizens with human dignity and rights.

References

Bhandari, Manas (2009). 'Prasanga Shiva o Lingopasana, Varnaparichay', Kolkata, November–December.

Chakravarty, Uma (2006). *Everyday Lives, Everyday Histories: Beyond the Kings and Brahmanas of Ancient India*, Delhi: Tulika Books.

Chattopadhyay, Deviprasad (1998). *Lokayata Darshan*, Kolkata: New Age.

Choudhury, Sujit (2002). *Prachin Bharate Matri Pradhannya: Kinbadantir Punarbichar*, Kolkata: Papyrus.

Roy, Arundhati (2010). 'Aranyer Din Ratri' (Hindi), Kolkata, June.

Sharma, Ramsaran (1999). *Ancient India*, Delhi: NCERT.

18

Baby Factories

An Emerging Form of Violence against Women and a Violation of Women and Children's Rights

JESSICA EZEKIEL-HART

Abstract

Baby factories, a rapid growing business outfits in Nigeria are churning out hundreds of babies for illegal adoption and for some other unknown purposes. Violence against women takes various forms, but the incidence of baby factories is a new phenomenon. The women are often unmarried young adults/adolescents who mistakenly get pregnant out of wedlock and in an attempt to avoid stigmatization, end up in these 'maternity homes' or 'orphanages' (factories operated under various pseudo names). They are given the cover they require at the expense of turning in their babies for ridiculous stipends. Some of these factories use all manner of coercion to hold their victims captive and use them to breed more babies. Hitherto, some articles on violence against women reiterate that men are the perpetrators of violence, but in this case, women appear to be more culpable. They own the factories and employ men as sales agents and in some cases, use them to impregnate their inmates. The devastating effects on the well-being of these women and children constitute a violation of their human rights. This paper attempts to examine the relevant laws which are meant to protect the rights of women and children. It also suggests the way forward in such situations.

Keywords

Baby Factories, Violence, Violation of Rights, Women.

Introduction

The task of nation-building is tough. The challenges are pervasive and sectorally interconnected and often at the base of it all is corruption, a concept that is as old as the world and which has received varied definitions. Broadly, it can be defined as a perversion or a change from good to bad. Specifically, corruption or corrupt behaviour involves the violation of established rules for personal gain and profit (Sen, 1998). Corruption is an effort to secure wealth or power through illegal means, private gain at public expenses; or a misuse of public power for private benefit (Lipset and Lenz, 2000). It threatens the rule of law, democracy and human rights, undermines good governance, fairness and social justice, distorts competition, hinders economic development and endangers the stability of democratic institutions and the moral foundations of society.

Corruption takes different forms such as bribery, fraud, embezzlement, extortion, favouritism, and nepotism. On a holistic approach, it can be divided into political corruption, bureaucratic corruption and electoral corruption. No country is immune to it, they only operate at various degrees. That is to say that corruption is endemic to all government and it is not peculiar to any continent, religion and ethnic group. It cuts across political systems. The leaders and the led young and old, men and women are engaged in it. In Nigeria, it is pandemic having eaten deep into the fabric of the nation (Dike, 2008). This paper will present the immense negative impact it makes in violating human rights as can be seen in the prevalence of baby factories, an emerging phenomenon of violence against women and a violation of women and children's rights.

This paper begins with a clarification of some concepts. It then takes a look at how baby factories operate and what is fuelling this phenomenon. Among other things, it examines the relationship between the attitudes and beliefs of different dominant groups and the establishment of baby factories. It also elaborates on the relevant laws which are meant to protect the rights of women and children achieving their purpose and suggests a way forward.

Baby Factories

UNESCO (2006) reports that human trafficking is the third most common crime in Nigeria behind fraud and drugs. Human traffic is bad but more despicable is the traffic of innocent and helpless babies. These babies are produced in obscure and often unhygienic environment under various pseudo names such as orphanages, maternity homes, clinic, etc. These appellations give a sense of legality and professionalism where in fact their operations are illegal and are often run by quacks. Babies who are produced in these factories are sold to the highest bidder. Usually baby boys are more expensive than baby girls which is expected in a patriarchal society. Operators care more about profit than the motive of the buyer which may range from the harmless to the diabolical. Both buyer and seller exhibit such morally bankrupt behaviour that they do not care about what happens to the biological mothers of these babies. A large number of these babies are sold locally but the police suspects that children have been sold to Europe and the USA.

In recent years the media is inundated with large number of factories, where security operatives are busted. The following reports prove this:

> Nigerian Police has uncovered a series of alleged baby factories in recent years, notably in the Southeastern part of the country.

> In May of 2011 in South Eastern Abia State, Police freed 32 pregnant girls who said they have been offered to sell their babies for between 25,000 and 30,000 naira (about $191) depending on the sex.
>
> Other 17 pregnant girls were discovered ... in October 2011 under similar circumstances. (african.howzit.msn.com) Ejinkeonye (2013)

Being that Nigeria is consistently ranked as a highly corrupt nation (Lipset and Lenz, 2000), it is safe to conclude that there may be far more factories than are made public. Ejinkeonye (2013) notes that even among the country's security officers, anti-corruption operatives and judicial officers are among many whose penchant to corruptly amass wealth surpasses that of the corrupt public officers they are mandated to check. Terese Christianson of 'Expressen' against women, a grassroots initiative which highlights abuses and oppression against women while empowering them, also infiltrated several baby factories in the south eastern part of Nigeria with hidden camera. Pretending to buy a baby, she was assured by the sellers that they could arrange court orders and deal with the police. For them, court is no problem, they will handle it. They also have all the documents from the Ministry of Social Welfare, the ministry responsible for legal/legitimate adoptions. All these are government functionaries.

Why and How Baby Factories Operate

In a country with little emphasis on sex education, unwanted adolescent pregnancies occur quite frequently. Such pregnancies bring unqualified shame and embarrassment, not only to the ladies involved but to their entire families. Their future is sometimes jeopardized as pregnancy stops their education if they are students and abortion has continued to be illegal. Different reactions to unwanted pregnancies can be noticed among some ethnic groups in Nigeria. Some groups are more sympathetic to victims than others, many parents in the South South and South West of Nigeria will do whatever they can to accommodate and possibly send back their girls (if they are still in school) to another school to complete their schooling. Other ethnic groups particularly in the South East who claim to hold marriage in a very high esteem, tow such hard line that can result in the social exclusion of victims from society. To avoid this embarrassment desperate unmarried pregnant ladies hide away in some obscure 'clinics' or 'orphanages', deliver, dispose of the babies and return to the society as if nothing has happened. These dubious homes sometimes lure these frightened and devastated ladies to their facilities on the pretext that they render social services to ladies with peculiar needs. Thereafter the ladies are forced to turn over their babies for stipends while they in turn sell the babies to desperate buyers at exorbitant prizes, sometimes a hundred times more. Official reports also confirm that these homes often hold these ladies captive and use them repeatedly to produce babies hence baby factory is a thriving business especially in those parts of the country where unwanted pregnancy outside wedlock is a serious taboo (Agbu, 2003).

There are other conditions that promote the success of baby factories. A lot of blame is being heaped on poverty and unemployment. While it is true that the rate of poverty and unemployment is high nationally it is not true that the south east which is yoked with these factories is the poorest region, neither does it have the highest unemployment rate. Even if it does, poverty should not take humanity from man. In fact, this region is among the most educationally advanced and they are known to be very industrious. Their involvement in baby factories therefore may better be explained in their astuteness for making money. Christianson who pretended to buy a baby recorded that the owners of the factories were very elated to see great potential to make huge amount of money from Home of Hope, an organization which she informed them she represents and which wants to have business relationship with the factory. They lighted up when she introduced business and dollar, and admitted that church delegates from Germany come there to give them money.

Stigma against infertility drives desperate women to patronize these factories. Male and female reproductive capacities are said to be on the decline. A hospital in Abia State in the south east region recorded 53 per cent infertility in 2011 and in 2012 infertility related matters rose to 60 per cent. This condition, it is believed, is reaching a desperate level even among young couples. Delay in child bearing, possibly as a result of schooling, infection and long distance relationship are among the common reasons for infertility. These conditions are widespread nationally and not limited to any geographical area. Baby factory operators are simply more business minded and they are able to cash in on the principle of demand and supply. If there were no buyers, there would be no babies to sell; these buyers avoid open adoption which will show them up as barren or infertile. Sellers adopt different strategies in dealing with this category of clients. While some women would pay and collect, others who are blinded by their desperation are duped into thinking that they are pregnant. Women in this group are injected with substances which get them bloated up giving a deceptive appearance of pregnancy. Such 'pregnant' women are never managed by any other doctor or nurse except the original 'doctor' or 'nurse' (the factory owner) who enabled them to get 'pregnant', neither can their babies be delivered elsewhere except at the factory. On an agreed date, the 'pregnant' woman would go to the factory and return with a baby which she would claim she delivered. Sometimes the absurdity is pathetic. Women are known to have returned home the same day after 'delivery' with babies whose umbilical cords have fallen off already. Hell is let loose if an unsuspecting husband or an extended family member discovers this (Duru and Ogbonnaya, 2012).

A crucial fact which must not be overlooked in the emergence and continuation of this phenomenon is the breakdown of values and ethics. The entrenchment of strong values and ethics are pivotal for development; they are central to any organization. But Nigeria, since independence, has had constant episodes of political and economic instability and leadership patterns which have resulted in the erosion of nation's traditional value systems. One visible effect of the Nigerian Civil War and the subsequent long era of military rule is a reckless quest for quick money – a lifestyle that has seriously impaired fundamental values of honesty, commitment, contentment, sanctity of life, discipline, etc. Baby factories, therefore, are run primarily by a network of people who have the same interest to make quick money at whatever cost. After all corruption conveys a dangerous and wrong lesson which debunks the merit of honesty, handwork and the rule of law. Overnight people who could hardly afford a meal begin to flaunt corruptly amassed wealth and the society raises no questions. Brazen display of wealth from unexplainable source encourages dubious people to dabble into unethical means of making money too. Instead of a reprimand, society showers praises on known crooks who make fat donations at public functions while those with honest and modest income are ridiculed (Dike, 2008).

The 2004 National Economic Empowerment and Development Strategy (NEEDS) recognizes this very important need of restoring the fundamental values which have been weakened over the years, hence, value reorientation is one of the imperatives on which NEEDS is anchored. But the different institutions such as family, religion, education, police, judiciary, etc. are all mired in one crisis after another. Family ethos is broken down; education is reduced to schooling with demoralized teachers who can hardly mentor their students, and several institutions have been compromised (Federal Government of Nigeria, 2004).

Baby Factories and Violence against Women

Baby factories can safely be classified as violence against women taking into consideration, the devastating effects on the health and well-being of these women. Situations which arise from coercion, arbitrary deprivation of their children and the deprivation of their own liberty in cases where these ladies are held captives against their will amounts to violence. For violence against women refers to any act or threats of acts intended to hurt or make women suffer physically, sexually or psychologically (Richters, 1994). Baby factory fits into this definition. But while many articles on violence against women suggest that men are the perpetrators of this violence (Sen, 1998), this paper argues differently.

Traditionally violence against women are violent acts against women purely because they are women and it arises as a result of patriarchal gender constructs. But in the case of baby factories women are the main culprits. Maternity homes and orphanages are nearly always owned and definitely manned by women. As absurd as it is, a man or few men may be recruited to impregnate several girls in the factory. Men may serve as security personnel to prevent the girls from escaping to expose the factory. They may be recruited to canvass for and negotiate prices with buyers. The whole idea of baby factories can be classified as violence against women by women, of women who have economic power against those who do not have.

According to World Health Organization (1997) typology table, violence against women begins from conception through the life circle. In the pre-birth state, sex-selective abortion type of violence occurs, that is, a female foetus is more likely to be flushed out than a male foetus if the need arises. In the same way, infancy and girlhood have their own peculiar types of violence such as female infanticide, sexually and psychological abuse, incest, child prostitution to mention a few. For adolescents and adulthood, types of violence consist but not limited to economically coerced sex, whereby sex is exchanged for money, incest, sexual abuse/harassment in the workplace, rape, forced prostitution, trafficking in women, and abuse of women with disabilities. Baby factory seems to be a recent entrant and there may be other types that are yet to be documented.

Baby Factories as Violation of Women's Rights

Having established that baby factories are violence against women, this paper argues that any form of violence against women is a violation of their rights. Women rights are those rights and entitlements claimed for women and girls of many societies worldwide. These rights may be supported by laws, local customs and behaviour. Much as they differ from broader notions of human rights, it is no longer acceptable to discuss women's rights as separate from human rights. Ongoing advocacy presents human rights as women's rights and women's rights as human rights. Human rights are everyday rights of all human beings given by God and guaranteed under international treaties. Women's rights connote that women who are part of the human race have their rights covered by the definition of human rights. Therefore, women's rights are human rights peculiar to women individually and collectively. Women's rights are highlighted because of the historical and traditional subjugation of women in many societies. This subjugation is more pronounced in patriarchal societies where it is shrouded in cultural, structural and religious systems.

Whether as women's right or human rights these rights are important indicators to understand global well-being. Gender equality furthers the cause of child survival and development for all society and should never be under played. Healthy, educated and empowered women have healthy, educated and confident children. Gender equality does not only empower women to overcome poverty and live full productive lives, it also enhances better lives for the children, families and countries. Gender equality, therefore, is not only morally right; it is a prerequisite to human progress and sustainable development (UNICEF, 2007).

The Universal Declaration of Human Rights (UDHR), 1948 envisaged women's human rights but the articulation of women rights framework came into being in 1979 with the International Convention on Elimination of all forms of Discrimination Against Women (CEDAW). To reaffirm and clarify the above, the 1993 United Nations World conference on Human rights in Vienna specifically states that 'human rights of women and the girl-child are an inalienable, integral and indivisible part of human rights. Consequently, it behooves all governments to ensure the protection of human rights which subsumes women's rights.

This observation gave rise to several United Nations declarations, yet in spite of these many years of advocacy and involvement of many feminist activist organizations, the issue of violence against women still remains one of the most pervasive forms of human rights violation worldwide.

Nigeria and Women's Rights

Nigeria adopted the UDHR and ratified a plethora of international and regional treaties protecting human rights in general and women's rights in particular. For instance, the protocol which was adopted on 11 July 2003 by the African Union (AU) sought to strengthen, promote and protect women's rights. By signing this protocol Nigerian women are guaranteed the right to dignity, the right to life; freedom from harmful practices which negatively affect the human rights of women, integrity and security of persons, equal rights in marriage; equal rights in cases of separation, divorce and annulment; the right to equal protection and benefit of the law, the right to participate in political and decision-making process; the right to peaceful existence and participation in promotion and maintenance of peace; the right to education and training; equal opportunity in work and career advancement; the right to health, including sexual and reproductive rights the right to adequate housing; the right to healthy environment; the right to sustainable development, etc.

The obligation of the Nigerian Government under the protocol which would ensure that women enjoy the rights mentioned above would be for government to take such positive actions by enacting appropriate legislature that would prohibit all forms of violence against women; to guarantee that no marriage takes place without free will, and between consenting adults; provide budgetary and other resources necessary for effective implementation, etc. This has not happened due to reasons which may be shrouded in cultural and religious systems. The overwhelming control of patriarchal interest, arising from the patriarchal structure of the Nigerian society, a structure characterized by the subjugation of women remains a stumbling block. The National Assembly (the body responsible for making laws) has continued to dodge passing the bill on abolition of all forms of discrimination against women in Nigeria and other related matters. There is also no bill prohibiting violence against women. In fact, the protocol is yet to be domesticated and the necessary legislature that would bring to pass government obligations and undertakings under the protocol are yet to be enacted. This is a shade of corruption. Falk, an actor, noted that in order to appear righteous among comity of nations, for reasons associated with pride and public opinion or for whatever other reasons, governments are often eager to endorse standards of human rights despite their unwillingness to uphold these standards in practice. It is not surprising, therefore, that the provisions of the protocols recognizing and guaranteeing the rights of women are yet to attain a commensurate levels of improvement in the lives of Nigerian women (Odigie-Emmanuel, 2010).

Child's Rights Law in Nigeria

The Federal Republic of Nigeria comprises 36 states and one Federal Capital Territory (Abuja). She also has three tiers of government – federal, state and local levels. According to Nigeria's Constitution, law pertaining to children's Rights Act must be adopted by individual state legislature to be fully implemented. Though each state has its own government, law and judiciary, federal authority defines and monitors the implementation of this very policy. Like women's rights, children's rights are those benefits which accrue to them because they are part of the human race. Children's rights pay particular attention to the rights of special protection and care to minors. Further interpretation of child's rights include the enforcement of their freedom from physical, mental, psychological and emotional abuse; though what constitute abuse is a matter of debate.

Nigeria as a signatory to the Convention of the Rights of the Child (CRC) has passed the Child's Rights Act into law at the Federal Level, through the law appears to have different levels of acceptance and implementation among states in the federation. Some states have passed the bill into law; some are cautiously considering it, while others have blatantly refused to do so. This is so because the states and local governments represent a diverse range of ethnic groups and customs. Moreover, apart from passing the Child's Rights Act 2003, there is no instrument at the national level that truly enforces the adoption of the bill by various State Governments, instead, in many states, child protection activities are carried out by Non-Governmental Organizations (NGO).

It is vitally important also to note that in discussing children, little or no attention is paid to unborn babies and infants. So inadvertently this class will be highly prone to abuse. No wonder they are treated as commodities/ merchandise.

Baby Factories as Human Trafficking

Overlooking the interest of unborn babies and infants forces a new look at the scope of people trafficking in Nigeria and human trafficking is a serious violation of human rights.

Article 3 of Palermo Protocol, an additional protocol to the UN convention against trans-national organized crimes which aim at preventing and punishing trafficking in persons has defined trafficking in persons as:

> The recruitment, transportation, transfer, harbouring, or receipt of persons by means of threat or use of force or other forms of coercion, of abduction, of fraud, of deception, of the abuse of power or of a position of vulnerability of the giving or receiving of payment or benefit to achieve the consent of a person, having control over another person for the purpose of exploitation. Exploitation shall include... other forms of sexual exploitation, forced labour or services, slavery, servitude or the removal of organs. (UN, 2000)

The literature on trafficking of persons in Nigeria presents women and children as high risk victims. Girls and women are trafficked for forced prostitution. Boys are trafficked primarily to work as forced bondage labourers, street peddlers and beggars who make returns to their masters. Girls are trafficked for domestic services, street peddling and commercial sexual exploitation. What are infants trafficked for? Not much is known yet, nevertheless on the basis of the definition above baby factory can easily fit into the trafficking model which is:

1. The act – ladies with unwanted pregnancies are recruited and harboured in the factories.
2. The means – once they are lured into the factories all the instruments of force, threat and coercion are used to 'imprison' them until they are delivered of their babies and give them up at some ridiculous stipends.
3. The purpose – primarily exploiting for monetary gains to factory owners. There are also hints for ritual purposes.

This paper, thus, reveals that baby factory is another dimension of human trafficking. The dimension and categorization of human traffic continue to multiply by the day (Agbu, 2003). But while series of arrests have been reported in the media hardly any prosecution, much less convictions have been heard of people involved in trafficking. Is it that these people are not breaking any law? Certainly they are; for there are laws governing trafficking in persons and since baby factory is a dimension of human trafficking, the law should apply to it too. However, non-application of the law may be a result of corruption (Dike, 2008). A compendium of laws with little enforcement is as good as nothing.

Conclusion

Nigeria is one of the countries that has refused to legalize abortion. It, therefore, follows that even the unborn baby has a right to live. But the multiplication of baby factories is rapidly and pathetically demeaning, if not demonizing the country's image among the comity of nations. In recent times, unscrupulous business people register Non-Governmental Organizations with Corporate Affairs Commission claiming they are rendering social services. But, behind the façade, are heinous hideouts where ladies with unwanted pregnancies hide until they deliver, dispose of the baby and reintegrate into the society. In more heinous cases, ladies are held captives and used in producing more and more babies for sale by the factories owners. What the factory owners pay the biological mothers is often less than 0.5 per cent of what they sell. Among the conditions which fuel this trade are high rate of infertility, stigmatization of barren women, poverty, unemployment, the love of money, stigmatization which comes with pregnancy outside wedlock, change in value system, the law and practices of adoption which are unduly bureaucratic and lengthy, a situation which offers an excuse to source babies from the black market (baby factory). While legal adoption have well articulated procedure and conditions, the illegal adoption has no such rules, therefore buyers can do whatever they want with the babies, to the extent that factory operators assure potential clients that they have the backing of security operatives.

Several times the media reported that police had bust one baby factory or the other. While celebrating this feat, the general impression is that of a tip of the iceberg – there are far many more factories (Duru and Ogbonnaya, 2012). Security operatives may claim to know little of the locations of these factories but if pregnant ladies and buyers of babies know where these factories are located, security operatives should not claim ignorance because they all live in the same communities. Unfortunately lack of reliable and continuous data does not allow for a clear picture, though the media is frequently bombarded with stories of baby factories.

Child's rights law exists to safeguard children, their well-being and their individual rights. Babies have the right to life. In fact, the future of teenage girls and their babies is being destroyed for when dignity which is the foundation of other human rights is denied, a person may suffer from different kinds of trauma – physical, emotional, psychological etc. Section 34(1a) of the Nigerian Constitution provides that every individual is entitled to respect for the dignity of his person and accordingly no person shall be subjected to any form of inhuman treatment ... while Section 34(1b) disallows any person to be held in slavery or servitude.

The Way Forward

The following suggestions prove the way forward. They are:

1. Since the perpetrators of this crime live among other people in the society, the cooperation of the citizens in the area for information gathering cannot be over emphasized.
2. Traditional rulers must be involved in fishing out the culprits and in the elimination of those aspects of culture which give rise to undue stigmatization.
3. Intensive and extensive campaign on the ills of baby factories must be taken by all stakeholders, governments, Non-Governmental Organizations, etc.
4. As a highly religious nation, moral and religious studies should be taught at all levels in our schools.
5. Christian clergymen and their Muslim counterparts should also contribute their quota in inculcating moral lifestyle among the adherents.
6. Parents and guardians should not be adjudged blameless. They should desist from encouraging their girls to make money not minding how.
7. Corruption which is the root cause should be confronted with the tenacity, tactical approach and dynamism that is demanded.
8. There is need for value re-orientation in Nigerian society where wealth and people of questionable characters should not be celebrated.
9. Busting the factories is not enough, let those who are guilty be prosecuted and convicted.

References

Agbu, O. (2003). 'Corruption and Human Trafficking: The Nigerian Case', *West African Review*, 4(1).

Bakare, O. (2014). *Daily Independent Newspaper*, 13 May.

Dike, V.E. (2008). 'Corruption in Nigeria: A New Paradigm for Effective Control'. Retrieved 1 July 2012 from www.africaeconomicanalysis.org.

Duru, E.J. and Ogbonnaya, U.M. (2012). 'Combating Human Trafficking in Nigeria: An Evaluation of State Policies and Programmes', *Mediterranean Journal of Social Sciences*, 3(3).

Ejinkeonye, U. (2013). 'Kill Corruption before it Kills You', *The Nigerian Voice*, www.ugowrite.blogspot.com africa.howzit.msn.com.

Ezekiel-Hart, J. (2013). 'Dealing with Alternative Sexual Orientation in Schools and Homes in Nigeria', *African Journal of Education and Technology*, 4(1).

Ezema, M. (2002). 'Global Financial Institutions Options for Poverty Reduction', *The Guardian Newspaper*, 10 July.

Federal Government of Nigeria (2004). National Economic Empowerment and Development Strategy (NEEDS), Abuja: Government Press.

Krantz, G. and Garcia-Moreno, C. (2006). 'Violence against Women', *Journal of Epidemiology and Community Health*, 59(10). Retrieved 10 March 2014 from www.jstor.org/stable.

Lipset, S.M. and Lenz, G.S. (2000). 'Corruption, Culture and Markets', in E. Harrison and P. Huntington (eds), *Culture Matters: How Value Shapes Human Progress*, New York: Basic Books.

Newswatch Magazine (2011). 'The Booming Baby Market in Igboland', 8 August, 16–22.

Odigie-Emmanuel, O. (2010). 'Assessing Women's Right in Nigeria', *Pambazuka News*. Accessed on 15 November 2015 from fpif.org/assessing-womens-right-in-nigeria.

Okeke, U. (2016). Women's UN Report Network (WUNRN), www.wunrn.com.

Oloja, M. (2002). 'How Civil Servants Engage in Corruption', *The Guardian Newspaper*, 21 April.

Onoinbholo, F. (2008). 'Nigeria Country among World's Highest in Human Trafficking', *Daily Independent (Lagos)*, 22 December.

Richters, J.M. (1994). *Women, Culture and Violence: A Development, Health and Human Rights Issue*, Leiden: Women Autonomy Centre (VENA).

Sen, P. (1998). 'Development Practice and Violence against Women', *Gender and Development*, 6(3). Retrieved on April 2014 from www.jstor.org ...4030497.

UN (2000). Protocol to Prevent, Suppress and Punish Trafficking in Persons, Especially Women and Children.

UNESCO (2006). 'Human Trafficking in Nigeria: Root Causes and Recommendation', Policy Paper No. 14, 2.

UNICEF (2007). Report on State of World Children.

World Health Organization (1997). Violence against Women: Definition and Scope of the Problem. Retrieved 30 November 2013 from http://www.whoint/gender/violence/v.4pdf.

19

Maternal Health of Women under National Rural Health Mission

A Study in the Central Region Districts of Odisha

RANJIT KUMAR DEHURY AND JAGATABANDHU MOHAPATRA

Abstract

Odisha is classified as one of the 'High Focus States' under NRHM for the low status of health infrastructure. Among the three Revenue Divisions, the maternal health of central division is alarming. To bridge the gap, a lot of programmes under NRHM are functioning in Odisha. The present study evaluates the situation of maternal health in central region districts of Odisha. Further the study would analyse the health infrastructure to address various issues of maternal health. An analysis of the secondary data about the districts and its sub divisions was done to understand the health service infrastructure in the region. The findings indicate a shortage of buildings, consumable goods, valuable drugs and basic amenities in the thrust areas. Lacking is public health infrastructure makes it difficult to provide expected quality of health in general and maternal health in particular. The study recommends for up-gradation of health centres particularly appointment of pharmacists, purchase of drugs as per the local needs, and provision of dedicated space for OPD patients and storage of drugs. Social determinants of health in tribal areas, especially improvement of living conditions, women leadership, education, money and other resources should be equitably distributed.

Keywords

Maternal Health, Central RDC Odisha, JSY, NRHM

Introduction

The birth rate in India is very high, i.e. 27 million, and maternal death is estimated at about 1,17,000 per year in the world. There are several reasons for the high maternal mortality rate in India including non-availability of obstetricians and skilled birth attendants in rural areas (Mavalankar, 1999; Mavalankar and Rosenfield, 2005; George, 2007; Mavalankar, Vohra and Prakasamma et al., 2008). While globally, maternal and child mortality rate is declining, the pace of decline in India has not been sufficient to attain Millennium Development Goals (MDGs) 4 and 5 (Lozano et al., 2011). The MDG 5 has targeted to reduce the maternal mortality rate (MMR) up to 109 per one lakh births between 1990 to 2015. For smooth governance of maternal health the 30 districts of Odisha have been grouped in three different divisions, i.e. Northern, Southern and Central. Each division has 10 districts. Each division is headed by Revenue Divisional Commissioner (RDC) and Inspector general of police (IGP). The central region districts are Mayurbhanja, Baleswar, Bhadrak, Kendrapara, Jagatsinghapur, Cuttack, Jajpur, Nayagarh, Khordha, Puri. The major tribal community is found in Mayurbhanja district whereas minor tribal community is found in other remaining nine districts.

Maternal Health

Health indicators in India have not yet demonstrated an eye-catching improvement parallel to the national growth rates. However, the present health system has the advantage of wide network of health facilities across the country (Zodpey and Negandhi, 2008). According to the report of WHO, 2000, India was placed at 118 rank among 191 member countries of World Health Organization (WHO) on overall health performances so the initiations of public health by the Government of India was a way of success among other countries of the world. The performance in the field of maternal health is also lagging. Motashaw (1997) reported 28 per cent of world's birth and 46 per cent of maternal death in India, Pakistan and Bangladesh. Such high maternal mortality rate (NMR) in India are due to medical reasons, non-availability of obstetricians and skilled birth attendants in rural areas (Mavalankar, 1999; Mavalankar and Rosenfield, 2005; Mavalankar, Vora and Prakasamma et al., 2008). The maternal mortality rate is in a declining state globally where as the declining state is not sufficient in India to attain Millennium Developmental Goals (Lozano et al., 2011) causing a moral urgency of reinvigorating effort. The Government of Odisha has taken steps to reduce MMR to 119 by the end of the 11th plan period by promoting ante-natal and post-natal care. Although the number of women receiving institutional deliveries has been increased over the years (from 36.8 per cent in 2004–05 to 71 per cent in 2008–09). On total coverage, it is still a distant dream (NRHM, 2012).

Need for the Study

It is a matter of fact that the assessment of the activities of antenatal check-up as well as Janani Surkhya Yojona is quite necessary to observe the progress activity of NRHM in Odisha. Especially the scientific assessment of structures and processes of health care delivery could be able to improve the maternal health. Implementation of various programmes mainly depends upon the infrastructural component and functionally by active involvement of the key health workers. The decision made by the physicians and compliance with government protocols are the most important factors which significantly impacts the programme. Furthermore, it is also necessary to study the perspective of the beneficiary for assessment of the programme's congruence with the culture and needs of the local people. Lastly, the assessment of HMIS has the potential to uncover the lacunae in the existing system. This paper evaluates the situation of maternal health in the central region districts of Odisha.

Objectives

The objective of the study was to monitor and evaluate maternal health programme in central region districts of Odisha by using medical and non-medical parameters. This involves the following:

1. Evaluating the functionality of health centres of central region district of Odisha in accordance with Indian Public Health Standards (IPHS).
2. Assessment of the antenatal check-ups in promoting the institutional delivery and health seeking behaviour among the people.

Significance of the Study

The study assumes significance in the context of the effective implementation of maternal component of NRHM by teaching them various preventable factors of maternal death, as a result of which the maternal deaths can be reduced to a greater extent. It is difficult to assess the relative contribution of antenatal and post-natal care. There are several factors that are involved in the assessment process. These are immunization programmes, iron prophylaxis, early detection of preeclampsia, education, advice and preparation for transport and safe delivery, etc. These elements may also affect the pre-natal and post-natal cares. Proper monitoring of maternal death depends upon the adequate reporting of the maternal deaths and the causes of death.

The Study Area: Odisha

Odisha as an Empowered Action Group (EAG) state, one among the 18th high focussed states of NRHM programme, has made a significant investment under NRHM scheme for maternal and child health. Implementation of HMIS with the help of National Health Systems Resource Centre (NHSRC) – New Delhi to improve the Maternal and Child Health after the launching of NRHM assumes significance in this context.

Methodology

In order to evaluate maternal health, descriptive and evaluative survey methods were used. Primary data was collected using quantitative and qualitative methods. Focus Group Discussions (FGDs) and Key Informant (KI) interview techniques were used to collect information on the development and implementation. The Health Management Information System (HMIS) data was analysed for the comparison of different regions of Odisha in terms of registered pregnancy, antenatal check-up and institutional delivery. District and Sub-District level secondary data were analysed to know the overall situation of the health infrastructure of the district. The modified version of the Indian Public Health Standards, 2010 was used to assess the infrastructure in terms of manpower, availability of drugs and consumables and administrative support at PHCs.

Findings and Discussion

The shortage of buildings, drugs and consumables, and basic amenities are glaring in the study districts. The Antenatal Check-Up (ANC) registration is increased but early registration is a distance dream in that region. Further, ANC registration is not commensurable with record of institutional delivery. There is huge reluctance to adhere to the norms of 4 mandatory ANC check-ups.

Maternal Mortality Rate of Different Regions of Odisha

The maternal mortality rate is shown in Table 1 as can be seen there have been higher maternal deaths (128) and the mortality rate which is equivalent rate which is equal to that of the state (Figure 1).

Figure 1

Maternal Mortality Rate (MMR) of Odisha in Comparison to Different Administrative Divisions

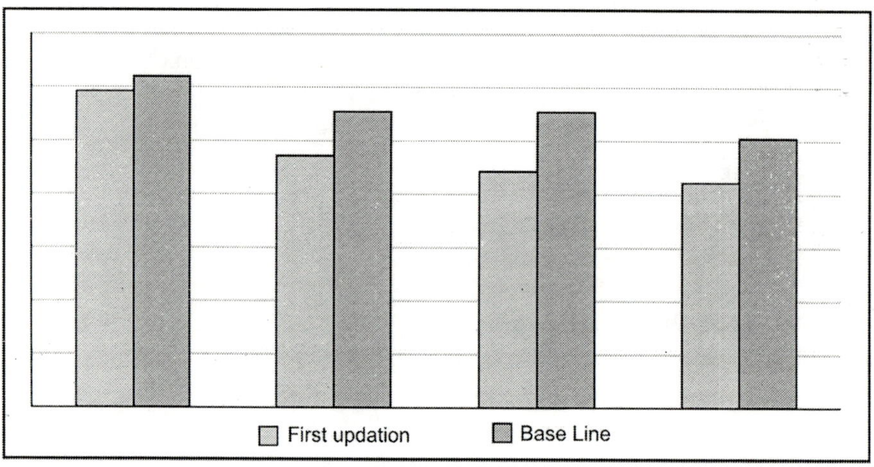

Source: NRHM Odisha (2013).

General Backward Condition of the State

Backwardness of Odisha, a state with high MMR, has implemented the NRHM to actualize MDGs. It has a geographical area of 1,55,707 sq km with a population of nearly 41.9 million (Census, 2011), and is considered to be one of the less developed states of India with regards to agriculture, industry, and other social sectors. About one-tenth of the tribal population in India resides here. The State is one of the poorest state in the country with 46 per cent of its population is below the poverty line (BPL). This accounts for nearly 15 million poor in rural

Table 1

Maternal Mortality Rate (MMR) of Odisha

State/Commissioner/(District)	*Sample Female Population*	*Sample Live Birth*	*Maternal Death*	*MMR*	*95% Confidence Interval*		*Maternal Mortality Rate*	*Life Time Risk (%)*
					Lower Limit	*Upper Limit*		
Odisha	5,31,560	1,11,390	308	277	246	307	19	0.67
Northern Division (Bargarh, Jharsuguda, Sambalpur, Debagarh, Sundargarh, Kendujhar, Dhenkanal, Anugul, Sonpur, Balangiri)	1,96,353	37,936	96	253	202	304	16	0.57
Central Division (Mayurbhanj, Baleshwar, Bhadrak, Kendrapara, Jagatsinghapur, Cuttack, Jajpur, Nayagarh, Khordha, Puri)	2,27,875	46,452	128	276	228	323	19	0.65
Southern Division (Ganjam, Gajapati, Kandhamal, Baudh, Nuapada, Kalahandi, Rayagada, Nabarangapur, Koraput, Malkangiri)	1,07,332	27,002	84	311	245	378	26	0.91

Source: NRHM Odisha (2013).

areas and three million in urban areas of Odisha (Government of Odisha, 2010). To redress this situation, it is recognized as a member of Empowered Action Group (EAG) (Maternal Mortality Report, 1997–2003; Maternal Mortality Bulletin, 2004–06).

Trends of MDG

In pursuance of MDGs, the Government of India has devised policies to improve maternal health. The National Health Policy 2002 focusses on some of the salient issues of maternal health. The survey by Registrar General of India (RGI) shows there is a gap of 30 points between the MDG 5 targets for the year 2015 based on the base year 1990 and its likely achievement for the same year pertaining to maternal health. The deliveries attended by skilled birth attendant are only 60 per cent as against full coverage. Table 2 shows the details of these trends.

Table 2
Analysis of the Trends on Goal 5 of MDG in India

Items	*Baseline Position (1990)*	*MDG Target (2015)*	*Likely Achievement (2015)*	*Situation (year)*
MMR	437	109	139	212 (2007–09)
Deliveries attended by skilled birth attendant	33%	100%	60%	52 (2007–08)

Source: Office of the Registrar General of India (2011).

Despite this, the MMR of Odisha has not shown significant progress. According to Sample Registration System (SRS) survey, the MMR has decreased from 358 to 302 from the period 2001–03 to 2004–06. Further, there is a reduction of 303 to 258 from the period 2004–06 to 2007–09. The drop in MMR between the two periods has slowed down from 55 to 45 points. Table 3 below shows the slowed process.

Table 3
Maternal Mortality in Odisha

Year	*Sample Female Population*	*Live Births*	*Maternal Deaths*	*MMR*	*Drop in MMR in Survey Years*
2001–03	2,54,176	914	75	358	00
2004–06	2,56,956	21,118	64	303	55
2007–09	2,72,797	20,616	53	258	45

Source: SRS Survey, Registrar General of India (2009).

Paucity of Basic Facilities

The shortage of buildings, drugs and consumables, and basic amenities are dazzling in the study districts. There is inadequate supply of electricity connections, piped water supplies and health care centres in the districts. Even, existing PHCs absence of ECG and X-Ray machines for proper diagnostic services are the major causes for the failure of public health approach.

Inequitable Distribution of Health Infrastructure

To combat this slow process, health infrastructure in the State is getting upgraded. Some initiative for the renovation of buildings, procurement of drugs and supply of consumables to bridge critical gaps has been initiated but still there is an urgent need for infrastructure up-gradation.

Manpower shortage is the biggest hurdle in the expansion of NRHM aimed at revitalizing primary and secondary care in rural India. To overcome this problem, the Ministry of Health and Family Welfare (MoHFW) in consultation with Medical Council of India (MCI) is framing the strategy for better manpower planning.

Gaps in Health Care Infrastructure

The Antenatal Check-up (ANC) registration increased but early registration is a distance dream in these regions. Further, ANC registration is not commensurable with record of institutional delivery. There is huge reluctance to adhere the norms of 4 mandatory ANC cheek-ups. Community Health Centres are also lacking in basic diagnostic and ambulance services making the tribal pockets inaccessible. The tribal dominated block shows poor performance in terms of total registered Antenatal Check-ups. There is a gradual decrease in ANC percentage from first to fourth. Compliance with IPHS standards needs serious attention to ensure safe delivery. The IPHS standard provides enough scope for availability of quality services in a public health care institutions. Women fallout from regular ANC visits due to several reasons. Additional effort is required for capacity building of front line workers (ASHAs, ANMs, health workers etc.) to track ANC progress by the use of HMIS. This will make home visit regular, effective and meaningful particularly in remote tribal communities.

Structural Issues Affecting the Maternal Health

Primary Health Centres (PHCs) take care of both public health concerns and medical care and as such are geared for improving reproductive health. WHO has laid special importance on developing PHCs, making them scientifically sound, socially acceptable and technologically viable. The strategies that PHCs adopt need to be accessible and cost-effective to ensure full participation of the community (WHO, 2004). Such structural improvements can strengthen the reproductive health programmes.

The Government of India has taken steps to maintain Indian Public Health Standard (IPHS) at PHCs level by improving the standard of PHCs. That's why, draft guidelines were prepared and published in 2006. Again in 2010, the guidelines were modified and revised. But no changes have been marked in the availabilities of health services at PHCs level. So, it is necessary to assess the successful percentage of maternal care at ground level.

Provision for assessment of services in PHC is made by government for the promotion of maternal health. A Facility Assessment Tool was developed by the Ministry of Health and Family Welfare, Government of India, to assess the PHCs in terms of availability of assured services. The services are: outdoor patient's services, in-patients services, 24-hour emergency services, referral services, antenatal care, intra-natal care, post-natal care, newborn care, and medical termination of pregnancy, management of reproductive tract infections/sexual transmitted infections and immunization. All these services affect maternal health (MoHFW, 2005).

One of the major reasons for the poor quality of services at the PHC is lack of capital investment. The NRHM has made some efforts to strengthen necessary service delivery in rural areas. Provision for capital investment has been made by the government for up-gradation of the existing PHCs to comply with IPHS norms.

A study by Murthy and Barua (2004) found that most medical deaths occur during perinatal and post-natal period. Further the death cases belong to high risk groups, high parity, socially disadvantaged, mothers, not receiving pre-natal care. There is evidence of lack of transport facilities, poor referrals and inadequate preparedness at the referral centres. The findings suggest that most of the deaths cases could be avoided if the health system is improved and accessible to all.

Studies have reported about the hidden potential of maternal health care services in India. The major function of maternal care service is to identify and monitor pregnant women as well as to establish a good rapport between women and paramedical workers. The coordination between pregnant women and providers of health system (Doctor, Nurse, ASHA, Anganwadi workers etc.) can uplift the acceptance of family planning at rural areas. The programme of antenatal care not only provides preventive interventions, but also provides nutrition, health education, postpartum care and family planning services (Govindasamy et al., 1993).

The analysis clearly indicates the acceptance of family planning methods by the currently married women who utilized the antenatal care. It is an encouraging fact that the contraceptive acceptance was higher in case of village women having no health facilities than in urban and sub-urban women having more health services. The above facts were established that the coordination between health staffs during the antenatal and post-natal care may increase the degree of acceptance of family planning methods by pregnant women in villages. One may agree that the improvement in antenatal care service is more fruitful than the increasing of the level of education.

ANC Registration Increased but Early Registration is a Distance Dream

A comparison between registered pregnancy between the year 2010–11 and 2011–12 shows the increasing trend of total registered pregnant women for ANC, but the decreasing trend of registration within the first trimester for these districts. This may be due to low level of awareness activity for availing of antenatal services in the early stage.

Increased Number of Non-Skilled Birth Attendant (Non-trained SBA)

The study focussed on a major point that the number of non-skilled birth attendants (Non-trained SBA) is more than that of the trained SBA (Doctor/Nurse/ANM) in these districts.

Non-Payment of Incentives to Mothers for Home Delivery

The percentage of mothers, who were paid JSY incentive, for home deliveries to total reported home deliveries is very low in case of these districts. Though there is provision for JSY incentives for home delivery, there is lack of proper mechanism for the payment of JSY incentive for those deliveries.

Decrease in Home Deliveries and Transportation

There is a decrease in home delivery and increase in institutional delivery in these districts. Similarly, poor transportation facility is a major barrier for women beneficiaries to avail institutional care. This is evident from low turnout in OPD and IPD services.

Anaemia and Pregnancy

Anaemia during pregnancy is one of the major causes of maternal morbidity, mortality and reproductive wastage in the world including India. Anaemia is the most common nutritional disorder in the global scenario since time immemorial. As per World Health Organization Report, prevalence of anaemia in pregnant women in developed and developing countries was 14 per cent and 51 per cent respectively and 65–75 per cent in India. Among South Asian countries, India contributed about 80 per cent of the maternal deaths due to anaemia.

A cross sectional study on 180 number of pregnant women in costal Odisha during antenatal period attending two major hospitals revealed an alarmingly high incidence of 71.1 per cent of anaemia. This indicated very poor maternal and child health care in this region. Several epidemiological studies showed that both low and high haemoglobin (Hb %) concentrations are associated with an increased adverse birth outcome. Therefore, foetal death, intrauterine growth retardation, preterm delivery and low birth weight are the final outcomes of the imbalanced haemoglobin concentration (Balgir, Panda, Panda and Ray et al., 2011).

The study revealed that dietary pattern and health seeking behaviour are the main behavioural risk factors associated with pregnancy. Dietary restrictions are often imposed on women. Food taboos are culturally defined and can adversely affect the health of women during pregnancy. There are several risk factors which are associated with the problem of anaemia during pregnancy. These are cultural food taboos, socio-economic status and literacy level among women. In some areas, there is a wrong notion about eating of pepper, i.e., Pepper eating causes with sores all over the body and red eyes in born babies.

Daily activities of pregnant women are treated in same way as they are in a non-pregnant state in some areas, which is not a wise decision. The pregnant women should continue their daily activities which gives the best support for smooth delivery. In some areas the family members have an unfavourable look towards the pregnant women which puts a negative impact on pregnant women and her psychological aspects.

Lack of Awareness

Although JSY popularized deliveries at home by trained birth attendants in remote areas, there were no such abnormal cases for the month under consideration. Lack of awareness among the people on basic information about safe motherhood, and superstitious attitude are considered to be major causes for maternal morbidity and mortality happening in the districts.

Evidence suggests that there exists a positive relation between empowerment of women and nutrition status of women in Odisha (Ali, 1995). Apart from this, lack of education, information and some cultural practices also affects the health status of a pregnant women. The present study also marked that some family members have some blind beliefs that the early child-bearing women must have the nutritional deficit and poor health status.

Women Education, Decision-Maker and Women Leadership

Improvement of women education, independency to women for taking own decisions regarding health condition is quite necessary now-a-days. Empowerment of women is very much essential for the society in taking decisions independently on health matters. However, there has been limited research on the influence of women's autonomy on decision-making regarding maternal health and utilization of preventive or curative health care services.

ANC Status in this Region

ANC registration increased but early registration is a distant dream. A comparison between registered pregnancy between the year 2010–11 and 2011–12 shows the increasing trend of total registered pregnant women for ANC; but there is a decreasing trend of registration within the first trimester in the State of Odisha.

Conclusion

ANC is mandatory for the pregnant women. The number of ANC check up is gradually increasing but a short fall of ANC is found in the study. There are several reasons involved for women fallout from regular ANC visits. Thus, the study recommends for the continuous tracking and follow up ANC at individual level is quite necessary. It is also evident from the low turnout of OPD and IPD services that transportation is the major barrier to avail institutional care by women beneficiaries. Furthermore, additional effort is required from the health workers like ASHA, ANM, etc. to uplift the progress of ANC by using HMIS. Additional effort includes regular home visit and convincent effort for the beneficiaries is necessary for the upliftment of ANC. In addition, the improvement of living condition, education, money transaction by the NRHM are also the major factors for the maintenance of maternal health care system. Lastly, proper maintenance of records and equal distribution of cash is quite important to place maternal health care programme at a suitable level.

References

Ali, Almas (1995). 'Health and Nutrition Status of Women in Orissa', in B. Singh and N. Mahanti (eds), *Tribal Health in India*, New Delhi: Inter-India Publications.

Bajpai, N., Sachs, J.D. and Dholakia, R.H. (2009). *Improving Access, Service Delivery and Efficiency of the Public Health System in Rural India: Midterm Evaluation of the National Rural Health Mission*, New York: USA Columbia University.

Balgir, R.S., Panda, J., Panda, A.K. and Ray, M. (2011). A Cross-Sectional Study of Anemia in Pregnant Women of Eastern Coast of Odisha. *Tribal Health Bulletin*, Vol. 17 (1 and 2), January and July, pp. 1–7.

Balk, D. (1994). 'Individual and Community Aspects of Women's Status and Fertility in Rural Bangladesh', *Population Studies*, 48(1): 21–25.

Basu, S. (1995). 'Health Status of Tribal Women in India', in B. Singh and N. Mahanti (eds), *Tribal Health in India*, New Delhi: Inter-India Publications, 18–38.

Govindasamy, P., Stewart, M.K., Rustein, S.O., Boerma, J.T. and Sommerfelt, A.E. (1993). *High-Risk Births and Maternity Care Demographic and Health Survey*, Comparative Studies No. 8, Columbia, Maryland: Marco International Inc.

Husain, Z. (2011). 'Health of the National Rural Health Mission', *Economic and Political Weekly*, 46(4): 53–60.

Jha, P. and Shing, L.K. (2010). 'Causes of Neonatal and Child Mortality in India: A Nationally Representative Mortality Survey', *Lancet*, 376(1): 1853–60.

Lozano, R., Wang, H., Foreman, K.J., Rajaratnam, J.K., Naghavi, M., Marcus, J.R. and Murray, C.J.L. (2011). 'Progress towards Millennium Development Goals 4 and 5 on Maternal and Child Mortality: An Updated Systematic Analysis', *Lancet*, 378(1): 1139–165.

Ministry of Health and Family Welfare, Government of India (2005). *Mission Document National Rural Health Mission*, New Delhi: Manager of Publication.

Motashaw, N.D. (1997). 'Root Causes of Maternal Mortality: Infancy to Motherhood', *Journal of Family Welfare*, 43(2): 4–7.

Murthy, N. and Barua, A. (2004). Non-medical Determinants of Maternal Death in India, *Journal of Health Management*, 6, 47–61. Available at http://jhm.sagepub.com.

World Health Organization (2004). *Developing Health Management Information Systems: A Practical Guide for Developing Countries*, Geneva, Switzerland.

Zodpey, S.P. and Negandhi, H.N. (2008). 'Contemporary Issues in Public Health Governance: An Indian Perspective', *Indian Journal of Public Health*, 52(2): 96–99.

20

Shedding Shyness

A Perspective from Tamil Nadu

JOSEPHINE SELLE JEYANATHAN AND A. SHENBAGAVALLI

Abstract

Healthy citizens are the greatest asset of a country. The statistics from World Health Organization (WHO), National Cancer Registry Programme (NCRP) and Population Based Cancer Registry (PBCR) records alarming rates of breast cancer prevalent in India. It shows breast cancer equally risky as cervical cancer and if it continues to grow, it might become the number one cause for death among women. As early detection is the only protective mode, oncologists and radiologists advise that every woman must get regular screening tests done after the age of 35. Currently, mammography is considered to be the gold standard diagnostic and screening tool for the human breasts. Similarly, Thermal Infrared (IR) Imaging is also being used for breast screening which is non-painful, non-intrusive and causes no discomfort to the patient. Rural medical camps in and around Kovilpatti in the southern district of Tamil Nadu were organized in collaboration with Indira Gandhi Centre for Atomic Research (IGCAR), Kalpakkam, for age groups from 20 to 60 years.

It, thus, becomes mandatory and good for every woman to shed her shyness and immediately report to the doctor even the smallest cyst she feels in her body. Mortality among female citizens of India can thus be successfully irradiated.

Keywords

Breast Cancer, WHO, NCRP, Mammography, Thermography, IGCAR

Introduction

Breast cancer is caused due to the uncontrolled growth of abnormal cells which form a tumour in the breast. Breast cancer tumours may grow for months or years without causing symptoms or any sign of breast cancer. Most breast cancers develop in the milk duct, known as ductal breast cancer. Breast cancers that develop in the lobes are known as lobular breast cancer.

Although breast cancer is the second most common cancer in all India (Figure 1), the recent data from the Atlas of Cancer in India project (https://canceratlasindia.org) and a study to assess nationwide patterns of cancer incidence across urban and rural parts of the country suggest that breast cancer is highly common in metropolitan cities (Figure 2).

Figure 1

Different Cancers Prevalent among the Female Citizens of India

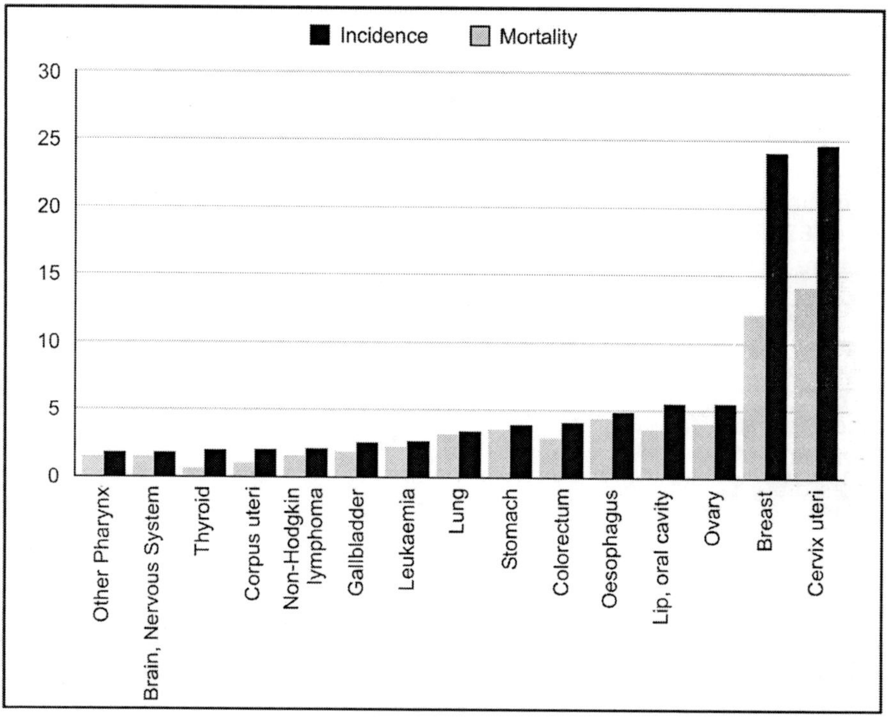

Figure 2

Breast Cancer Most Common in Metropolitan Cities

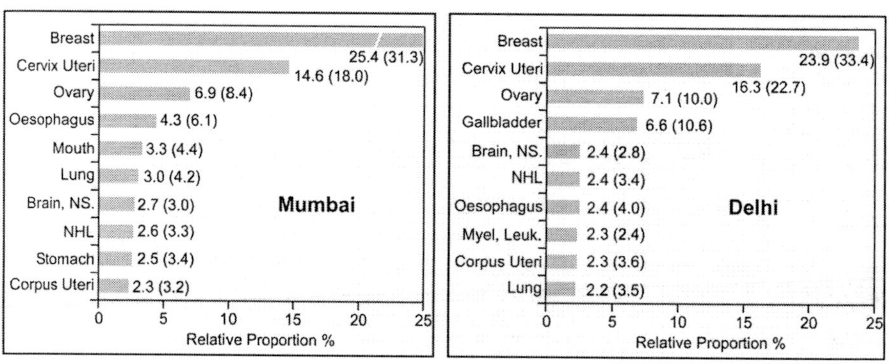

Figure 2 (cont'd...)

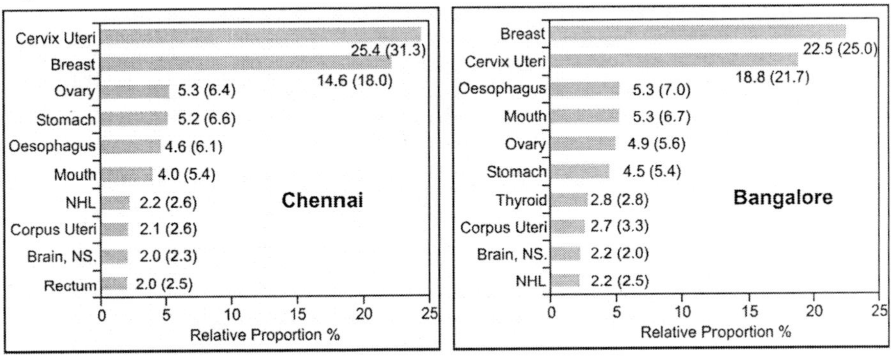

The Population Based Cancer Registry (PBCR) had recorded the incident and mortality rate which is depicted in Table 1. The statistics show that more than one lakh women were diagnosed of breast cancer in the year 2008 out of which 82 thousand women died in the same year. The five-year prevalence for women, prone to be diagnosed of this cancer is predicted to be increased by 30 per cent (http://www.ncrpindia.org/Cancer_Atlas_India). The Indian Council for Medical Research (ICMR) has analysed for different cancer sites in India for different time interval. Table 2 shows that breast cancer is likely to overtake cervical cancer after 2015. The ratio at which the women are prone to breast cancer in urban areas is 1: 22 and in rural areas is 1: 60 in her whole lifetime. Dr David Forman, Head of International Agency for Research in Cancer (IARC), states that this drastic rise is partly because a shift in lifestyle is causing an increase in the incidence and partly because clinical advances to combat this disease are not reaching many women.

Table 1

Estimated Incidence, Mortality and 5 year Prevalence in Women by PBCR

Cancer	*Incidence*			*Mortality*			*5-year Prevalence*		
	Number	*(%)*	*ASR (W)*	*Number*	*(%)*	*ASR (W)*	*Number*	*(%)*	*Prop.*
Lip, Oral Cavity	36,365	4.7	5.5	23,470	4.9	3.6	65,437	3.9	11.1
Nasopharynx	1,500	0.2	0.2	1,062	0.2	0.1	3,708	0.2	0.6
Other Pharynx	11,747	1.5	1.8	9,603	2.0	1.5	19,847	1.2	3.5
Oesophagus	31,663	1.4	4.9	28,152	5.8	4.4	22,523	1.3	3.9
Stomach	26,043	3.4	3.9	23,954	5.0	3.6	26,239	1.3	4.6
Colorectum	27,294	3.5	4.1	19,570	4.1	2.9	46,259	2.7	8.1
Liver	10,556	1.4	1.6	9,966	2.1	1.5	5,578	0.3	1.0
Gallbladder	17,013	2.2	2.6	12,126	2.5	1.9	20,687	1.2	3.6
Pancreas	6,075	0.8	0.9	5,218	1.1	0.8	3,414	0.2	0.6
Larynx	4,644	0.6	0.7	3,013	0.6	0.5	10,432	0.6	1.8
Lung	22,428	2.9	3.5	20,457	4.2	3.2	14,809	0.9	2.6
Melanoma of Skin	1,310	0.2	0.2	651	0.1	0.1	3,311	0.2	0.6
Breast	1,72,975	22.4	24.1	82,638	17.1	12.1	5,18,723	30.7	90.6
Cervix Uteri	1,73,917	22.5	24.6	95,871	19.8	14.1	4,51,968	26.8	78.9

Cont'd...

...*Cont'd*

Corpus Uteri	13,771	1.8	2.1	6,659	1.4	1.0	50,676	3.0	8.9
Ovary	38,798	5.0	5.5	27,334	5.7	4.1	84,588	5.0	14.8
Kidney	5,392	0.7	0.8	3,557	0.7	0.5	10,957	0.6	1.9
Bladder	6,136	0.8	0.9	3,411	0.7	0.5	14,936	0.9	2.6
Brain, Nervous System	13,390	1.7	1.8	10,416	2.2	1.5	19,364	1.1	3.4
Thyroid	14,552	1.9	2.0	4,147	0.9	0.6	56,505	3.3	9.9
Hodgkin Lymphoma	4,074	0.5	0.5	2,300	0.5	0.3	9,627	0.6	1.7
Non-Hodgkin Lymphoma	15,059	2.0	2.1	10,691	2.2	1.5	19,969	1.2	3.5
Multiple Myeloma	4,242	0.5	0.7	3,907	0.8	0.6	7,112	0.4	1.2
Leukaemia	21,093	2.7	2.7	17,210	3.6	2.3	17,670	1.0	3.1
All cancers (excl. non-melanoma) skin cancer	7,72,036	100.0	110.8	4,83,134	100.0	71.7	16,88,591	100.0	294.8

Incidence and mortality date for all ages. 5-year prevalence for adult population only.

ASR (W) and Proportions per 1,00,000.

Table 2

Projected Cases of Cancer for Selected Sites and Selected Time Period in India (2008–10, 2015 and 2020)

Site of Cancer	*ICD–10 Code*	*2008*	*2009*	*2010*	*2015*	*2020*
Female						
All Sites	*Coo-C96*	*4,98,773*	*5,07,990*	*5,17,378*	*5,63,808*	*6,14,404*
Tongue	C01-C02	7,687	7,829	7,974	8,689	9,469
Mouth	C03-C06	14,402	14,669	14,940	16,280	17,741
Hypopharynx	C12-C13	4,620	4,706	4,793	5,223	5,691
Oesophagus	C15	17,755	18,083	18,417	20,070	21,871
Stomach	C16	12,458	12,689	12,923	14,083	15,347
Colon	C18	10,675	11,276	11,896	15,206	19,014
Rectum	C19-C20	9,005	9,172	9,341	10,180	11,093
Liver	C22	7,564	7,943	8,334	10,412	12,795
Gallbladder	C23-C24	17,839	18,169	18,505	20,166	21,975
Larynx	C32	3,894	3,966	4,039	4,401	4,796
Lung	C33-C34	13,009	13,250	13,494	14,705	16,025
Brest	C50	84,805	87,693	90,659	1,06,124	1,23,634
Cervix	C53	1,00,088	1,01,938	1,03,821	1,13,138	1,23,291
Corpus Uteri	C54	14,314	14,579	14,848	16,181	17,633
Overy	C56	29,386	29,929	30,482	33,218	36,199
Brain NS	C70-C72	11,232	11,440	11,651	12,697	13,836
Thyroid Gland	C73	11,329	11,538	11,751	12,806	13,955
NHL	C82-C95-C96	11,696	11,913	12,133	13,222	14,408
Lymp. Leuk.	C91	5,703	5,808	5,916	6,447	7,025
Myeloid Leuk.	C92-C94	11,070	11,770	12,492	16,363	20,828

Source: Time Trend in Cancer Incidence Rates, 1982–2005. National Cancer Registry Programme, ICMR, April 2009.

The average age of breast cancer patients has been reported to be 50–53 years in various population-based studies done in different areas of the country. A significant proportion of Indian breast cancer patients fall below 35 years of age. Young age is usually associated with larger tumours and high number of metastatic lymph nodes (Shavers et al., 2003: 135; Mathew et al., 2004). There is a significant difference in the survival rate in developed and developing countries mainly because of a lack of early detection programmes and inadequate resources for treatment (Coleman et al., 2008: 735). Early detection of cancer greatly increases the chances for successful treatment.

There are two ways for early detection of cancer, i.e. education to promote early diagnosis and screening. Screening refers to the use of simple tests across a healthy population in order to identify individuals who have disease, but do not yet have symptoms. The objective of the study was to promote awareness about breast health among the female citizens in the southern districts of India. Screening programmes using mammography and ultrasonography along with IR imaging were adopted at free of cost for the women of all age groups.

Different Modalities for Breast Cancer Detection

Some of the modalities used in the cancer detection are used for screening and for diagnostic purposes as well. Imaging instruments used for screening must be cost effective and efficient enough to reach the masses. When breast cancer has been detected in the screening tests, further evaluations are performed using diagnostic modalities. Adjunctive modalities are also used by the doctors and oncologists for additional confidence in their initial diagnosis. Widely used modalities in breast cancer detection are mammography, breast ultrasound, magnetic resonance imaging (MRI), Positron Emission Tomography (PET) and thermography.

Mammography

Mammography is the gold standard technique used for breast imaging. It uses low dose amplitude X-rays to examine the breast. This method is good for detecting Ductal Carcinoma In Situ (DCIS) and calcifications as they appear brighter in the mammogram. Mammography can has decreased mortality rate by 30 per cent in screening programmes (Kerlikowske et al., 1995: 151). Though it is difficult to detect cancer at early stages, it can be combined with additional screening tests to reduce the death rate from breast cancer (Kopans, 2004: 490). The conventional mammography technique was modified into digital mammography to produce 3D views of the breast (Wu et al., 2003: 370). The digital mammography has given an increased sensitivity rate from 0.43 to 0.62 even on dense tissues.

Breast Ultrasound

Ultrasound imaging is mainly used to detect the location of suspicious breast lesions. The ultrasound transducer send high frequency sound waves into the breast tissues and sensors are used to detect the reflected sound waves. The 2D real time images are displayed on the monitor. The ultrasound imaging has little evidence to support in breast screening as it gives false positives and false negative outcomes (The and Wilson, 1998: 449). The study conducted in Japan in 2009 has given similar performance as mammography in detecting breast cancer. Tohno E., Ueno E. and Watanabe H. et al. (2009: 20) have suggested after the study that combination of ultrasound and mammography is suitable for breast screening in Japan.

MRI

MRI makes use of hydrogen nucleus which contains water and fat for imaging purpose. The magnetic property of the hydrogen nucleus enables the production of detailed images from any part of the body. The patient under MRI imaging is placed in the magnetic field and radio frequency waves are applied to create high contrast images of the breast. The MRI is used to monitor vascularity associated with neoangiogenesis (Leach, 2001: 24). MRI imaging has become a popular diagnostic technique nowadays to evaluate the tumour response to treatment. Schnall M.D. (2001: 18) proves that MRI can yield early detection results of certain high risk population with advance Tesla magnets and improved spatial and resolution (Lehman and Schnall, 2005: 217). MRI is most useful for women with high risk of breast cancer, is effective for evaluating dense breasts, helps to evaluate inverted nipple, allows the simultaneous evaluation of both breasts, helps to determine whether lumpectomy or mastectomy is the best treatment and most importantly it is non-invasive. The limitations of this technique are that it cannot diagnose ductal carcinoma in situ (DCIS), slow to process the images (30 mins to one hour) and very expensive.

PET

Positron Emission Tomography (PET) is a nuclear imaging technique. The radionuclide capsules are introduced into the human body and the gamma rays that are emitted from them are detected. Malignant tumours contain high glucose metabolism compared to the normal cells and, hence, this characterizes between them in three-dimensional PET images. But PET is known to be expensive and yields poor resolution images. Moreover, the patients are exposed to radiation but PET is being used frequently to predict the treatment response in many cancers (Fass, 2008: 115).

Breast Thermography

The metabolic rate of cancerous and pre-cancerous breast tissue is higher compared to the normal tissues. This results in high vascularity by developing new blood vessels known as angiogenesis. As a result, the temperature surrounding the cancerous tissue is higher, the variation in the skin temperatures were studied and examined to detect early signs of cancer (Gautherie and Gros, 1976: 140). Thermography technique is painless, non-intrusive and a very important advantage is that it can be used on young women even with denser tissues which pose difficulty while viewing in x-ray mammography. Moreover, thermography is very useful in detecting histological pathologies in pregnant and lactating women as they need not face any ionizing radiation. Digital Infrared Thermal Imaging (DITI) camera is used to obtain infrared images and these images are called as thermogram. The camera converts the infrared radiation emitted from the skin surface into electrical impulses that are visualized in colour on a monitor. This visual image graphically maps the body temperature and the spectrum of colours indicates an increase or decrease in the amount of infrared radiation being emitted from the body surface. Since there is a high degree of thermal symmetry in the normal body, even slight asymmetries can be easily identified.

Figure 5

Five Thermal Imaging Positions: Front, Right Oblique, Left Oblique, Right and Left Sides

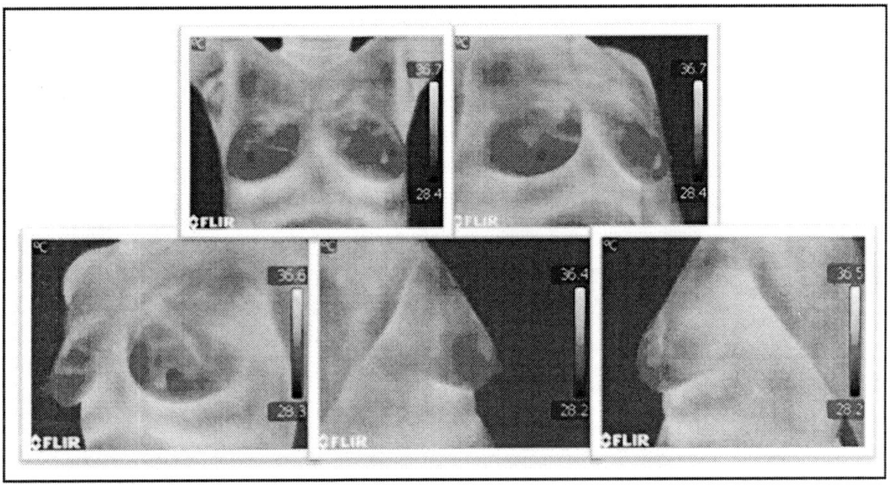

Currently thermography is widely used for accurate breast cancer detection. Ng EYK (2009: 852) says that thermography is a promising tool for mass screening as it can diagnose breast cancer at least ten years in advance. However, both analysis and interpretation of thermograms depend on the analyst.

Screening Procedure for Thermography

There is no such universally accepted acquisition protocol for breast thermal imaging. Hence, clinics and hospitals in other countries assumed different protocols and patient positioning while imaging. The scanning procedure begins with filling personal health related forms. The patient will be asked to sit in a cool room (68°F.) alone for 15 minutes, upper body undressed and shoes/stockings removed, to equilibrate. After this brief waiting time, the candidate is positioned in front of the imaging system so that the surfaces of the breasts, upper chest, and under arms are imaged. A series of images is taken for a baseline study. The patients are made to stand in five views as shown in Figure 5. The technician operates the equipment from outside of cool room for privacy and temperature maintenance. The images are captured in real-time from an ultra-sensitive medical infrared imaging camera and sent to a sophisticated computer for storage and analysis (the images are kept on archival media for precision comparison of future images so that the breasts can be monitored over time). Sophisticated computer programmes allow the doctor to check temperature values, perform vascular analyses, and do dynamic thermal subtraction studies (see Figure 6).

Figure 6

Computerized Medical Infrared Thermal Imaging Setup

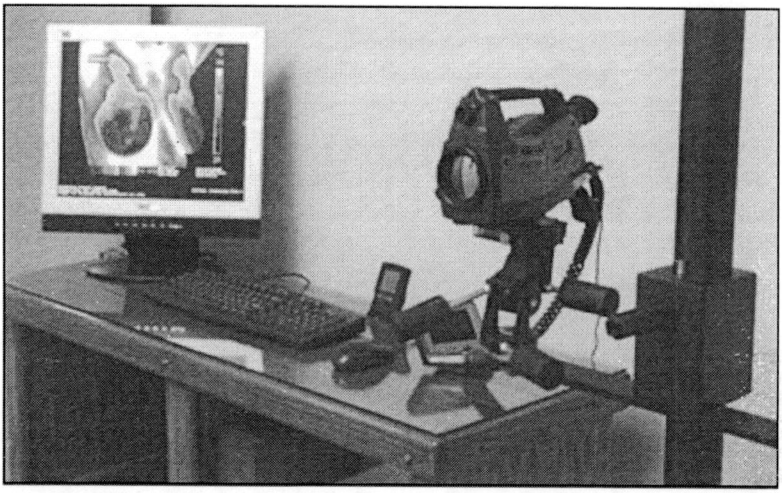

Courtesy: breastthermography.com

Early Detection Means Life

Breast cancer being the most common cancer in women, the risk increases with age (American Cancer Society, 2000–2010). Risk is also higher in women whose close relatives have had the disease. Women without children, and those who have had their first child after age 30, also seem to be at higher risk. The uniqueness of thermography is the ability to detect thermal signs that may suggest a pre-cancerous state of the breast, or signs of cancer at an extremely early stage. However, it does not have the ability to pinpoint the location of a tumour nor can it detect 100 per cent of all cancers. Moreover, its role is in addition (an adjunct) to mammography and physical examination, the tests complement each other. Since it has been determined that one in eight women will get breast cancer, every possible means is sought to detect cancers where there is the greatest chance for survival. Proper use of breast self-exams, physician exams, breast thermography, and mammography together provide the earliest detection system available to date. If treated in the earliest stages, cure rates greater than 95 per cent are possible (Gautherie, 1983: 53).

The Study

Considering these facts that many Indian women are less aware of breast cancer, screening camps were initiated in and around rural areas of Kovilpatti, Tamil Nadu. In collaboration with Indira Gandhi Centre for Atomic Research (IGCAR), Kalpakkam, series of free screening camps were organized to promote awareness on breast health and the importance of regular screening. The later sections describe the work done so far in conducting the medical camps.

Mass Screening Camp

The first medical camp was carried out in a rural village Nalattinputhur at Sharda Government Higher Secondary School. Women of all ages participated in screening. Dr R. Gomathi, Aarthi Scans Centre, Kovilpatti, presided over the camp in order to consult the participants attending the camp.

Figure 7

In the Picture: Dr K.N.K.S.K. Chokalingam (Director) and Dr P. Subburaj (Principal) of National Engineering College, Kovilpatti had Presided Over the First Medical Camp along with Dr Gomathi, Aarthi Clinic

The IR imaging for the women was carried out in one of the classrooms of the school. The total number of people were 195, out of which 20 were suspected abnormalities in the IR reading. These candidates were further subjected for mammography to the scan centre.

Figure 8

Dr Gomathi, Aarthi Scans Centre, Kovilpatti Consulting a Patient

Figure 9

People from the Nearby Villages at the Venue for the Medical Camp

The second camp was organized for the college staff members of K.R. Mills, National Engineering College, K.R. Arts College and Lakshmi Ammal Polytechnic (LAP) College. The female staff members were given an orientation programme related to breast screening and seriousness of breast cancer. Those having suspected lesions and cysts were subjected to mammography and breast ultrasound for further investigation.

Figure 10

First Picture: Digital Infrared Imaging camera was demonstrated to the staff members.
Second Picture: Candidates were made to fill health history forms and sign the consent forms before they were screened by IR imaging

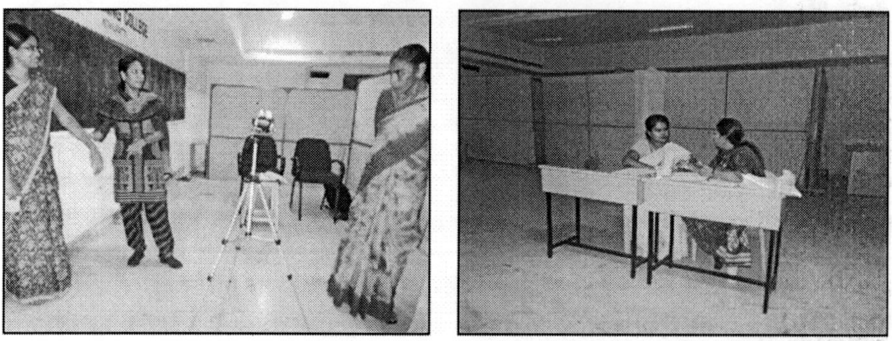

The next camp was organized in a scan centre where three modalities such as IR imaging, mammography and breast ultrasound were available. Dr V. Uma Maheswari, Madurai Medical College, Madurai; Dr C. Rani Chakravarthi, LITTI Scans, K. Pudur, Madurai. Dr R. Pandia Rajalakshmi, Radiologist, Madurai were present in the camp.

Figure 11
The General Public were Notified In and Around LITTI Scans, Madurai

Figure 12
High Court Judge D. Geetha Participated in the IR Screening

Figure 13

An Article Regarding the Camp was Published in Indian Express Newspaper on 22 April 2013

'Shed Shyness and Get Screened'

A free medical camp for women organised by the National Engineering College in Kovilpatti underway in Madurai on Sunday | EXPRESS

Express News Service

Madurai: Women should shed their shyness to to get tested for breast cancer, said experts at a special medical camp for women, especially for breast cancer. It was organised by National engineering college (NEC), Kovilpatti along with Litti scan centre, K Pudur, here on Sunday.

Speaking at the camp at the scan centre, V Uma Maheswari, general surgeon and gynaecologist, said prevalence of breast cancer remains at the same level, but it can only be cured or controlled with early detection. Some people would shy away from getting screened for it and some others would not give it any attention if they found it a problem.

Breast cancer does not show any early symptoms, so it is in every woman's interest to get checked for it. There are many procedures like physical scan, ultra scan, thermal scan and mammogram and it is easy to confirm the disease, said Maheswari, who is also HoD of community medicine at Madurai Medical College.

Women should check themselves five days after the period, if they found any changes, she said.

Talking to Express, A Shenbagavalli, professor of ECE department, NEC, said that "we are organising such camps to reach out to illiterate women, especially rural people, as they lack in awareness about cervical, breast or uterus cancers. It is our third medical camp; we had two camps in Kovilpatti areas."

The programme is funded by Indira Gandhi Centre for Atomic Research (IGCAR), Kalpakkam.

IR imaging is regardless of gender as breast cancer affects not only the women but even the men. Figure 14 shows a male patient, who had confirmed breast cancer being screened through IR imaging.

Discussion and Conclusion

Breast cancer is indeed a disease with no specific cure, and its treatment can be less aggressive and effective only if it is diagnosed in time. Such a life threatening disease requires immense research in developing modalities that can help in early detection and find a possible cure. A system that can increase high quality of screening tools and supporting programmes to improve the treatment must be ensured to every woman. Thermography is a non-invasive, radiation free and non-painful modality. Although it can be used as breast cancer detection tool, it

Figure 14

A Male Candidate (age 61) who had Come for Screening had Confirmed Breast Cancer. Right bottom is the thermogram showing high temperature on his left chest

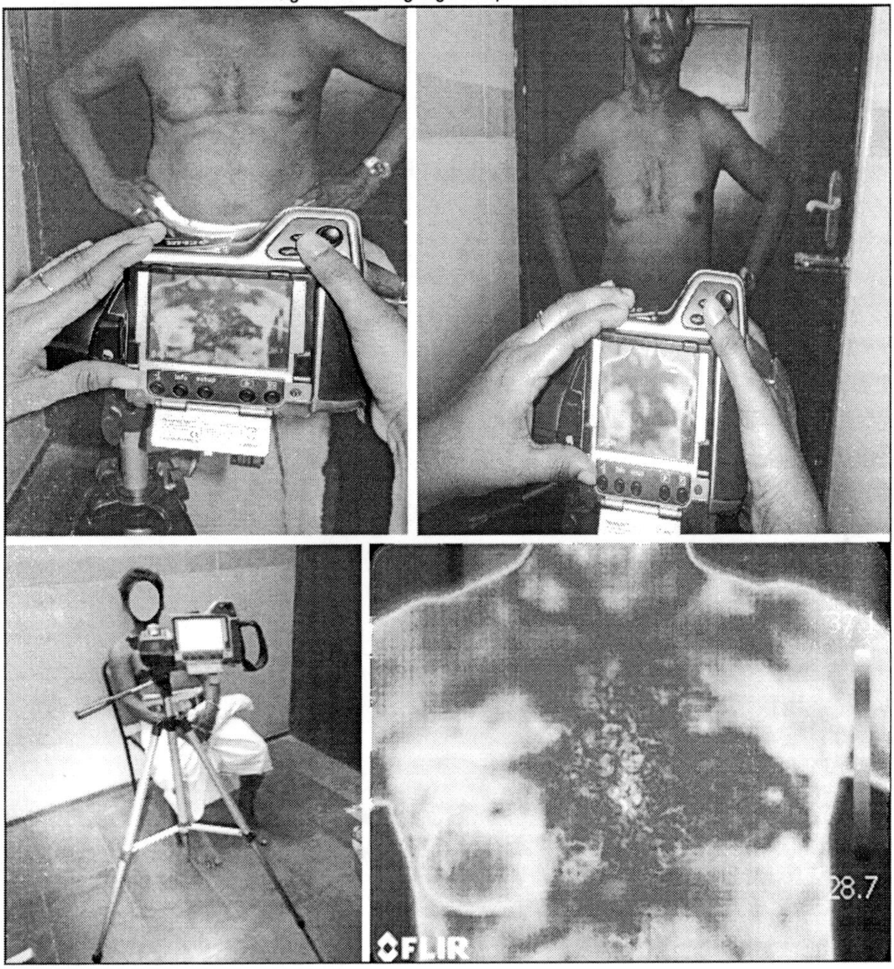

is not accepted on par with the gold standard tool, mammography. Studies however showed the sensitivity of thermography in detecting breast cancer as 83 per cent, while the combination of thermography and mammography had 95 per cent sensitivity. Thermography, thus, cannot be used as a stand alone but it is a complimentary screening technique in breast cancer detection (Kennedy et al., 2009). Further, more research work must be carried out to develop this modality by bringing standardized protocols for image acquisition for clinical effectiveness and examine all the aspects in the use of thermography on pattern recognition.

This paper attempted to signify the importance of IR imaging and its effectiveness to detect cancer as early as possible. Efforts should be directed to enhance the diagnosis of breast cancer using thermograms to complement the gold standard mammography, added with computer vision so as to reduce the subjective interpretation involved by the medical fraternity. Ultimately, the larger goal of making women shed their shyness should be ensured to reduce the female mortality in India.

Acknowledgements

The authors thank IGCAR, Kalpakkam for research grant, Dr B. Venkatraman, AD, RSEG and REG, IGCAR, Kalpakkam, M. Menaka, Scientific Officer E, QAD, IGCAR, Kalpakkam, Dr M. Jayashree, Chief Radiologist and DAE Hospital deserve credit for their support in the study

References

Amalu, W.C., Hobbins, W.B., Head, J.F. and Elliott, R.L. (2006). 'Infrared Imaging of the Breast: An Overview', in *Biomedical Engineering Handbook*, Chapter 25, Boca Raton, FL: CRC Press, 1–36.

American Cancer Society, 2009–2010. Breast Cancer Guidelines and Statistics.

Ammer, K. and Ring, E.F.J. (2006). 'Standard Procedures for Infrared Imaging in Medicine', in *Biomedical Engineering Handbook*, Chapter 36, Boca Raton, FL: CRC Press, 1–14.

Bray, F. (2012). 'Cancer Incidence and Mortality Worldwide: Sources, Methods and Major Patterns in GLOBOCAN 2012', *International Journal of Cancer*, 136(5).

Bray, F., Ren, J.S., Masuyer, E. and Ferlay, J. (2013). 'Estimates of Global Cancer Prevalence for 27 Sites in the Adult Population in 2008', *International Journal of Cancer*, 132(5): 1133–145.

Coleman, M.P., Quaresma, M., Berrino, F. et al. (2008). 'Cancer Survival in Five Continents: A Worldwide Population-based Study (CONCORD)', *Lancet Oncol*, 9: 730–56. http://www.canceratlasindia.org.

Fass, L. (2008). 'Imaging and Cancer: A Review', *Mol Oncol*, 2: 115–52.

Gautherie, M. (1983). 'Thermo Biological Assessment of Benign and Malignant Breast Diseases', *Am. J. Obstetrics and Gynecology*, 147(8): 861–69.

Gautherie, M. and Gros, C. (1976). 'Contribution of Infrared Thermography to Early Diagnosis, Pretheraputic Prognosis and Post-irradiation Follow-up of Breast Carcinomas', *Med Mundi*, 21: 135–49.

—— (1980). 'Breast Thermography and Cancer Risk Prediction', *Cancer*, 45(1): 51–56.

Gros, C., Gautherie, M. and Bourjat, P. (1975). 'Prognosis and Post-therapeutic Follow-up of Breast Cancers by Thermography', *Bibl Radiology*, 6: 77–90.

Kennedy, D.A., Lee, T. and Sealy, D. (2009). 'A Comparative Review of Thermography as a Breast Cancer Screening Technique', *Integrative Cancer Therapies*, 8(1): 9–16.

Kerlikowske, K., Grady, D., Rubin, S.M., Sandrock, C. and Ernster, V.L. (1995). 'Efficacy of Screening Mammography: A Meta-analysis', *JAMA*, 273: 149–54.

Kopans, D.B. (2004). 'Sonography Should Not be Used for Breast Cancer Screening Until its Efficacy has been Proven Scientifically', *American Journal of Roentgenology*, 182: 489–91.

Leach, M.O. (2001). 'Application of Magnetic Resonance Imaging to Angiogenesis in Breast Cancer', *Breast Cancer Research*, 3: 22–27.

Lehman, C.D. and Schnall, M.D. (2005). 'Imaging in Breast Cancer: Magnetic Resonance Imaging', *Breast Cancer Research*, 7: 215–19.

Mathew, A., Pandey, M. and Rajan, B. (2004). 'Do Younger Women with Non-Metastatic and Non-inflammatory Breast Carcinoma have Poor Prognosis?', *World Journal of Surgical Oncology*, 2(2).

Ng, E.Y.K. (2009). 'A Review of Thermography as Promising Noninvasive Detection Modality for Breast Tumour', *International Journal of Thermal Sciences*, 48: 849–59.

Ng, E.Y.K. and Sudharsan, N.M. (2004). 'Numerical Modeling in Conjunction with Thermography as an Adjunct Tool for Breast Tumour Detection', *BMC Cancer*, 4: 1–26. http://www.ncrpindia.org/cancer_atlas_india/index.aspx.

Ring, E.F.J. and Ammer, K. (2000). 'The Technique of Infra Red Imaging in Medicine', *Thermology International*, 10: 7–14. http://www.pbcrindia.org/index.aspx.

Schnall, M.D. (2001). 'Application of Magnetic Resonance Imaging to Early Detection of Breast Cancer', *Breast Cancer Research*, 3: 17–21.

Shavers, V.L., Harlan, L.C. and Stevens, J.L. (2003). 'Racial/Ethnic Variation in Clinical Presentation, Treatment, and Survival among Breast Cancer Patients under Age 35', *Cancer*, 97: 134–47.

Suri, J.S. (2010). *Performance Evaluation Techniques in Multimodality Breast Cancer Screening, Diagnosis and Treatment*, New York: American Scientific Publishers.

The, W. and Wilson, A.R. (1998). 'The Role of Ultrasound in Breast Cancer Screening: A Consensus Statement by the European Group for Breast Cancer Screening', *European Journal of Cancer*, 34: 449–50.

Tohno, E., Ueno, E. and Watanabe, H. (2009). 'Ultrasound Screening of Breast Cancer', *Breast Cancer*, 16: 18–22.

Wiecek, B., Wiecek, M., Strakowski, R., Jakubowska, T. and Ng, E.Y.K. (2011). 'Wavelet-based Thermal Image Classification for Breast Screening and Other Medical Applications', in E.Y.K. Ng, Y. Chen and L.N. Ung (eds), *Performance Evaluation Techniques in Multi-modality Breast Cancer Screening, Diagnosis and Treatment*, Bota Racon, FL: CRC Press.

Wu, T., Stewart, A., Stanton, M., McCauley, T., Phillips, W., Kopans, D.B., Moore, R.H., Eberhard, J.W., Opsahl-Ong, B., Niklason, L. and Williams, M.B. (2003). 'Tomographic Mammography Using a Limited Number of Low-dose Cone-beam Projection Images', *Medical Physics*, 30: 365–80.

Index